Fraud Upon the Court

Reclaiming the Law, Joyfully

Mary W Maxwell, PhD, LLB

FRAUD UPON THE COURT

by Mary W Maxwell
pp. 320, includes index
Set in Garamond 13

Print (ISBN-13): 9781634240123

Keywords: writ of error coram nobis, Pat Tillman, April Gallop, Bill Windsor, grand juries, Lyndon Barsten, William Pepper, Troy Davis, judicial treason, Brice Taylor, National Guard Bureau, Maret Tsarnaeva, Martin Bryant, Gerry Docherty, Mae Brussell, civil RICO, Laurent Louis

Published by:
Trine Day LCC
PO Box 577
Walterville, OR 97489

www.TrineDay.com
publisher@TrineDay.net

First Edition
10 9 8 7 6 5 4 3 2 1

Printed in the USA
Distribution to the Trade by:
Independent Publishers Group (IPG)
814 North Franklin Street
Chicago, Illinois, 60610
312-337-0747
www.ipgbook.com

2

To
the Sisters of Notre Dame de Namur,
my elementary and high school teachers,
who were unfailing in their generosity and
personal discipline, and who considered
integrity and high ideals
to be part of the flora and fauna of this world

Thank you, Sisters, for doing without, for us.

Other Books by This Author

Human Evolution (1984)

Morality among Nations (1990)

The Sociobiological Imagination (editor) (1991)

Moral Inertia (1991)

Prosecution for Treason (2011)

Consider the Lilies (2013)

A Balm in Gilead (2014)

Truth in Journalism (co-author) (2015)

Websites:

ProsecutionForTreason.com

maryWmaxwell.com

YouTube Channel:

Mary W Maxwell

Publisher's Foreword

You're searching for good times
But just wait and see …
  — Jerry Ragovoy, "Time Is On My Side"

How can we expect to get up each morning, when the world we left the day before is awash with cruel insanities?

We are living in a very troubled time, one permeated by ends-over-means agendas, many implemented through psychological warfare methods that then exacerbate natural dilemmas creating extreme division and dysfunction.

A tightly controlled "national debate" plies it trade, the earth revolves around the sun, and we wake up in the morning further down the road. To where?

I implore the reader to work on understanding our human condition; do not be afraid to enter into conversation with those with whom you do not agree. Do not be afraid to make a mistake or read something you do not agree with. Sometimes, only by following a false lead can we recognize true ones.

I do not always concur with my authors – but then, exploring truth and the world around us is not about orthodoxy, or lock-step group-think. We must always challenge our commonly-held beliefs, our leaders, ourselves.

Mary W Maxwell does just that. She looks at the world through a unique perspective of sociobiology and law. Mary is bold, unafraid to venture into untried areas. She speculates, with facts behind her, about known covert technologies, and the proverbial corrupting tendency of "absolute" power. *What would you do if you could?*

Mary is very hopeful that you will do the right thing, and be a responsible steward of our history and future. She asks us to understand our heritage and use the Law to take back our country from the corruption, ignorance and treason that enslave our common destinies.

George Washington once remarked, "Government is not reason; it is not eloquence; it is force. Like fire, it is a dangerous servant and a fearful master." Here, in *Fraud Upon the Court*, we find explorations and exposés of "a fearful master."

Onward to the Utmost of Futures,

Peace,

Kris Millegan
Publisher
TrineDay
July 22, 2015

Message Published by Troy Davis in 2008

I want to thank all of you for your efforts and dedication to Human Rights and Human Kindness. In the past year I have experienced such emotion, joy, sadness and never-ending faith. It is because of all of you that I am alive today. As I look at my sister Martina I marvel at the love she has for me and of course I worry about her and her health, but, as she tells me, she is the eldest and she will not back down from this fight.

As I look at my mail from across the globe, from places I have never ever dreamed I would know about and people speaking languages and expressing cultures and religions I could only hope to one day see first hand, I am humbled by the emotion that fills my heart with overwhelming, overflowing Joy. I can't even explain the surge of emotion I feel when I try to express the strength I draw from you all, it compounds my faith and it shows me yet again that this is not a case about the death penalty, this is not a case about Troy Davis, It is about the Human Spirit to see Justice prevail.

So Thank you, and remember I am in a place where execution can only destroy your physical form but because of my faith in God, my family and all of you I have been spiritually free for some time. ... I want you to know that the trauma placed on me and my family, as I have now faced execution and the death chamber 3 times, is more than most can bear. Yet as I face this state sanctioned terror, I realize one constant: my faith is unwavering.... You inspire me ... you add to my strength, my courage. We must dismantle this unjust system city by city, state by state, and country by country. I can't wait to stand with you, no matter if that's in physical or spiritual form, I will one day be announcing:

"I AM TROY DAVIS AND I AM FREE."

TABLE OF CONTENTS

What times we live in!

My father was a young adult in the 1920s, a time when major intellectual breakthroughs were occurring every year. When browsing a library shelf, in various disciplines, I give a fond pat to any books from the 'Twenties.

Who, someday, will be patting the books of our era? Will there still *be* books? Will there be writers? What is the likely future situation for our children? Can we have an influence on it?

When I was young I certainly did not expect to become a writer. And although this is my ninth book, I never think of my vocation as having to do with writing, but with solving urgent problems. If it turns out that I am just imagining these crises, all well and good. Who needs 'em? But whilst they still seem real to me I'll have a go at them.

The book at hand started out as a project to help someone get the hell out of Death Row where he was unfairly stationed. But nowadays I feel that many of us are stationed on a sort of Death Row. Are we *unfairly* there? Probably not. I think we deserve what is happening to us – at the hands of the Powers That Be – as we are steadfastly ignoring it.

In this book I try to find as many ways as possible for folks to deal with it. They could, of course, contemplate the miracle of life! The bounties of earth! The unlimited possibilities for love! But here one will find only chatter about *the law*. I think law can be our best friend.

It seems that a serious handicap, built into our DNA, is the lack of means for grouping together against a baddy, if that baddy is Daddy. We don't like to say our leaders are doing harm. It's impolite and embarrassing to say it. So say it!

Please read the chapters in any order you like, perhaps even backwards. Get in touch with me if this stuff turns you on!

ACKNOWLEDGEMENTS

My first thank you has to be to Martina Correia, who is no longer with us. She was Troy Davis' beautiful older sibling, who took the role of protector to great heights. Martina was very persuasive. And so completely alive! It was one of the real pleasures of my life just to be in touch with her.

My next thank-you is to my editor Shiva Jade. She happens to be the granddaughter of my beloved late husband George, so, needless to say, I am thrilled to see any of his traits in her. Turns out she's got George's editing skills. Nothing gets past her. I'm not referring to errors of punctuation, but to ill-considered ideas. Wow – out of the mouths of babes.

I say *gracias* to Ailsa for indexing this book, and Craig for artwork. I thank two members of the Fourth Estate, who know the value of their role, and the serious obligations it brings. The first is Rayelan Allan. She let me to be an 'agent' at her website, "Rumor Mill News." That authorizes me to upload articles from Australia, bypassing the need to wait for daybreak in the US to get editorial imprimatur.

The other person is publisher Kris Millegan, who, like Raye, is partly Native American. I'll bet that's got something to do with it. They just aren't into "spin." Kris, you carry a big load in this world. And don't let me forget Jennifer Byrne, Paul Carter, and Robert Haupt who let me publish at *The Age*. Robert died too young.

I am thankful to Australia for harboring me since 1980. My gratitude flares up when I think of the help given to me by Prema, Kane, Cam, and Louis, each of whom has tried to keep me on track. My law professors Greg, John, and Horst, made me feel welcome. Janie introduced me to the maxims.

During the worst of times, I was salvaged by a message from His Honour, Justice David Bleby, retired judge of the Australian Federal Court. His lecture in Adelaide on July 4, 2011 said to me -- 'in so many words':

"Go for it, Mary. Hang on to the law. Believe in it. She'll be right, Mate."

Mary W Maxwell   Adelaide, August 9, 2015

US Federal Law Mentioned in This Book

United States Constitution:

Federal Statutes, with United States Code Reference (USC):

Civil Actions:

Criminal Trials:

I hold this truth to be self-evident, that if you give ten men the reins to run the whole world – secretly – they will run it according to what they need for themselves.

After all, why should they do otherwise? Why look at, say, the needs of the people? Since their own helmsmanship is a secret, they lack one of the main incentives to act nobly, namely the incentive of getting credit, of being thanked and admired. They will proceed selfishly.

Am I saying that human nature is, overall, more bad than good? No. I am not saying anything about human nature overall. I'm analyzing a particular scenario, one which I think actually exists. I believe there is a small coterie of guys up there today who run our planet as though there were no sovereign nations, no human history, no cultural values.

They live in the raw, so to speak. Take my "self-evident truth" a bit further. What if the ten men (ten is just a guess) were each from different cultures. Would they bring their background preferences to their day's work? If one guy up there were from India and one from Pakistan would they be having a go at each other?

Of course not. They are too busy surviving. "Uneasy lies the head that wears a crown," as Shakespeare said. Very uneasy lies the head that has to concentrate every minute on what will happen to him if he gets caught for what he's been doing. Most of what he's been doing is criminal, per the laws of any of the nations he fiddles with. It could be firing-squadsville for him tomorrow and he well knows it.

I feel sorry for those ten jerks. The dedication of my book *Prosecution for Treason* says "To our prodigal sons, Come home! Come home!" Not that I expect them to apologize and be restored to the bosom of society. It's unlikely they would do that, and even more unlikely their victims would be nice to them. Still, I think it would pay for us to stop fearing them and understand that they are in a bind.

Their bind is killing us and, worse, it is killing the biosphere. They are so worried about their position – it's my claim that all that motivates them now is survival – that they will do anything, or instruct their minions to do anything, to keep them from falling of the perch. Logic can show that this means ecological disaster.

The book at hand is about only one institution of society, the law. At present, the men in charge of the world have applied their genius to decimating this wonderful institution. If you don't believe me now, I think you'll believe after reading some of the chapters. The judicial system no longer functions in a free way. Its black-robed elite have developed a blind spot to issues that would normally engage them. They are truly under the sway of the aforementioned secret rulers. It is *sooo* pathetic.

Clearly a main preoccupation of the judiciary nowadays is to prevent the punishment, or even the exposure, of the secret rulers (and thereby of their fantastic crimes). So I have gone about showing how we would normally proceed, *were it not for that blockage.*

You will therefore find me old-fashioned, non-innovative, boring. I am so boring it is unbelievable. (Check the frontispiece of the Conclusion, Chapter 25.) I am rah-rah the past. This book is strewn with law maxims, which I take to be both a record of the clear thinking of our forebears, and a kernel of what humans relations are all about.

Here is an example of a law maxim: *Minatur innocentibus qui parcit nocentibus.* Sparing the guilty threatens the innocent. Boy, is that ever true! Here's another: *Suppressio veri, expressio falsi.* A suppression of truth is equivalent to a lie.

Are the maxims in Latin because they come from ancient Rome? Nope. They're in Latin because law was done in Latin even in the courts of England until a few hundred years ago. I presume that was because of the power of the Church. (As to why Jesus' message should have a base in Rome, that is anyone's guess. WWJS?)

My fave maxim is, of course, this one: *Lex non deficere potest in justitia exhibenda.* The law cannot fail in dispensing justice. Ahem. Can we make the legal profession live up to that? What is the authority of a maxim? I believe it has long been considered that a maxim so sums up the principles that it can be called into service as an authoritative comment.

I hear you ask "Does a maxim have standing?" I would like to know "Does 'standing' have standing?" We in the law field are too devoted to precedent and formality. Any existing precedent or formality came from human beings; it does not reside in the sky.

Among the maxims, some merely guide a judge in particular kinds of cases: *Lex succurrit minoribus.* The law assists children. Some show how to evaluate testimony: *Allegans contraria non est audiendus.* A person making contradictory allegations should not be listened to. Others show how to think about reality: *Necessitas non habet legem.* Necessity has no law.

That last one may come to be needed soon. If there is no other way to get around today's blockage in the courts, people may have to take the law into their own hands. But, I say, we shouldn't think we are quite there – yet.

Walk with me down a very happy road. The restoration of sensible law. It CAN BE DONE.

chapter one

Court of the King's Bench, under Henry the Eighth

PART I. HAPPINESS IS...THE LAW!

1. Anybody for Law School?

Law is the subject's birthright. Want of right or remedy is all one.

– Sir Edward Coke, *Institutes of the Laws of England* (1628)

Typical lawyer jokes on the Internet:

Why do they bury lawyers 20 feet under? Because deep down they're good people.

One woman to another: "I'm glad it's finally over. My lawyer got the condo, his lawyer got the beach house and the two cars."

Part I celebrates law. One of the reasons life is wonderful is that humans are a social species. This means we are not loners. There is some biologically-given structure to the whole tribe, with a set of predictable relationships. A part of the background of human society is law. No need to argue about where it came from -- it came from "us."

Law distinguishes *Homo sapiens* from any other animal species. We can think up ways to get around the perennial problem of individuals mistreating each other in their desperate contest for survival. We can, and routinely do, use words and ideas to set up compromises or even brilliant solutions to problems.

Moreover, "the law" has become an intellectual discipline in itself. Scholars know how to design very fine points of justice. Perhaps this is because the brain shoots out a supply of opioids when a person is dealing with high principles. There must be, within the human species, some sort of drive toward the use of abstract notions – this is true even in pure mathematics.

At the moment, the call for help within the law field has to do with a certain degradation of judicial behavior. That can be easily corrected, in fact I think it's odd that it came about.

Imagine the following system of law as a dream, and then realize that it is already concrete!

1. Two citizens have grievances with each other. "He didn't return the money I lent him." "She hit my cat." They can take it to a judge. It will be determined who should compensate whom.

2. In the above case, if Party A needs to look at some of Party B's records, the court may order "Discovery." That means B will be required to open his records for A.

3. An accused person doesn't have to "take the stand." Also, if he's kept in jail without charges, his family can seek a writ of *habeas corpus* ("You have the body"), to set him free.

4. Witnesses can lie. But a cross-examination can shake their story. They can also be charged with perjury for lying. It's up to a jury to evaluate a witness's credibility.

5. A citizen who knows that a crime has been committed can "lay an information" with police or with the court.

6. A person can ask the court for an injunction, such as a restraining order, to prevent a bad thing from happening.

7. If a state legislature or executive sees something amiss in society, it can conduct an investigation with open hearings.

8. If a person is accused of murder and pleads guilty, she is nevertheless given a trial, in case her guilty plea was coerced.

9. If a person dies in odd circumstances, a coroner's inquest will be held. This should deter secret murders.

10. A person may strike someone in self-defense or in defense of another person. At trial they may be acquitted.

11. A defendant may plead "diminished responsibility" if another person coerced her to commit the crime.

12. Legislatures mustn't enact laws that violate basic rights or that offend the national or state constitution.

13. In a civil action, a person who accuses someone of willful harm can ask for punitive damages (triple amount).

14. A governor can grant a pardon to a state convict.

15. Citizens can take to their state licensing boards any complaint about an unethical lawyer, including a judge

16. One can ask a state legislature to impeach a bad judge.

17. Anyone who thwarts the judicial process can be charged with the crime of obstruction of justice. No official has 'immunity' re this crime -- or any crime.

18. A civil action can be brought for abuse of process, if for example financial pressure is used to harm a case, or if a suit is brought for the purpose of harassment.

19. Spoliation: If you destroy records the jury can infer that you had something to hide. Maxim: *Omni praesumuntur contra spoliatorem.* All things are presumed against the one who destroys.

20. Many judicial rulings depend on the common law, where the legislature has not enacted a statute. Federal law is codified at the "USC" -- the United States Code.

Mission Statements of Five Law Schools

Stanford Law School's basic mission [is] dedication to the highest standards of excellence in legal scholarship and to the training of lawyers [to] diligently, imaginatively, and honorably serve their clients and the public; to lead our profession; and **to help solve the problems of our nation and our world.**

The University of Virginia School of Law strives to uphold Thomas Jefferson's conviction that lawyers have a special **obligation to serve the public interest** and is committed to upholding its founder's ideal of public responsibility to nurture the civic virtues that support it: **integrity, civility, and service.**

Boston College Law School. We search for opportunities to instill in our students the **moral** and ethical application of law. Our commitment is to **foster new insights** through research, to impart knowledge and to **critically** evaluate the role of legal institutions. [The book at hand should be a bestseller at BC Law.]

University of Chicago Law School aims to train well-rounded, critical, and **socially conscious thinkers and doers.** The cornerstones that provide the foundation for Chicago's educational mission are the **life of the mind**, participatory learning, interdisciplinary inquiry, and an **education for generalists.** Learning the law at Chicago therefore is a passionate -- even intense – venture.

Northeastern University Law School. Our mission - to fuse theory and practice with ethical and **social justice ideals** so students understand what lawyers do, [and] how they should do it. [We help] reflect critically upon law and its **impact on** individuals, enterprises, and **communities.** We value intellectual inquiry, critical thinking, vigorous exchange and **testing of ideas.** We are devoted to the pursuit of social justice. We believe we have an **obligation to advocate** for individuals and groups who are underrepresented, **less powerful or less economically secure domestically and abroad.** [Emphasis added]

OPINION - We Are in Extreme Trouble

Those mission statements cast a very wrong impression.
No student gets taught such ideals as:

1. Help solve the problems of our nation (Teachers would ask if you've forgotten to take your meds if you said something like that.)

2. Nurture the civic virtue of integrity (Oh come on.)

3. Critically evaluate the role of legal institutions (Has any law school even uttered the term "creeping police state"?)

4. Develop the life of the mind. (Nice idea, but...)

5. Feel an obligation to act for the less economically secure... abroad. (That is a plainly dishonest claim.)

Sorry but law students need to interview their deans and find out why the advertised ideals are not present in the curriculum! I'm not recommending that those mission statements be dumped, but be lived up to. Society needs them.

When you turn the page you will come to the story of Pat Tillman, football star turned soldier. You won't fail to see that the Congressional hearing that discusses his death was *surreal*.

After that, there's a chapter about Bill Windsor, a modern day Lone Ranger. Judges have misused law to punish Bill's for his civic virtue. Bill's time in jail is made particularly difficult by the fact that he has extreme claustrophobia.

Yet none of the incidents to be described can compare with the frightening fact that the public is not reacting. Law professors are "on hold." I searched Google Scholar to see if there has been any criticism of the Marathon bomber case. Wouldn't you know it, some journals have asked whether the Tsarnaev boy should have been read his Miranda's. Nothing about the trial being a total farce.

I think we'd better all go to Chicago Law School and learn to be "socially conscious thinkers and doers" – and pronto.

chapter two

The brothers Tillman, Army Rangers in Afghanistan in 2004.
Pat on left, Kevin on right.

Marie Tillman, Pat's widow

Mary Tillman, mother

2. Investigations and Congress's Hearing on Tillman

If I should die, think only this of me
That there's some corner of a foreign field
That is forever England.

   -- Rupert Brooke, *The Soldier* (1915)

Criminal trials are one way for people to find out what happened; investigations are another. You will be shocked to read, below, how Congress handled the inquiry into the killing of Pat Tillman. This soldier died of two close-together bullet wounds in the forehead that were fired at him at close range in Afghanistan by – wait for it – Americans.

A book by Pat's mother, Mary Tillman, *Boots on the Ground by Dusk,* provides what we need to know. A Humvee (a tank-like truck) had broken down. The leader decided to split the men into two groups (known as 'serials'). One serial was sent into a town to get the Humvee repaired, the other, Pat's serial, went on ahead, with a plan that they would meet up "by dusk."

Pat's group saw fire, and Pat realized it was Americans who were firing on him, so he threw a smoke grenade to indicate he was a "friendly." Yet they continued to shoot. The back of his skull was blown off. One other man died, an Afghan soldier who was working with the US.

It is a pity that the media told a different story. They said Congress asked for an investigation into the fact that during Pat's funeral he was lauded for dying heroically, "but it was really from friendly fire." Much was made of that, and of the fact that he had given up his career as a football star to join the Army "in response to 9-11"

Few people still know of the far more important issue, which his mother spent years uncovering, that the killing of Pat was planned and carried out from on high. Stunning, eh?

On Witnessing the Murder of Pat Tillman

Sworn testimony by Specialist Bryan O'Neal, US Army, to the Committee on Oversight, House of Representatives, 4/24/07:

"We had started to receive fire from a GMV [ground mobility vehicle]. At first, it was short, sporadic.... I looked and saw that it was friendly fire coming toward us. Pat asked me, basically, what was going on....

And it didn't take long before those in the GMV who were stopped at the time, to dismount and open up on us with the 50-caliber machine gun and a 240-Bravo machine gun – and basically shot at us in waves, or bursts of rounds. At that time, I felt myself become limp.

And I got down. I had no cover, and there was nothing blocking my sight watching the people at the Humvee [a tank-like truck] shooting at us. I know Pat ... was able to get himself behind some cover. But it was not much. [We were]...yelling, screaming.

[Pat popped a smoke grenade] to signal the troops down in the GMV that we were friendlies. And after he had done that, the firing ceased in the truck.

So we had both believed at that time that the shooting was over. ...[Soon] they moved into a better position...in the GMV and started shooting at us again.... I could hear Pat calling, 'Stop shooting. I'm Pat f-ing Tillman. Stop shooting.' ...And it abruptly stopped, with him calling for help. And it wasn't too long after that before the truck had moved out."

REPRESENTATIVE WAXMAN: "Did you have any doubt at that time that it was friendly fire that killed Pat Tillman?"

O'NEAL: "No, sir, I am 100 percent positive that was friendly fire. ... When our medic came up to come assist us, he asked what happened, and I tried to let him know."

WAXMAN: "Who is he? Could you identify the name?"

O'NEAL: "That would be Sergeant Anderson. [He] asked me what happened. I tried to let him know, but our squad leader told me basically just don't say anything at that time."

Gossip among the Troops and Brother Kevin

Brother Kevin was in Serial Two on the same mission as Pat. After Pat's burial in California, Kevin returned to Fort Lewis. There, Sergeant Baker told Kevin that it was he, Baker, who had shot, in the chest, an AMF soldier who was standing near Pat and Bryan O'Neal. (AMF's are Afghans working with the US military.)

Later, Colonel Bailey went to the family home and explained that the decision to split the two serials had been made by Lieutenant David Uthlaut. Uthlaut misheard and **thought they said dusk, not dawn.**

Eventually Pat's mother Mary collected all the information we need to realize that the death was not 'friendly fire' (a term that connotes accident). It was deliberate murder. She published it.

The Autopsy Report

Pat's young widow, Marie, and mother Mary received the autopsy report. The gist of it was this: Pat's clothing had been thrown away, but that is against the rules when a solder dies *in situ*. This caused Mary to know that there was foul play. After much quizzing, she learned that the clothes *can* be thrown away if the man is wounded, but does not die in battle.

She noticed that the autopsy report mentioned a mark on his body from where they defibrillated Pat. Thus Mary Tillman cleverly deduced that her son, even though very dead, was defibrillated in order that there would be justification for dumping the clothing!

She figured that the clothing would reveal – and later the doctors confirmed this – that his uniform was studded with green marks, indicative of American bullets. So someone needed to get rid of that incrimination evidence.

Note: in a court, this would be called 'guilty knowledge,' as why defibrillate a man whose head had been blown off? (On the same theme, companion Bryan O'Neal was whisked off to Ranger School so no one could talk to him. Why do that?) We can ask who made those particular decisions!

Interestingly also, mother Mary noted that the signature of the autopsy was dated July 22nd – very odd since Pat died on April 22nd. When she inquired, she was told that the first doctor had been unwilling to sign! Hooray for him!

Summary. Pat Tillman was murdered. Amazingly, Congress massaged the issue in such a way that it was merely the lying about heroism that needed to be addressed, rather than the murder. Even when O'Neal testified (you can see this on Youtube, he's in uniform and speaking clearly to the Congressmen) that Pat was shot by men who stepped out of a GMV tank, *no Congressmen showed any response! They all play dumb!*

As a result of sleuthing for four years, Pat's mother figured out that the damaged Humvee was part of the setup. She also realized that the order should never have been given to have boots on the ground by *dusk*. Rather, the military should follow its normal procedure of quoting the time, e.g., "1800 hours" for 6PM. The word dusk was used deliberately to mess up the traveling arrangement by which the two serials would coordinate. The clincher is a Pentagon document that reveals a conspiracy. On page 213 of her book, Mrs Tillman says this:

> He then told Jones about what happened as it was described to him, but he made one unusual statement in talking about the AMF soldier who accompanied Pat. Here is what he said. I'll underline the statement:
>
> "When they [the AMF soldiers] heard the trail serial make contact, my understanding was that all the AMF soldiers stayed with the vehicles minus one guy. That one guy dismounted and moved with Corporal Tillman. When he positioned himself on the ridgeline, he <u>was to be south</u> of Corporal Tillman."

What did he mean "was to be" south of...?"

The family demanded a hearing. It took place in 2007 and began with O'Neal's testimony. Please read my chastising of Congress:

IN CONGRESS April 24, 2007
(with a fictitious interactive by Mary W Maxwell)

Chairman Henry Waxman: ... We are focused on Corporal Tillman's case because the misinformation was so profound and persisted so long. In seven investigations into this tragedy, not one has found evidence of a conspiracy by the Army to fabricate a hero, to deceive the public or mislead the Tillman family ...

> **MM.** Who needs evidence of a "conspiracy"? It's plain fact.

At our last hearing, Specialist Bryan O'Neal testified. O'Neal was standing next to Corporal Tillman during the fire-fight. He knew immediately that this was a case of friendly fire.

> **MM:** This is horrendous, Chairman Waxman. O'Neal said that men got out of a US Army tank and shot Pat dead. The autopsy showed two bullet holes in the center of Pat's forehead. It was a murder that must have been ordered by the brass. What's with you? Why aren't you investigating it?

Waxman: But Specialist O'Neal told us something else: [that] after he submitted his [first] statement, someone else rewrote it. This unnamed person made significant changes that transformed O'Neal's account into an enemy attack. We still don't know who did that and why he did it. Our focus has been to look up the chain of command, but that has proved to be as confounding as figuring out what happened to Specialist O'Neal's witness statement.

> **MM:** Balderdash! All Congress has to do is subpoena the staff members who saw O'Neal's first report. They need only be told that perjury is a jailable offense. Now watch Rumsfeld and others claim they don't remember.

Waxman: ...What doesn't make sense is that weeks later, in the days before and after the Defense Department announced that Corporal Tillman was actually killed by our own forces, there are no e-mails from any of the 97 White House officials about how he really died. The concealment of Corporal Tillman's fratricide caused millions of Americans to question the integrity of our government, yet no one will tell us where and when the White House learned the truth.

> **MM**: That's *your* job, Waxman!!! You get paid for 'oversight.'

Waxman. General Kensinger refused to appear today. His attorney informed the committee that General Kensinger would not testify voluntarily, and, if issued a subpoena, would seek to evade service.

> **MM.** It will take you less than a day to impeach him. Also, as you know, it is a crime to 'default' when asked to testify at a Congressional investigation. You do know that, right? A crime.

Chairman Waxman: The committee did issue a subpoena to General Kensinger earlier this week, but U.S. Marshals have been unable to locate or serve him.

> **MM**: Has anyone tried looking in Tora Bora?

Chairman Waxman: Fortunately, we do have the other two recipients of the P-4, General Abizaid and General Brown, here this morning.

> **MM**: Tell police to detain them for questioning now.

General Myers: ... When I learned that General McChrystal had initiated an investigation, that was – that was good for me. I know he had worked for me before. I knew his integrity. I said, this is good. We will learn the truth.

> **MM**: When I heard it was McChrystal I went Oh, no!

Mr. Davis Mr. Secretary, thank you for being with us today. How and when did you learn that Corporal Tillman had been killed?

Mr. Rumsfeld: I don't recall precisely how I learned that he was killed. It could have been internally, or ... through the press.

> **MM**: Lying to Congress is a crime, Rummy. See 18 USC 1001.

Mr. Davis of Virginia: Do you remember did you take any action at the time that you learned that he was killed? ...This could be highly publicized and of concern to a lot of people.

Mr. Rumsfeld: The only action I can recall taking was to draft a letter to the family.

> **MM**: Liar! No person at Cabinet level would ever be the drafter of such a letter. There are thousands of bereaved families.

Mr. Davis of Virginia: OK. Before he did so, were you aware that President Bush was going to reference Corporal Tillman in a correspondents' dinner speech on May 1st?

Mr. Rumsfeld: No.

Mr. Burton: I am sorry, Mr. Chairman, I am late. Mr. Secretary, it is nice seeing you again. When you said to Secretary White keep his eye on [Tillman], you meant that he has potential?

Mr. Rumsfeld: I wouldn't know that. I just think here is man who is serving his country, and gave up a good deal to do that.

Mr. Burton: You didn't single him out asking for progress reports or anything like that?

Mr. Rumsfeld: No. Of course not.

> **MM**. Pants on fire at this time.

Mr. Burton: OK. Thank you very much.

Chairman Waxman: Let's see, the next one in line is Mr. Hodes.

> **MM**: Ahem. I ran against Hodes in New Hampshire in 2006.

Mr. Hodes: Thank you, Mr. Chairman. Gentlemen, as I understand it, there have been at least six different investigations into this matter. It appears that each of those investigations had serious flaws. First there was Captain Scott's investigation, completed within 2 weeks of the incident. Second, Colonel Kauzlarich's investigation -- I don't know whether I have butchered his name -- which was finished on May 16, 2004. The DoD IG [Inspector General] concluded that these two investigations were, "tainted by the failure to preserve evidence, a lack of thoroughness, and the failure to pursue investigative leads."

> **MM**: I see. Have they been dismissed from their positions then? Why do we have Inspectors General anyway?

Mr. Hodes: Third was an investigation by General Jones. But the IG was unable to determine who doctored key witness statements....

> **MM**: Why not call Michael Chertoff? Call the KGB! Call somebody!

Mr. Hodes: An Army Criminal Investigation Division... report inexplicably concluded there were no rules of engagement violations, even though there was a friendly fire fatality... Do you all, Gentlemen, agree that it should not take six different investigations, 3 years, congressional investigations, and millions of taxpayer dollars to address the significant failures that have occurred in this case?

> **MM**: Great! The man from New Hampshire is about to nail them for the murder. Hang on! Get ready for it!

Mr. Rumsfeld: Absolutely. **General Myers**: Agree.

General Brown: Yes, sir. **General Abizaid**: Agree.

Mr. Hodes: Secretary Rumsfeld, the approach of ordering a series of military investigations that are limited in scope and that do not address the question of what top officials knew appears to be the Department of Defense's MO when it really doesn't want accountability.

> **MM**: Excellent point! Now he's going to get them for sure...

Mr. Hodes: When the allegations of abuse at Abu Ghraib arose in 2004, the Pentagon took the same approach. First, there was the Taguba investigation, limited to the conduct of the military police at Abu Ghraib .... Third was the Army Inspector General's investigation, which focused on interrogation practices without examining the role of top Pentagon leadership.

Mr. Secretary, do you see the parallels here? Do you see why some would think that in the case of both Abu Ghraib and in the Tillman investigation there were deliberate efforts to avoid accountability? And if you see that, the manner in which this serial kind of narrow investigating, never answering the questions about who at the top knew...

> **MM**: Perfect! This is the moment. This is historic! The tables are about to turn on the wicked imposters at the Pentagon. Go, Hodes!

Mr. Hodes: ...what do you think ought to be done so that the American people can be assured that the top leadership in this country… is accountable?

> **MM**: *Mein Gott!* He dropped the ball. It's a Clay Shaw *déjà vu.*

Mr. Rumsfeld: Congressman, I don't obviously agree with your characterization of the history of this. There was an independent panel that looked at Abu Ghraib….

Mr. Hodes: What should be done about it?

Mr. Rumsfeld: I don't know. I wish I had some brilliant answers.

Mr. Hodes: Thank you. I see my time is up.

> **MM**: Can't the Granite State send somebody better than that?

Mr. Davis of Illinois: So you disagree with General Craddock. Thank you very much.

Mr. Rumsfeld: I can't do that. General Craddock is a terrific officer. I don't know what he said. I don't know the context.

Mr. McHenry: Thank you, Mr. Chairman. I appreciate you all testifying today. …I think we all should highlight… that there was a man involved here. And I say this to my colleagues and I say to all, there was still heroism involved in this incident. …I think that is what this hearing should be about, that valor in the battlefield of putting himself in harm's way, not about pointing fingers after the fact.

> **MM**: So far as I can discern, this hearing is not about valor. No. Nothing valorous is involved here.

Mr. McHenry: I think this has been much covered, that there were screw-ups in the bureaucracy. And I think everyone agrees. I don't think there was a cover-up. I think there was a screw-up, and that has had a lot of coverage.

> **MM**: That's not true. Read Mary Tillman's *Boots on the Ground by Dusk*. There was a massive, complicated cover-up. Who is Represntative McHenry trying to absolve?

Mr. Lynch [presiding]: … And as you may remember, Specialist

O'Neal was with Corporal Tillman on that canyon road near Manah. And Specialist O'Neal went back to Salerno, a couple of days after the firefight, and actually he wrote a witness statement. ... But then something happened. Someone rewrote that statement and the revised version – we had Specialist O'Neal in, and we showed him the statement and we asked, Did you write this part? No, I didn't. Did you write this part? No, I didn't. So folks wanted to honor the memory of Corporal Tillman. And he was a hero; the minute he put on that uniform.

> **MM**: I don't honestly think putting on a uniform can make a person a hero. What about General Myers, for example? He wears a uniform.

Mr. Lynch: [Pat] was an American hero, and nothing changes that. But we owe it to our servicemen to accurately account.

> **MM**: After we murder them.

Mr. Lynch: So I ask you, can anybody here on this panel explain how that happened? Explain to the American people?

Mr. Rumsfeld: I – needless to say, it happened the way you've described it and the way the various investigations have reported it. It happened in the field that somebody took somebody else's words and altered them. I have no idea who did it.

> **MM**: Bailiff, cuff him. Oh! wait, here is Professor Myers now.

General Myers: It would be extremely difficult to divine that. I haven't seen how the words were altered, but it is inappropriate and inexcusable. But I don't know why.

Mr. Lynch: General Abizaid, good to see you again, sir.

> **MM**: I can't believe he just said that. And the Tillmans are sitting right there! Is Mr. Lynch is trying to rub it in to them?

General Abizaid: Sir, it is good to see you as well.... Again, no excuses can be offered, but I can tell you a couple of facts. General McChrystal reported the incident in a forthright and in a timely fashion.

> **MM**: His wife should restrict his privileges for saying that.

Mr. Murphy: ... Thank you very much for being here today. I [went] this year to Iraq and Afghanistan; and frankly, as someone who has never worn the uniform or fired a gun or been shot at, I left there with a deep ... unconditional sense of appreciation for what our men and women are doing there. And I thank you for your role in leading them.

> **MM:** Excuse me, did someone say someone was *leading?*

General Myers: ...No, the matter should have been handled by the Army. And it would not – I mean, I don't think it would have occurred to me to say, Gee – I mean, this was not – unfortunately, not the first fratricide, not the first death.

> **MM:** Now I see why Pat's Dad wrote to the brass as he did.

Chairman Waxman: You have been here a long time. I appreciate your taking the time to be with us. We are obviously trying to find out what went on. That concludes our hearing today, and we stand adjourned.

> **MM.** Chairman, I'll send you a copy of the parchment, OK?

> Note to citizens: you can hold both Generals McChrystal and Myers to account for the murder of Pat Tillman, can you not? It is you who pay their salaries and retirement pensions.

Revolving Door. General Richard Myers is currently on the boards of United Technologies and Northrop and chairs Oneida Financial. He was in charge of America's air defenses on September 11, 2001, and arranged the war in Iraq. He holds the Colin Powell Chair of Leadership, Character and Ethics (you can't make this stuff up). His Medal of Freedom says "for his contribution to our nation's freedom and security."

chapter three

Starring in the movie *Lawless America:*

Bill Windsor

Mona Gudbranson

Diane Booth
with son Vincent

Christopher
Payne

Don Acree

John Lobianco

Katherine
Connor

Lisa Baldwin

Shirley Blome

3. Bill Windsor Is Your Courthouse Ombudsman

Arms and the man I sing, who, forced by fate
And haughty Juno's unrelenting hate,
Expelled and exiled, left the Trojan shore.
Long labors, both by sea and land, he bore;
And in the doubtful war, before he won
The Latin realm and built the destined town,
His banished gods restored to rights divine,
And settled sure succession in his line....

-- Virgil, *The Aeneid* (19 BC), translated by John Dryden

Bill Windsor is an American chap who believes that when there is an urgent problem to be solved, somebody had better get to it.

Many years ago a company called Maid in the Mist sued him over something that he had nothing to do with, so he had to learn how to defend himself in court as a "pro se" litigant, that is, without an attorney. Eventually, he heard from folks who had been out-and-out persecuted by the judicial system. In 2012, he went on tour of 49 states to talk to anyone who had a complaint. The result is his riveting Youtube show, Lawless America.

On February 5th, 2013, Windsor arranged for persons in his videos to meet in a room near the Capitol building. He invited all 535 members of the Legislature, and their staff, to this gathering. NOT ONE showed up. He also had no luck luring the media!

Courts have done their new trick: they've misused the law to punish Windsor. When he stopped uploading videos in 2013 I thought they might have killed him. (Standard office procedure.) I also considered that they may have hypnotized him. (SOP.) In 2014 we learned that he was only in jail, thank God, for "disobeying a court order." His next court date is September 28, 2015, in Missoula, Montana. I hope many citizens show up for him. He's our guy.

Complaints by Seven of Lawless America's Interviewees
These are NOT verbatim quotes, I am paraphrasing:

John Lobianco (NY). My dear Dad is 90 years old. I've been his best friend for years, but am now **prevented from visiting him**. A guardian, appointed by the court as part of a scheme to get Dad's money, is the legal decision-maker and has decided to exclude me. It is unbelievable and heartbreaking.

Diane Booth (HI). In California, I was told that I had to put my son on the medication Ritalin. I refused. To avoid having the state take my son from our home, I escaped with him to Canada and became a refugee, seeking political asylum. **The FBI came up and stole my son.** I haven't seen him in years and cannot locate him. Vincent, if you hear this, please get in touch with Mother.

Shirley Blome (MT). At age 65, I was accused of embezzling $100,000 from a car dealership where I was the accountant. I had all the ledger books to prove my innocence but **was not allowed to show them in court.**

Lisa Baldwin (NC). Our son has Chronic Fatigue Syndrome. He **was kept away from us for 5 months** when doctors accused both myself and my husband of having the psychiatric problem known as Munchausen Syndrome! Luckily, for 7 years I have been audio-taping all our visits to doctors, and can perfectly prove my case about the threats that doctors frequently make.

Christopher Payne (NM). My nephew, wrongly in prison today, was clearly used **as a substitute for the actual murderer** of an old lady.

Katherine Connor (LA). My teen son, accused by a teacher (!) of indecently exposing himself to her, is in prison. **Every legal move I make gets me the run-around.** It is a nightmare.

Don Acree (TN). My elderly Dad, a physician, is kept drugged by his second wife, whom I suspect is CIA. I assume he is on Scopolamine, to make him forget what he knows about her crimes. They **prevent my seeing him in the nursing home.**

Grand Juries

Bill Windsor promotes grand juries, the citizen-initiated kind. Serving in these, in America's early days, was a normal duty of citizens. (The jury that tries a case has 12 members and is called a *petit* jury. This other kind is called *grand* because it has up to 23 members.) Historically, the grand jury was empanelled to serve for two years, and was authorized to look around and see where crime was occurring. Grand juries also had general tasks, like seeing if bridges and roads were in good order. Any citizen could alert that jury about suspected crime, of course.

Once it finds what looks like a crime, a grand jury can interview anyone it chooses. This must be done in secrecy to protect reputations. If it issues an indictment, the state must then try that person. Many states have fiddled with this, putting the attorney general *over* the grand jury! So when citizens get called to serve, they are told that they are 'helpers' to the government. No way, Josephine! If you are called you should stand your ground.

Bill Windsor recommends that you look up the rules in your state to see if citizens are prevented from accessing the members of the grand jury. (See his website for some states' rules). If you can't access your grand jury, you **ask a court to make a declaratory judgment against that unconstitutional practice.**

As emphasized in Maxwell (2011), it is perfectly legal for you to form an *informal* grand jury right now. This should make you be confident about your own "sovereignty." The people of the US *are* the sovereign. Your group can't issue indictments or make offers of immunity, but you can practice how it's done.

How Bill Got in Trouble in Montana

Briefly: years ago Bill was contacted by Crystal Cox who is a Montana "online journalist." She said a man named Sean was harassing her. Bill stood up for her. Then, Bill claims, Sean shot at him on the highway and has admitted, in an email, that he did so. Naturally, Bill then asked for a protective order against Sean. It was not granted. Perhaps Crystal's issue was, from the beginning a trap set for Bill.

From lawlessamerica.com:

"Bill's life has been threatened many times. A University of Montana employee, **Sean Boushie, Boushie**, attempted to murder Bill Windsor. Boushie then falsely claimed that Bill stalked him, threatened him with a gun, and a host of other lies. Corrupt courts gave Sean Boushie a Temporary Order of Protection. It expired on September 16, 2013, but corrupt Montana and Texas folks pretended it still existed, and a bench warrant was issued. Bill Windsor was put into the **Ellis County Texas Jail** illegally for 53 days as a political prisoner -- held for extradition. Then unlawfully held in the Ada County Idaho Jail for 35 days, and then illegally handed over to two Missoula County Montana Sheriff's Deputies on March 25, 2015. He was held there for 46 days (a total of 134 days behind bars). He won bond on May 9, 2015.

The State of Montana has filed five criminal charges against William M. Windsor for sending a Tweet, publishing the name of the would-be killer four times, sending a legal notice email to a University of Montana attorney, and filming the movie and the pilot for a TV show that will expose Montana as the most corrupt state in the country. 'Law enforcement' had website **LawlessAmerica.com** removed from the Internet.

It contains over 1,400 articles exposing corruption. Bill Windsor worked with a friendly offshore hosting company to return the website to the Internet outside. He wasn't so lucky when Facebook removed the movie page falsely claiming it promoted nudity ... or when AT&T canceled the email that he used on everything related to the movie for years falsely claiming he violated their Terms of Service."

Bill, age 66, says he could have been the Granddad of many of the inmates. They called him "School" as is he is old-school. He felt fond of them and helped a few get bail.

Note: Bill can bring a civil action – and no doubt he will – against his tormentors for malicious prosecution, false arrest, and false imprisonment. He still loves the law.

Proposed Legislation, by Bill Windsor
[at LawlessAmerica.com]:

1. All court proceedings shall be recorded, and all parties shall have the right to do their own recording of all proceedings.

3. Judges must address all points raised by all parties in every court decision.

9. "Motion practice" must be minimized. Judges must hold conferences and allow attorneys and *pro se* parties to communicate important issues directly to judges.

10. Judges may not dismiss a case or enter summary judgments when a jury trial has been requested. [Yay!]

18. Campaign contributions are not allowed for funding judicial campaigns.

24. Each county shall have grand juries, and citizens will be able to directly present charges of government misconduct and corruption to a Special Grand Jury.

26. All judicial misconduct complaints will be handled by a Special Grand Jury. The judiciary will cease 'policing' itself.

27. All attorney misconduct complaints will be handled by a Special Grand Jury. The (Bar Association) will cease being the sole means of 'policing' attorneys.

75. **No person may be named a vexatious litigant without a finding by a jury.** (This is brilliant. See Appendix T.)

Note: the above is not yet law.

chapter four

Long line of Japanese-Americans waiting to be interned. Approximately 100,000 were US citizens. Executive Order 9066, which was approved by Congress, called for martial law in some areas of Arizona, California, Oregon, and Washington.

Fred Korematsu who objected to the above, later got Presidential Medal of Freedom from President Bill Clinton in 1998

4. Fraud Upon the Court and Coram Nobis

No Man is wise at all Times, or is without his blind Side.

   -- Desiderius Erasmus, *The Alchymyst* (1497)

All truths wait in all things,
They neither hasten their own delivery nor resist it....
Logic and sermons never convince,
The damp of the night drives deeper into my soul.
(Only what proves itself to every man and woman is so.
Only what nobody denies is so.)

   -- Walt Whitman, *I Celebrate Myself* (1855)

What if there were a magic way to get rid of a bad court ruling? Well, there is. It's called Coram Nobis. It's based on the concept that the court **has a sacred duty to prevent anything fraudulent from hampering its work.** So, if any officers of the court (judges, clerks of court, and attorneys) do something that precludes justice, this can nullify the case! Makes perfect sense when you think of it. The relevant maxim is: *Fraus et lex numquam cohabitant.* Fraud and law do not dwell together.

Hardly anyone knows about this remedy. I would not have learned of it but for Sherman Skolnick's writing on the Net about "fraud upon the court." He was a lay lawyer in Chicago whose sense of social responsibility was magnificent. He personally invented a "Committee To Clean Up the Courts" and had several bad Illinois judges jailed. Who would have thought that possible?

The way to right the wrong doesn't consist of appealing. Rather, you ask the original court to undo what it has done. One should file a Writ of Error Coram Nobis. (The Latin words mean "mistake before us" or "in our presence.") It came to us from English common law. Congress statutorily underwrote it in 1911, in the All Writs Act. You can find the particulars at 28 USC 1651.

In 1944, the **S**upreme **C**ourt **O**f **T**he **U**nited **S**tates (acronym: SCOTUS) explained why fraud upon the court must not be tolerated. This is from the Hazel-Atlas case:

> "Tampering with the administration of justice in the manner indisputedly shown here involves far more than an injury to a single litigant. **It is a wrong against the institutions set up to protect and safeguard the public,** institutions in which fraud cannot complacently be tolerated consistently with the good order of society." [Emphasis added]

Great! Another uplifting remark was made by Justice Joseph Story way back in 1827. Luckily, the Fifth Circuit court cited it in the 1959 Carter O'Neal case:

> "Every court must be presumed to exercise those powers belonging to it, which are necessary for the promotion of public justice; and we do not doubt, that this court possesses the power to reinstate any cause, dismissed by mistake." [Wow]

Naturally the judiciary must refrain from engaging in fraud! Or we'd **be asking government to fill the role of thug,** right?

Current Judicial Behavior Is Pretty Embarrassing

Many courts in the US accept without question the rotten tactics that have been used during preparation of a case. Prosecutors often load the charges, quite awfully, in order to push the accused into accepting a "plea bargain." This cuts out the well-established institution of trial-by-jury! A judge can also mock the spirit of the law by dismissing cases "on a technicality." Her job is to sort out the conflict between two parties. For this, she needs to hear the case and judge its merits.

How To Start a Writ of Error Coram Nobis

The beauty of **coram nobis** is that it is informal, and that it is sent to the original court – no one needs to file an appeal. It's free! As long as you have a sense of the court being an entity greater than the persons who work in it, it will be easy for you to feel that you are doing the court a favor by filing a coram nobis. After all, you are coming to the rescue of the court's integrity. It's akin to filing an *amicus curiae* brief as a "friend of the court."

More Authorities for the Notion of Fraud-Upon-the-Court

In *Bulloch v. United States* (1985), the Tenth Circuit Court said:

> "Fraud upon the court is fraud which is **directed to the judicial machinery itself** and is not fraud between the parties or perjury. ... It is where the court or a member is corrupted... or **where the judge has not performed his judicial function**, thus where the impartial functions of the court have been directly corrupted." [Emphasis added]

In *Kenner v. C.I.R.* (1968), the Seventh Circuit Court said:

> "A decision produced by fraud upon the court is not in essence a decision at all, and never becomes final."

Shock city, eh? You will find more examples on the websites ballew.com and LouFisher.org. Professor Fisher wrote a whole book about an unsuccessful attempt to use coram nobis in the Reynolds case. It involved state secrets, and you know how peeps get glassy-eyed over that. (Note: the tendency to get glassy-eyed is a real problem for law today.)

In appendix K, you will find the Writ of Coram Nobis I sent to a court in Savannah, Georgia. It was rejected on the basis of its having been emailed. Next time I will use a postage stamp.

Korematsu: Mistreatment of Japanese Americans

In 1942, an American-born man, age 23, Fred Korematsu, tried to get past the rule that said 'Japanese' must not wander out of curfew territory on the West coast. He had an American girlfriend of Italian descent, and wanted to be with her. He was caught and jailed. This was done in accordance with Executive Order 9066, written by President Franklin Roosevelt. It ends with these words:

> "I hereby further authorize and direct the Secretary of War and the said Military Commanders to take such other steps as [they] may deem advisable to enforce compliance...." [Oh-oh.]

Of course only a legislature, not a president, can make law. But a wartime Congress obliged, with Public Law 503, making it a crime to disobey a commander. For that crime, Korematsu was arrested, tried, and convicted. Oddly, in 1980, someone wanted to do something about this old case. President Carter created a 'commission' to investigate the wartime practice by which Japanese-Americans had been interned in camps. The commission concluded with a report, entitled "Personal Justice Denied," a typical goody-goody name for such a report.

Earlier, in 1948, the Japanese Americans who had had their homes and businesses appropriated were compensated, per an Act of Congress. This foreshadowed the gift to all to the 9/11 survivors, of an average of $1.8 million each, as explained in Kenneth Feinberg's book, *What Is Life Worth?*

Later, in the 1990's, Congress ended up paying each of the Japanese sufferers $20,000. But first a hurdle had to be cleared. Payment to the kin of Korematsu could be seen to violate the separation of powers -- the judicial branch having said that the internment of Japanese Americans was lawful and was justified. It looks as though a bit of fiddling with the Korematsu decision was needed!

Lo and behold, just when "Personal Justice Denied" was published, in 1983, Peter Irons, a law professor in San Diego, happened to find, in government records, some proof that FDR knew that the West coast residents had been loyal to America! This proved that the original prosecutor in Korematsu had withheld information favorable to the accused. That is a no-no. (Since the 1963 ruling in *Brady v Maryland,* prosecutors must hand over exculpatory data.)

Peter Irons and colleagues then thought of petitioning the court for the very rare writ of coram nobis, to set the judicial case aright. They went to a district court where, lo and behold, the man in charge happened to be Judge Marilyn Patel.

In 1984 she 'set aside' the conviction. Uncharacteristically, the US Attorneys did not put up much of a rebuttal to the claim that our government had defrauded the 1942 court by hiding some data. Judge Patel ruled as follows:

Two factors make the particular stance of this case unusual. The government has neither interposed any specific objection nor put any facts in controversy. Furthermore, this is not a matter which will ultimately be decided by a jury. Where the function of the court is to act as a factfinder or exercise its discretion, more leeway to take judicial notice is justified....

In light of these concerns, the court finds it proper to **take judicial notice** of the purpose of the Commission [the one that wrote Personal Justice Denied]... and substance of its conclusions. Judicial notice of these facts may be used to inform the court's determination of **whether denial of the motion would result in manifest injustice....** [Fabulous!]

The government has also failed to rebut petitioner's showing of timeliness. It appears from the record that much of the evidence upon which petitioner bases his motion was not discovered until recently.... **There is thus no barrier to granting petitioner's motion for coram nobis relief.** [Emphasis added]

Template for Writ of Error Coram Nobis, by Mary Maxwell

To the Such-and-Such Court (must be the court at which the original error was made, not a later appeals court),

Regarding the Case of So-and-So, on _____ date. I humbly petition for a Writ of Error Coram Nobis, based on an error that occurred at trial and which constitutes fraud-upon-the-court.

Precedent: I cite the opinion of US Supreme Court in *Hazel-Atlas Glass Co. v Atwood* (1944). Justice Robert Jackson wrote:

"No fraud is more odious than an attempt to subvert the administration of justice. The court is unanimous in condemning the transaction disclosed by this record.... The resources of the law are ample to undo the wrong and to pursue the wrongdoer .... Remedies are available to purge recreant officers from the tribunals on whom the fraud was practiced. Finally..., to nullify the judgment if the fraud procured it .... Such a proceeding is required by settled federal law...."

(Per 28 USC 1651A, federal courts "may issue all writs necessary or appropriate in aid of their respective jurisdictions and agreeable to the usages and principles of law.")

In the Federal District Court of Northern California, in 1984, Judge Marilyn Patel set aside the 1942 conviction of Fred Korematsu. She did it on the basis that the prosecutor, the federal government, misled the court by not letting the court hear available exculpatory evidence about the wartime loyalty of Japanese-Americans.

In the case to which my petition relates, the Court was misled as follows: (Describe it as briefly as you can)_____.

I respectfully ask the Court to set aside the conviction [or any ruling] that was obtained by such error.

Signed on this _____ day of _____, year_____ , by
_____your name, _____ address.

Witnessed by_____, Justice of the Peace. Date: _____

Was the Patel Ruling Tongue-in-Cheek?

Why, after so many years, invoke the rare device of *coram nobis* for Fred Korematsu? I think the 1984 ruling may have been designed to make it OK for government to impose martial law in future. Judge Patel's closing statement was: **"Thus, the Supreme Court's decision stands as the law of this case and for whatever precedential value it may still have."** Hmm, that could explain why the US Attorneys cooperated by biting their tongue at the hearing – they were told to 'allow.'

If this interpretation be correct, this whole affair is great testament to 'precedent.' It says that someone figured it was *necessary* for a court to speak carefully, in order to end up with a reaffirmation of martial-law's acceptability.

Sky's the Limit for Future Instances of Coram Nobis

Keep in mind that the point is not to ask for a judgment to be overruled, rather to be set aside. No one can overturn a Supreme Court decision – which is a good thing, as finality of cases, known as *stare decisis*, is an important part of our mental security.

The best-known case in which the government lied, and thereby brought about a wrong decision by a jury, was Jim Garrison's trial of Clay Shaw in 1967. There was plenty of evidence to convict Shaw of being a conspirator in JFK's death. Imagine how that would have altered subsequent history. But the CIA denied that Shaw had used an alias of "Bertrand" and so jurors acquitted Shaw. Note, though, that a coram nobis only works if it is the *court* that lies.

Consider this: Wives of wrongly-convicted prisoners could start a Coram Nobis Club to look into fraud-upon-the-court. By the way, isn't it shocking to think that hundreds of thousands of wives in the US today haven't got their man at home – for years and years, perhaps a lifetime – because of prison? The wife is punished as surely as the prisoner!

Go, wives!

chapter five

Abu Ghraib. Newest American weapon: sexual humiliation. There is domestic law against torture, at 18 USC 2340, and there is domestic law against war crimes at 18 USC 2441.

| Samuel Alito | Sonia Sotomayor | Elena Kagan | John Roberts |
| Yale 1975 | Yale 1976 | Harvard 1986 | Harvard 1979 |

The four most recent appointments to the US Supreme Court. The other five are Clarence Thomas, Stephen Breyer, Antonin Scalia, Ruth Bader Ginsberg, and Anthony Kennedy.

Theologian Reinhold Niebuhr, author of Moral Man and Immoral Society (1932)

5. International Law Can Never Be

Nothing contained in the present Charter shall authorize the UN to intervene in matters which are essentially within the domestic jurisdiction of any state. – Article 2 (7)
-- The United Nations Charter (1945)

Three significant books related to international law are: *Moral Man and Immoral Society* (1932) by theologian Reinhold Niebuhr, *Ethics and Authority in International Law* (1996) by Alfred Rubin, and *The Biology of Moral Systems* (1988) by Richard Alexander.

Let's discuss Niebuhr first. Is man a sinner? Well, yes, that's a basic, biological fact. The reason we have the Ten Commandments (Do not hit, lie, steal, rape, etc.) is because we are likely, if not constrained, to hit, lie, steal and rape. The ability to get people to *obey* such commandments is likewise based on our biology. Since the young child craves approval, it is easy to train him to society's ways.

Morality only works within a group. We are not atoms in a huge population; we have communities. **They are the source of reward and punishment** for one's behavior. A stranger in the group is not trusted at first; he's not part of the system. Whole foreign groups just don't count, as we "don't know how they were brought up."

Niebuhr noted that a group does not feel moral constraint in its dealings with others. True, we may need to trade with another nation and may set up a relationship for that. But when there's enmity, we harm others with a viciousness not seen at home.

The title of Niebuhr's book, *Moral Man and Immoral Society,* implies that when you are acting for your nation you can happily take part in sin. You can do terrible things and feel good about it, as you are trying to save your nation. If fellow citizens tell you that you are wrong about this, you'll hate them and think they are being disloyal.

What Rubin Said. Alfred P Rubin, a law professor, at Tufts, came to similar ideas via his study of legal history. He argues persuasively that there has never been an authority for international law. The rule for treaties is Pacta sunt servanda -- compacts should be honored. But if powerful states decides not to keep a promise, how can anyone force them?

In domestic society, a court of law can make you keep your promise (or pay compensation for breaking it) but there is no enforcer, external to a nation. Sure, there are strong nations that can "enforce law" over weak ones. They can even get the weak ones to pay tribute. But if the weak ones make a moral appeal, they will be ignored. I believe the pretense that there is as law among nations is harmful. See my *Morality among Nations* (1990).

What Alexander Said. Richard Alexander, an entomologist at University of Michigan, was the first to see that we evolved with an ingroup-outgroup mentality. Many species are predatory and have other species as their prey. In *H sapiens* it is normal for individuals to prey on their conspecifics. Alexander observes that many of the nicer traits in humans evolved to suit inter-group competition: respect for one's leader, cooperation as a team in battle, and loyalty to one's own side with contempt for the other side. Recall Niebuhr's statement that we can act very selfishly for the nation, much more so than for ourselves!

The Hobbesian Dilemma. Political theorist Thomas Hobbes (1588-1679) noted that each nation has to arm itself, and steal resources, just to stay alive. If we started being nice-guy in a rough world we could get clobbered. Richard Alexander doesn't refer to the Hobbesian dilemma as such, but it fits his theory. I find that peaceniks do not get the point. They think the Hobbesian dilemma can be, and should be, intellectually wished away. But it cannot. It's permanent. I repeat: there IS no international law. It is a (deliberate) deception. The two courts at the Hague, the ICJ and the ICC, are fraudulent.

The ICJ. The International Court of Justice was a carryover from something that was begun at the 1919 Versailles Peace Conference that wrote up the agreements of nations (victors, that is) at the end of World War I. That conference tried to bring about a UN sort of arrangement where all the diplomats could meet – the League of Nations. It remained intact until Japan quit in 1934 over its desire to invade China.

Today the ICJ puts the trappings of a court on what is more realistically seen as the power structure of the world. How do I know? In 1986, Nicaragua went to the ICJ with a case against the United States for laying mines in the harbor at Managua. The court ruled in favor of the weaker state. So what did the stronger state do? It took its baseball bat and went home. That is to say, President Reagan withdrew the US from membership in the ICJ. Nicaragua was able to get 94 Yes votes in the UN General Assembly to urge the US to comply with the decision, involving monetary compensation. Three states voted No: US, Israel, and El Salvador. The matter then went to the UN's executive body, the Security Council. There, the US has veto power, so of course Nicaragua never got paid. So much for the word 'justice' in ICJ.

The ICC. In 1998 many states signed the Rome Statute -- peculiar name for a treaty; only a legislature can make a statute. It provided for an International Criminal Court to come into force on July 1, 2002. As of 2015, there are 123 state parties. Its jurisdiction is over members (the US is not a member). Its subject matter, the only crimes it can adjudicate, are: genocide, war crimes, crimes against humanity. As of 2017 it will also handle the crime of aggression. This court is a farce, as Article 16 of the Rome Statute says that when a member asks ICC to deal with a crime, it first goes to the UNSC. There the five great powers have a veto: US, UK, France, Russia, China.

Consider what happened at the ICTY, the International Criminal Tribunal for the former Yugoslavia. It held Slobodan

Milosevic, the leader of Serbia, as prisoner. When it appeared that he might speak against the great powers, in his defense, he died. Right there in his Hague cell. Suicide, you understand.

Universal Jurisdiction, Pinochet's Extradition

Some crimes are said to be enforceable by any state without regard to the location of the crime or the nationality of the suspect. A few years ago plaintiffs in Belgium threatened to bag Israel's leader Ariel Sharon if he entered Belgium. The government of Belgium then changed the rules, to prevent this.

In 1998 a Spanish magistrate indicted Augusto Pinochet (1915-2006) for torturing Spanish citizens in Chile. Pinochet was visiting London, so a request was made to the UK for extradition. He was detained for over a year while the House of Lords dealt with issues, such as: did Pinochet's holding the title Senator for Life give him the immunity of a sovereign (No); did an amnesty granted in Chile prevent indictment in Spain (No). Home Secretary Jack Straw nevertheless granted Pinochet the right to leave.

I do not disparage the efforts to deal as Spain did; I hope more will try this. Still, a crime that has universal jurisdiction can be tried domestically. See 18 USC 2441 for war crimes. Recently the UK tried soldier David Payne for war crimes probably to keep his case from the ICC of which Britain is a member!

World Government, as in the WTO or the IMF

It's hard to see World Government, as it has no visible headquarters (in the way that the European Union has at Brussels). It's highly secretive, with decisions made by a group of men, such as the Bilderbergers who attend annual meetings.

Their policies can be seen, however, in such products as the World Trade Organization, and the International Monetary Fund. A main goal is to weaken all national governments, such as by prohibiting Congress to pass certain laws! Note: Control of the money means the controllers can decide who will starve.

OPINION – Torture of Prisoners during 'War'

I regret the fact that there is such a thing as "the Geneva Conventions." They give citizens the false impression that there are constraints on behavior in war. The Geneva's are treaties signed in 1925 (and upgraded in 1949), based on the Hague Convention of 1899. It's better to have domestic law such as:

> 18 USC 2340A: (a) Offense -- Whoever outside the United States commits or attempts to commit torture shall be fined under this title or imprisoned not more than 20 years, or both, and IF DEATH RESULTS TO ANY PERSON FROM CONDUCT PROHIBITED BY THIS SUBSECTION, SHALL BE PUNISHED BY DEATH or imprisoned for any term of years or for life.
>
> (b) Jurisdiction -- There is jurisdiction over the activity prohibited in subsection (a) if -- (1) the alleged offender is a national of the United States; or (2) the alleged offender is present in the United States, irrespective of the nationality of the victim or alleged offender. [Emphasis added]

The Executive must supervise. (Constitution Article II, section 3: "He shall take Care that the Laws be faithfully executed.") But if Congress finds the Executive not doing its job, it can knock on the door of the White House and say "Do your job or be impeached, Buddy." In 2002 a DoJ counselor, John Yoo, "allowed" the president to torture al Qaeda men. When legal scholar Doug Cassel asked Yoo: "If the president deems he's got to torture somebody, including by crushing the testicles of the person's child, there is no law that can stop him?" Yoo answered "No treaty." But the law above is in force.

Indeed, it can be used to prosecute John Yoo who invented the 2002 torture memo, and Jay Bybee who signed it. Bybee, a former Eagle Scout and returned Mormon missionary, was then made a judge in the Ninth Circuit (i.e., Appeals) Court. This is completely intolerable. We must make inroads into holdback, the collusion of the executive and the judiciary.

April Glaspie Talks to Saddam about Kuwait. July, 1990

U.S. Ambassador Glaspie -- I have direct instructions from President Bush to improve our relations with Iraq. We have considerable sympathy for your request for higher oil prices, the immediate cause of your confrontation with Kuwait. (pause) As you know, I lived here for years and admire your extra-ordinary efforts to rebuild your country. We know you need funds. We understand that, and our opinion is that you should have the opportunity to rebuild your country. (pause

We can see that you have deployed massive numbers of troops in the south. Normally that would be none of our business, but when this happens in the context of your threats against Kuwait, then it would be reasonable for us to be concerned. For this reason, I have received an instruction to ask you, in the spirit of friendship -- not confrontation -- regarding your intentions: Why are your troops massed so very close to Kuwait's borders?

Saddam -- As you know, for years now I have made every effort to reach a settlement on our dispute with Kuwait. There is to be a meeting in two days; I am prepared to give negotiations only this one more brief chance. (pause) When we (the Iraqis) meet (with the Kuwaitis) and we see there is hope, then nothing will happen. But if we are unable to find a solution, then it will be natural that Iraq will not accept death.

Glaspie -- What solutions would be acceptable?

Saddam -- If we could keep the whole of the Shatt al Arab -- our strategic goal in our [1980-1988] war with Iran -- we will make concessions (to the Kuwaitis). But, if we are forced to choose between keeping half of the Shatt and the whole of Iraq [in Saddam's view, including Kuwait] then we will give up all of the Shatt to defend our claims on Kuwait to keep the whole of Iraq in the shape we wish it to be. (pause)

What is the United States's opinion on this?

Glaspie -- We have no opinion on your Arab-Arab conflicts, such as your dispute with Kuwait. Secretary (of State James) Baker has directed me to emphasize the instruction, first given to Iraq in the 1960s, that the Kuwait issue is not associated with America. (Saddam smiles)

No Nation Can See Its Own Atrocities

In 1990, the Bush Senior administration wanted us to go to war ("Desert Storm") in Iraq, and used many tales of Saddam's horribleness to get people interested. We all ought to be aware by now that atrocity stories are always used, and are believed. So we should stop falling for this. In 1997, a Canadian James Bacque wrote *Other Losses*, telling of terrible things Yanks did to the Germans after the war. The following is from an Amazon review of that book, submitted by jbrennick:

> "One of my WWII-casualty great-uncles on my German side (my father is Irish) had actually died in October 1946, a full year and a half after the end of the war. I was then informed that he had starved to death in a camp in France (after surviving years of hellish war), survived by his wife and child.
>
> So to suddenly stumble across this book was incredibly saddening & maddening, and to see that children suffered similarly long after the war was supposedly over was even worse. But it is true, and "the truth will out." And it is almost unknown. And it shatters the myth that only the "other" side's government is capable of mass murder. And now, I dislike Ike."

In regard to the preceding page's 1990 chat between Glaspie and Saddam, a month later when Saddam's forces actually attacked Kuwait, a British journalist got the tape, She walked up to April Glaspie in Baghdad, and said "You encouraged this aggression -- his invasion. What were you thinking?" Replied Glaspie: "Obviously, I didn't think, and nobody else did, that the Iraqis were going to take all of Kuwait."

That does not hold water. We can gauge from the transcript that the US wanted Saddam to do this so we could send troops over there. Wait for an amazing description, in Chapter 22, of the chicanery of a few members of the British upper class in making World War I happen because they wanted it to happen.

What Is Law, Anyway?

Last night I saw a remarkable video on Youtube (at NewsPoliticsNow11). A young mother was in a courtroom to deal with a simple divorce matter. The male guard told her she had to submit to a drug search (which is nonsense) and took her into a private room. Her modesty prompted her to object. She was then arrested. All of this went on in earshot of a lady judge. Many crimes are committed in the 10 minutes of the video, including that of the judge's obstruction of justice and misprision.

The victim more or less thought she was at fault, as there were armed guards and the venue was a "house of law." I mention this to note that we have an automatic reaction to law: we obey. That is a human instinct that can help our society be peaceful, but of course it means we can be taken advantage of.

Since this book is a veritable paean to law, I had better state that there are different kinds of law. This chapter has already gone to town on international law. As for domestic law, it should be divided at least into two kinds — that which is justifiable per the community's moral outlook, let's call that ordinary law, or, simply, *law*.

The other kind, which is mixed right in with it, is law that is predatory, or intended to keep people down. It's interesting that the English language, which has several words for almost every concept has got only the word "law" for both the helpful kind and the bad kind.

It follows that citizens have to be able to recognize, and have affection and respect for the good kind. Then they have to **be prepared to fight the other kind**. Bad law is just as much a harm-doer as brass knuckles. As a first step in sorting, we might say that the constitution is good law, as the people agreed to it, and it is in accord with oft-stated principles, and it has been fine-tuned by cases.

So whenever a law comes along, violating a constitution, it can be presumed to be unacceptable. Another interesting Youtube video, called "No Thanks" shows some men teaching the law to cops who have been pulling people over for unconstitutional searches. The video has had 4 million hits, thank God. We are generally not good at standing up to the law, so this role-modeling helps.

That proves that there are balances in society. Neuroscientist Antonio Damasio theorizes that cultures have a homeostatic mechanism to catch problems such as oppression. I do not know if he is correct, but with a huge population there will always be some individuals doing the kind of thing these roadside teachers are doing. And there will always be at least a few enlightened leaders who are allowed to make it to middle age. (Many, I think, get "taken out.")

As we saw in the Tillman chapter, there is something very odd going on whereby our representatives cannot do the obviously correct thing. And they would not even send a staff member to Bill Windsor's Washington meeting. But one of the 535, just one, bothered to oppose the president's claim that he had authority -- can you imagine it – to drone US citizens, without benefit of trial.

That is, Senator Rand Paul filibustered for 13 hours (no breaks allowed) to prevent confirmation of the nomination to CIA office of a person who condoned the said dronings.

A resistor

Senator Rand Paul

We are supposed to believe that a 757 jet, Flight AA77, got through this hole into the Pentagon.

Shanksville, P.A. Clearly, no "hijacked plane" landed at this site. See Appendix A regarding the "Let's roll" legend.

PART II. SOME STUNNINGLY BAD COURT CASES

6. The 9-11 Pentagon Case of *Gallop v Cheney*

The 19 savages who took the lives of thousands of Americans on September 11 were able to come here because we welcomed them.... How incredibly sick they must have been that they never, as far as we know, even for a moment, paused to reconsider the despicable, unconscionable and evil acts they planned to inflict on the people.
-- Ted Olson, First Barbara Olson Memorial Lecture (2001)

Know thyself. – Socrates (circa 390 BC)

Here in Part II the spotlight is on some bad court cases. How to make things go right? Part I laid out the beauties of our law, but Part II will show that law is routinely ignored by none other than the judicial branch of government! That's really frightening!

As we will see in the cases of Gallop, Desalvo, Gudbranson, and Ray, the executive branch is actually the criminal. Our reluctance to face up to that is a huge problem.

We think of the court as *neutral,* a referee able to sort out any conflict. It's essential that we make it work that way. Yet some judges 'work for' the White House. People tend to be forgiving about this, as they might forgive a person who practices family loyalty. But that is inappropriate in our system.

The Founding Fathers were well aware that the natural human tendency is for a ruler to grab maximum power. So, using Montesquieu's device of "checks and balances," they designed each of the three branches of government to act as a brake on the power of the other two. On the following page is Article III of the Constitution, of 1787, setting out the judiciary's powers.

> **Article III of the Constitution:**
>
> *Section. 1.* The judicial Power of the United States, shall be vested in one supreme Court, and in such inferior Courts as the Congress may from time to time ordain and establish. The Judges, both of the supreme and inferior Courts, shall hold their Offices during good Behaviour, and shall, at stated Times, receive for their Services, a Compensation, which shall not be diminished during their Continuance in Office.
>
> *Section. 2.* The judicial Power shall extend to all Cases, in Law and Equity, arising under this Constitution, the Laws of the United States, and Treaties made, or which shall be made…,
>
> *Section. 3.* Treason against the United States, shall consist only in levying War against them, or in adhering to their Enemies, giving them Aid and Comfort. No Person shall be convicted of Treason unless on the Testimony of two Witnesses to the same overt Act, or on Confession in open Court. The Congress shall have Power to declare the Punishment of Treason….

Gallop v Cheney – a Valuable Case to Sort Out 9-11

The proper place to sort out the crimes of 9-11 is in the courts. Any of the states that lost a citizen in the attacks can bring a prosecution. Of the many cases filed federally so far, all were 'required' to be handled by Judge Alvin Hellerstein.

Gallop v Cheney was filed by April Gallop against Vice President Richard Cheney, Secretary of Defense Donald Rumsfeld, and General Richard Myers of the US Air Force. Hellerstein assigned the case to Judge Denny Chin who dismissed it.

Gallop was a private in the Army, stationed at the Pentagon. On the famous day, September 11, 2011, she had just returned from maternity leave and brought her son Elisha to enroll him in the Day Care Center there. She was told to go to her desk first and soon the attack occurred. She and the baby were injured, but she says she saw no evidence of a plane having hit the Pentagon.

As you will see on the next two pages, Judge Chin made a mockery of her claim. She appealed; the Second District Court's three judges, one of whom is the cousin of the President George W Bush, upheld Chin's dismissal (see Appendix E).

Excerpt from April Gallop's Lawsuit
Prepared by her attorney William Veale, at Center for 9-11 Justice

[Plaintiff April Gallop] attempted to learn what the proper procedure would be if an attacker were seen in the sky approaching the Pentagon. It would be this:

First, since Cheney knew for 71 minutes that a plane was coming towards Washington, there should have been an alarm sounded within the Pentagon building so employees could run for safety. Indeed such alarms, complete with evacuation of the building, had been so common in the past that employees found them annoying.

Second, the jets that should have been scrambled were capable of going from their hangars to a height of 29,000 feet in three minutes, and were very capable of dealing with an attacker plane. Again, that was common practice: 67 times in the 9 months prior to 9/11, when aircraft went astray in the US, Air Force jets went aloft in response.

The thing that hit the Pentagon cannot have been a Boeing 757 for at least three reasons [she says]: <u>One</u>: the story that a hijacker named Hani Hanjour piloted the plane makes no sense. He was an amateur, and the 330-degree turn maneuver that was required is not only beyond his capability but beyond that of even a skilled pilot. <u>Two</u>: the nose of a Boeing contains radar equipment and therefore its outer shell is porous; it could not have made its way intact through the concrete wall (as Rumsfeld said it did).

<u>Three</u>: Gallop says: "as shown on CNN television, a large military aircraft, identified as an E-4B – the so-called 'Doomsday Plane', which carries the most complete and sophisticated military command and control apparatus – was circling above Washington at the time the Pentagon was hit. It was in a perfect position to coordinate the detonation and/or missile shot."

See Appendix E for dismissal of her appeal.

From Judge Denny Chin's Dismissal of April Gallop's 9/11 Lawsuit. Comments are by Mary W Maxwell:

I. "These affidavits [by theologian David Ray Griffin and physicist Steven Jones] only contain conclusory statements and personal opinions without evidentiary support."

Comment: Books by Griffin and Jones contain meticulous research and much evidence re 9/11.

II. "Plaintiffs concede that their complaint is alleged 'without reference to any binding or even analogous precedent.'"

Comment: How could a person get access to 'precedent' of government officials blowing up buildings?

"Factual allegations contained in the complaint, must be enough to raise a right to relief above the speculative level."

Comment: Ms Gallop is not "speculating" when she tells what is in the official 9/11 Commission report: Secretary of Transportation Norman Mineta stated that a young man in the White House kept coming into the room to tell Cheney how close the plane was getting, and asked if orders NOT to shoot had been changed. Cheney replied in the negative.

III. "Plaintiffs have provided no factual basis to support a meeting of the minds."

Comment: That is, one must show that the conspirators actually agree on things. Everyone knows that Cheney, Rumsfeld, and Myers work together. Is Judge Chin joking?

IV. "Plaintiffs assert that under the doctrine of equitable tolling, the statute [of limitations] was 'extended by additional acts of concealment in furtherance of the conspiracy.' The purpose of the time-bar... is to preclude the resuscitation of stale claims."

Comment: The issue is hardly stale, as the event of 9/11 is called upon constantly to support new legislation and foreign invasions.

Note: The judge called Gallop's claims "delusional and fantastic."

64

In Japan's Parliament Someone Demands the Facts

Mr. Yukihisa Fujita standing in front of microphone:
I would like to ask about the suspicious information being uncovered and the doubts people worldwide are having about the events of 9-11. ...There were more than 80 security cameras at the Pentagon but they have refused to release almost all of the footage.

A block away from the WTC, a building collapsed 7 hours after the WTC buildings were attacked. This is a 47-story building that fell in this manner (He drops and object to demonstrate), in five or six seconds. This building falls like something you would see in a Kabuki show. Also it falls while keeping its shape. Remember it was not hit by a plane.

I would also like to mention the put options. Just before the 911 attacks, i.e., on September 6th, 7th and 8th, there were **put** options put out on the stocks of the two airlines United and American. There were put options on Merrill Lynch, one of the biggest WTC tenants. Somebody had insider information.

Finance Minister Fukushiro Nukaga:
I know there have been reports about the points you raise. So we made it obligatory that people provide ID for securities transactions and for suspicious transactions to be reported and we made it a crime to provide money to terrorist organizations.

Mr. Fujita:
I would like to ask finance specialist Mr. Asao to tell me about put options. Could a few terrorists in Afghanistan and Pakistan carry out such a sophisticated large scale set of transactions?

Keiichiro Asao:
I understand put options are a deal to sell stocks at a fixed price. In this case someone must have had insider information to carry out such transactions because nobody could normally predict these airlines would have their planes hijacked. So, I believe this was certainly a case of insider trading.

Mr. Fujita:
We need to ask who the real victims of this war on terrorism are. I think the citizens of the world are its victims.

Note: In Appendix D see similar harangue in Belgian parliament.

Guilty Knowledge – GK

What is guilty knowledge? *Black's Law Dictionary* says: "This term is used when you know that an unlawful situation exists but you choose to ignore such as accepting goods you know are stolen." Judge Chin's unusual reasons for dismissing the case look to me like **GK**. I'm dragging in a little-used concept here to show how various actions evince guilt. On the previous page, a Japanese parliamentarian raises intelligent questions about 9-11. They are never raised by the US Congress. That's **GK**. Do any law journals analyze the Gallop case? *Nyet*. That's GK.

OPINION -- Introducing the Harrit rule.

While writing this book, I was puzzled how judges could shut their eyes to something as egregious as 9-11. It seemed that they either have a 'denial' problem, or are in bed with the baddies.

Professor Niels Harrit

Then my Gumshoe News editor, Dee McLachlan, reported on a lawsuit in Denmark. A professor of chemistry, Niels Harrit, at University of Copenhagen, had been called a "crackpot" by the media. He had claimed that WTC7 came down by controlled demolition (as anyone, including Blind Freddy, could see that it did). Ordinary law of libel would award the case to Harrit, as he could prove his science to be reasonable. I said "His case will be dismissed and not go to the merits." Why? "Because every judge knows not to discover that 9-11 was an inside job.

A week later, Matt Campbell's worthy case came up, in the UK. I foresaw that, it, too, would not be heard. I told Dee "That'll come under the same rule as Harrit's – no judge may adjudicate the merits of a 9-11 case as it could jeopardize the real killers, namely, our overlords." Soon I found myself using the phrase "the Harrit rule" to mean the way in which most people today turn off their brain rather than allowing the facts to seep in. (I don't mean Professor Harrit practices it; it was practiced on him by the Court.) It looks as if all university faculty are following the Harrit rule. This is pretty tragic since, if the human brain is the main way by which we can get out from under a crisis, and the brain is obeying some weird law, we are stuckaroo.

I recommend that you, as a citizen, try speaking truth to anyone. If it becomes clear you are getting nowhere, just chalk it up as a loss and try someone else, or some other method of communicating. Some folks may be just trying to protect their job, but some really cannot hear you. Please watch the Youtube video of Niels Harrit with BBC interviewer Michal Rubin. Tune in at the 50-minute mark. I don't suppose Rubin is deliberately trying to be difficult; he seems unable to listen to Harrit.

You Can Adjudicate 9-11

We are too timid, thinking if our court system won't work, we're out of luck. Nonsense, law students can easily run a trial of "John Doe," the US government employee who say, operated the remote control for attacking the twin towers.

You can use **circumstantial evidence**. Even in a case where there is paltry evidence, jurors must reach a verdict as best they can. Circumstantial evidence of 9-11 crime includes the FBI's involvement in theexplosions at the WTC in 1993, the Pentagon's failure to evacuate April Gallop's office when she was in danger, and the wording of the Larry Silverstein's insurance policy providing for "two separate terrorist attacks at the WTC." You should give the accused due process and empanel an objective-minded jury. Make a ruling.

What are we waiting for?

chapter seven

Boston police arrest Albert DeSalvo
(Photo from The Boston Strangler by Alan Rogers, PhD)

Boston at the time was undergoing "urban renewal." In 1957 the Boston City Council and Massachusetts Legislature created the Boston Redevelopment Authority, giving it:

"power to buy and sell property, and the power to acquire property through eminent domain, and the power to grant tax concession (under Massachussets General Law chapter 121A) to encourage commercial and residential development."

The Italian neighborhood in the North End gave way to the new Government Center.

7. It's Time To 'Forgive' the Boston Strangler

Disheveled, save his cap, he rode all bare,
Such a glaring eye he had, as a hare.
A Veronica plant he had sewn upon his cap
His wallet lay before him in his lap,
Brimful of pardons coming from Rome.

-- Geoffrey Chaucer, *The Canterbury Tales, Prologue* (1475)

This chapter is about the injustice done to the late Albert DeSalvo and members of his family. Desalvo was definitely not the Boston Strangler. It was not he who killed 13 single ladies in Boston from 1962 to 1964. Who then did the killings? Presumably the authorities. What? Wait till we get to Gudbransen's case and find that authorities in NATO actually admit to these things. So then, I hear you say, they can't be "authorities." Well, I'm glad you think that, but for now it's only a word quibble.

On the frontispiece page, you see me hint that an Italian was chosen to be set up the Strangler in order to give Bostonians a not-so-warm feeling toward that 'ethnicity,' in order that the urban renewal destruction of Italian homes in the North End could continue apace. The idea was not original with me, but I can't recall the source.

That sort of treatment of neighborhoods is now accepted. At a political science meeting in 2005 after Hurricane Katrina, I stated to my audience that Katrina was probably a real estate move, to get housing-for-the-poor out of New Orleans. No academic so much as looked askance when I said that!

Yet I think the purpose for constructing 'serial killer' Albert was the same as with other 'serial killers': take away people's security, sense of community, and trust. I was age 17 at the time in Boston and stopped going out after dark. We all did.

In *Prosecution for Treason* (2011), I argue that all serial killers are 'created.' Media reports of the killer's background are imaginary or exaggerated. Even if he had those traits he had them because they were pumped into him by some mechanism of mind control.

We'll see below the main means by which government was able to get DeSalvo convicted for the killing of several women. You may be surprised to hear that he was not tried for those murders but for another offense having to do with his being "the measurement man." Bostonians such as myself read the details in *The Globe* and fell for it all.

Simply Titillating

What did the measurement man purportedly do? He knocked on doors of single girls and gave them a line about being a talent scout for models. Then he took their measurements, a sort of soft way of having intimate contact. Later he "became addicted to killing women." (Yes, we did believe that!)

As far as I know, no one ever looked into the matter of such weird behavior. Is it really likely that he was able to choose the doors of women who did not have kids at home? Is a man with a sexual drive really able to limit his advances to taking measurements? Wouldn't some of the women have made a phone call to check his credentials?

There was also an incident that happened many years before the Strangler episode and which was used to nail DeSalvo. Let's call this 'the valentine silver dollar incident.' It seems that someone reported a burglary, from her home, of silver dollars. For some reason, red paint had been spilled onto those coins. Ahem, ahem. Later, when the real Albert DeSalvo was (allegedly) buying some Valentine's Day candy for his wife and child, he handed the salesclerk a silver dollar that had red paint on it.

Wouldn't you know it, a cop just happened to be standing in viewing distance! and just happened to know about the previous theft! DeSalvo was thus arrested as a thief. This became part of the background picture used to denigrate him. I picked up on it quickly as I have seen other cases in which a very implausible incident took place in the life of someone later 'patsified.' Think of the suffering such slander causes to the families!

Indeed, another thing that Albert was set up for was child molestation. (But he killed mainly old women – talk about eclectic sexual taste.) As he was leaving Germany, in the US Army, someone accused him of tampering with a 9-year-old girl. Later the charges were dropped, but the media had this data to work with "when needed."

There are many absurdities that would tip off any lawyer. The clincher is that the 'defense' attorney made a deal with the prosecution: he'd get DeSalvo to plead guilty to something other than the murders, but would 'mention' that he killed the women -- to get an insanity plea.

Any law student reading this may like to check old law journals to see if there was any criticism of the extremely unusual offer by the defense lawyer to have the accused confess to murders that were not part of the case. If not, does this mean the usual writers in law journals were too brainwashed to see it, or were too scared to discuss it? Or, God forbid, are part of the gig. I am a believer in the role of institutions. Persons in the law profession really do have responsibilities to society, not just to the clients on their office. (Remember the mission statements?)

Academic Demurral. Today, academics won't criticize the blatantly false Report of the 9-11 Commission. And in whole university departments of Environmental Science there is not even the odd lecture devoted to weather control. (Weather control isn't a woo-woo subject; you can look up commercial ads by companies that sell rainmaking services.)

I will now present a recap of a work by an academic, Alan Rogers, about DeSalvo. Rogers refrains from kicking up a fuss, but gives plenty of between-the-lines hints of his disapproval of the case. Thank you, Professor.

Albert DeSalvo – A Textbook Case

On these two pages I am paraphrasing *The Boston Strangler,* a booklet written by Alan Rogers, PhD, professor of history at Boston College, (who has also researched the anti-vaccination movement!)

1931 Albert is born in Chelsea, MA; father is a violent man.

1943 Albert and a buddy break and enter a house; Albert is sent to Lyman Reform School. [We should look at those schools.]

1948 He enters the army, goes to Germany, joins military police, marries Irmgard there; they come back to Fort Dix.

1958 He steals from a home some silver dollars stained with red nail polish and, on Valentine's Day, buys candy with them. A policeman happens to walk into the shop and notices. Albert is arrested, but charges are dropped.

1958 Just before leaving the Army, Albert is charged with molesting a 9-year old girl; he vigorously denies it.

1958 First baby is born, with deformity. Irmgard goes frigid. [I wonder if they arranged for the baby to be deformed.]

1960 A door-knocker in Connecticut pretends to scout for models, takes their "measurements", and fondles them.

1962 Anna Slesers, the first victim of Strangler, is found by her son who works at Lincoln Labs. Homicide detectives Sherry and Donovan inspect. Two weeks later, Nina Nichols, sister-in-law of the president of the Boston Bar Association, is strangled.

1962 CBS does an expose on police corruption. Thus the Commissioner is replaced. Ex-FBI man Ed McNamara gets the job.

1964 Man attacks woman in her home but does not kill her. When she describes his face, Cambridge cop says "That's Albert DeSalvo." He gets 2-year sentence for breaking and entering. Police notify the region, so the Connecticut con man is now thought to be Albert. Hence, a judge orders DeSalvo to stay at Bridgewater Center for Sexually Dangerous Persons.

1964 A few days later, George Nassar arrives there, suspected of having killed a gas station attendant by firing at close range. He chats with Albert, who tells him he did the 13 murders!

Nassar tells his attorney, 32-yr-old F Lee Bailey (who has just been in the news for defending Sam Sheppard). Bailey, an ex-Marine pilot, offers to become Albert's attorney. (Why?)

1965 Bailey makes a deal with Massachusetts Attorney General Ed Brooke, who is about to run for US Senate. The prosecution of Albert will not deal with the Strangler cases, only with sexual assaults and breaking and entering. Yet, "in order" to win a defense that Albert is insane, Bailey will mention the stranglings! (This, despite the fact that juries usually over-turn expert evidence about a man's insanity.)

1966 Albert enters a plea of Not Guilty to the assault cases.

1966 Bailey advises Albert to make a record of all bad things that go on at Bridgewater. (Why?) This "reform effort" leads to legislation to modernize the buildings at that prison.

1967 *Commonwealth v DeSalvo* begins. Judge Cornelius Moynihan agrees that the defense [!!] can mention DeSalvo's confession to 13 murders. Jury finds: guilty in assault cases.

1967 DeSalvo **escapes from prison**, over a 20-foot wall. Major manhunt enlivens the city. Two days later he is caught, and is transferred to maximum security at Walpole State Prison.

1973 Albert is stabbed to death in his locked cell. Two men are charged with his death but they somehow get off.

Note: Once the media has told us that someone is bad, it becomes hard to defend him. Your friends wonder how you could be sympathetic to such a lowlife. I assume that the media (run as psy-war by Tavistock?) has full knowledge of our human weaknesses. They know we will be unwilling to stand up for an accused.

Update: DNA allegedly shows Albert's involvement with the youngest victim. The book, *A Rose for Mary*, by Casey Sherman, had led to the exhumation of DeSalvos' body. (That book is, I am sure, part of the cover-up. Who has custody of evidence? Whose labs do the tests? The FBI. Don't believe what you hear!)

chapter eight

Morton Prince

Harry Harlow

Grandmothers of the Plaza, de Mayo

Blanche Chavoustie (left) with a friend

8. Amazing Goal: To Break the Mother-Child Bond

You who were darkness warmed my flesh
where out of darkness rose the seed.
All time lay rolled in me, and sense, ...
that nurtures still your crescent cell.

  I wither and you break from me;
yet though you dance in living light
I am the earth, I am the root,
I am the stem that fed the fruit....
    -- Judith Wright, *Woman to Child* (1949)

This chapter concerns the case of a mother whose children were removed by the state; it also looks into the larger matter of entities **that want to mess up the family**. For that we will need some background on what can loosely be called mind control.

Britain's Military Intelligence (MI6) has, for well over a century, been learning how human nature works, and how to control people without their realizing that they are being controlled. A high-tech method is to put an implant in the brain and send instructions to it. Blanche Chavoustie had that done to her.

But there are methods that don't require any equipment at all. You could, for example, take away a person's entire social support leaving him vulnerable. He will become obedient, or at least suggestible. The way to get him into that condition may include trauma, constant change, or pressure from a cult.

In 2010, I joined a private US Truth and Reconciliation Coalition, to help adults who had been mind-controlled as children in the MK-Ultra program in the 1950s. I can tell you that the CIA put our coalition out of business faster than a jack rabbit!

The 'Strategy of Tension' and the Meaning of NATO

In Brussels, Belgium, in the late 1980s, there were several shootings that happened to people in the checkout line of the grocery store and other shops. They mostly occurred in the Brabant district and are called "the Brabant supermarket massacres." Who do you think did it? Basically, the government did it. And what was the purpose? It was to stir people up, to make their daily lives full of tension. Honest. It lasted 3 years.

We know how the Brabant massacres occurred from the fact that they were allowed to continue when the police could surely have used video to catch the killers. Indeed a man of great height, nicknamed the giant, was one of the killers. Surely the police could catch a giant.

In 1949, the United States sponsored a treaty that produced a military alliance called NATO, which will be discussed in a later chapter. Here we are interested in one of NATO's amazing policies called a "strategy of tension."

In 2005, Daniele Ganser, a researcher at the Federal Institute of Technology in Zurich, Switzerland, published *NATO's Secret Armies*. He showed how covert operatives in Europe created false-flag incidents, such as the bombing of the Bologna Railway station that killed 75 people. One motive was to make the left-wing look bad (by attributing the violence to the "Red Brigades"), another was to make everyone expect bombings.

Mona Gudbranson, interviewed by Bill Windsor, 2012:

"My family was completely destroyed. I will never be whole again. All it took was one false call to an 800 number, which rings to a place which calls itself Child Protective Services -- and they are anything but. It was the beginning of the end for my daughter Ingrid Mae Bates and her children Brendan and Naomi and our family. I supported my daughter throughout this witch-hunt; all the endless appointments, meetings, court appearances, doctors, counsellings, groups, on and on, that the court ordered of her.

Whatever was demanded, Ingrid complied, as the clock continued to tick. I encouraged Ingrid to stay strong, everything would work out, she would get her children back, this is America, they will see. The truth will prevail. But in the end it all proved futile. "Why would they do such things?" you ask. Two words: *Federal money.* Title 4 funding. They [Congress] offer the states federal incentive bribes. When the system is set in place that is not a just system, and has no accountability, unlimited power, unconstitutional laws, total immunity, it is a very dangerous system. They created new statutes, committees and court-related jobs, new court-related industries. The more cases, the more grant money generated.

The worst abuse that we had experienced was at the hands of our government. It's a state-sanctioned kidnapping racket, signed with innocent blood. The late beloved two-time Georgia state senator Nancy Schaefer, and her husband Bruce, were silenced for their attempts to expose this corruption.

After five very long and difficult years it took its toll on my daughter they did everything in their power to physically destroy her. We had little or no money to hire a counsel, so we were at the mercy of their attorney pool. Judge William Aims from Courtland, New York's gavel rang out time and time again, case adjourned, case adjourned, case closed.

Sitting in that courtroom, shocked by what we were witnessing, goes way beyond comprehension. Attorney Ingrid Olsen threw her hands way above her head as if she scored the winning touchdown in the super bowl. I was shocked. I said to her, as we were ordered to leave the courtroom, "This is not a laughing matter, this is our family, this is our lives."

They stole everything precious to Ingrid. Days, months, years dragged by, my beloved Ingrid lost all hope. It's been almost seven years since I had to bury my daughter. I am outraged at why it was allowed to take place -- a blatant disregard for families *the very core of our society being destroyed from within.* The day my daughter died, I died.

Let us compare the kidnapping of American children (disguised as Protective fostering) with the 1970s in Argentina. In 2010, Jorge Videla, an ex-dictator, got a life sentence for his role in officially-sanctioned baby-snatching. An article by Marta Gurvich suggests what may have been the real motive for the whole operation:

> Bagnasco began investigating whether the baby-snatching was part of an organized operation and thus a **premeditated crime of state.** According to a report by the Inter-American Commission on Human Rights, the Argentine military viewed the kidnappings as part of a larger counterinsurgency strategy. **"The anguish generated in the rest of the surviving family** because of the absence of the disappeared would develop, after a few years, into a new generation of subversive or potentially subversive elements, thereby not permitting an effective end to the Dirty War," the commission said in describing the army's reasoning.... [Emphasis added] -- Consortium news.com August 19, 1998

Wow! Note the dishonesty of the term "counterinsurgency." The military supposedly had a strategy against insurgents. Yet in the remark about the continuation of the Dirty War, we see that it was considered *desirable* for there to be 'insurgents' (trouble-makers), as this allowed the military to keep chasing after somebody. *That's* what Videla wanted, a never-ending war.

In the US case involving Grandmother Mona, she seems to think the motivation is money. True, there are financial incentives for wrongdoing in this area, but keep in mind the finding about Jorge Videla: The baby-snatching in Argentina was intended to cause "the anguish generated in the rest of the surviving family."

Here in Part II of this book, the task is to examine judicial decisions, but very likely those decisions reflect World Government's desire to keep us destabilized. In 1928, HG Wells, who must have been an insider, wrote *The Open Conspiracy*. He said that our rulers want to put an end to the family, and the monarchy, and the church.

The Political Value of Wrecking the Family
Understandably, the powerful want to prevent members of society from being able to rely on one another. Since a family

is a natural entity, in which mutual reliance and protection is the norm, the family must be attacked.

This is easy to see in an extreme case, such as the way China, under Mao Zedong, demanded that each citizen place the Communist Party above the family. Recently in UK's *Guardian,* a man, Zhang Hongbing, told of his regret that he denounced his mother during Mao's era, which led to her execution. He says they were taught a song "Father and Mother are dear, but Chairman Mao is dearer; Sea and sky are big, but not as big as the Party's kindness." He says that when the Cultural Revolution came along in 1965 "the [old kind] of family affection vanished entirely."

What is a 'cultural revolution' if not the standard way that today's top bosses seek to eliminate any challenge, even if it means wiping out such a biological thing as family loyalty?

That this approach was not peculiar to the Chinese political scene can be seen in the fact that George Orwell wrote about it as standard procedure in his 'novel,' *1984.*

> ...The thing that now suddenly struck Winston was that his mother's death, nearly thirty years ago, had been tragic and sorrowful in a way that was **no longer possible.** Tragedy, he perceived, belonged to the ancient time, to a time when **there was still privacy, love, and friendship**, and when the members of a family stood by one another without needing to know the reason. His mother's memory tore at his heart because somehow, she had sacrificed herself to a conception of loyalty that was private and unalterable. [Emphasis added]

Morton Prince to Allen Dulles and No End in Sight

Allen Dulles was director of the CIA during the 1950s. He was personally involved in finding ways to break the mother-child bond in humans. For example, in 1940, he arranged for the Chavoustie family, his neighbors in Syracuse, New York, to subject their 2-year-old daughter Blanche to the mousetrap experiment. This meant she was to reach for a piece of bacon in a mousetrap, have her finger painfully caught, and go to Mom for help. Mom was instructed to do nothing to help or console the child! (How were they able to persuade Mom to do that? Probably by hypnosis.) The director of this was Morton Prince, founder of the Harvard Psychological Clinic!

Blanche Chavoustie then became a mind-control subject, receiving an implant of a stimo-ceiver from José Delgado. Such a stimo-ceiver, in an animal or human brain, gives the experimenter remote control of behavior. Delgado published dozens of articles openly in medical journals. Australian pediatrician Ross Adey also contributed to this field. Maybe he was was forced into it? Other persons with Delgado implants (but unrelated to the mother-child bond) are Robert Naeslund of Sweden (who has given up complaining) and Janine Jones: see Appendix Q.

A 1988 book by Michael Meiers entitled *Was Jonestown a CIA Experiment?* claims the Jonestown massacre in 1978 was a covert test. 'Reverend' Jim Jones, it is said, put something in the food *to make mothers lose attachment.* The test was to see if these cult members would "suicide" their kids when instructed. Some mothers did obey the instructions. Many did not. Just think: if Meiers' story is true, such a chemical is beknownst to the powerful.

Help! I am looking for Blanche Chavoustie. I traveled with her to Montreal and California in 2011. She hasn't been heard from by relatives and friends since 2012. She was in good health when last seen, age 73. Remember: she is still implanted with a brain remote-control item. If you have heard of her whereabouts please let me know.

OPINION - Noise for Mmes Gudbranson and Chavoustie
Are courts the answer? Well, first there has to be a law. It may come from legislation, or be "common law" – from the build up of jurisprudence, i.e. the decisions of past cases. Mona's judge ruled to take the daughter's children away (the second child was

snatched from the hospital two hours after birth!). Presumably state law required this, if the Mom was accused of harming her child. Still, His Honor could have seen that Ingrid Mae was complying with every governmental request. He should have smelled a rat. I place blame on the judges and believe they are the real blockage point of our troubles. We go to them to sort a problem. They are solemnly obliged to do their job. I'll argue in Chapter 14 that they otherwise commit treason.

Are doctors the answer? Certainly Blanche deserves to have doctors in America remove the brain implant. The fact that they won't touch it or even talk about it makes them, in my opinion, accessories after the fact to this heinous crime. What I am saying is that we have rule of law. When horrible things are happening, we find that a law is being broken. It's not good enough to say "And no one will fix it. Ho hum." Look instead to see if those who hold back on helping out are thereby committing a crime. I also say that the way around blockages is to make noise.

The Madres Made Noise and Estela Is Now Happy

Everyone has heard of the Mothers of the Plaza de Mayo. They held an outdoor vigil for years in Buenos Aires, demanding (futilely) that the government help them find their 'radical' sons and daughters who were arrested by death squads in 1977. Later they heard that 100 or more of their daughters had given birth and the babies were adopted. Estela Carlotto then searched for her grandson and found him recently, at age 38!

Hope springs eternal.

A grandmother of the Plaza de Mayo found her grandson

Balcony of the motel in Memphis. Rev. Martin Luther King, Jr, lies on the floor, shot. Who told these men to point to the shooter?

Left: Jimmy Ray, known to the world as "James Earl Ray, assassin," about to spend three decades in prison.

Right: Jerry Ray, brother of Jimmy, tells us what happened in a recent book: Memoir of Injustice.

9. The Shooting of MLK Was an "Act of State"

"We were saddened by the physical pain and suffering James Earl Ray endured during the last months...[and we feel] deep regret at the tragic failure of the criminal justice system to give him his day in court...There is abundant evidence of a major high level conspiracy in the assassination of my husband...."

-- Coretta Scott King, press release, 1998

Were you aware that James Earl Ray never had a trial re his alleged killing of Martin Luther King? The "physical pain" to which Mrs King refers was caused by Mr Ray being "shanked" in the prison yard. The wounds needed 77 stitches, and the blood transfusion contained Hepatitis C. He died having spent about 30 years locked up for a crime that was actually committed by government operatives.

Think I'm speculating wildly? What if a *jury* determined there was a conspiracy? Would that make you feel OK about believing it? Good. There *was* such a court decision in 1998, after Ray died. But media did not attend the trial and has since hushed it up. Hmm. Why would they do that? Isn't it a great media topic?

Two of James's brother's have written terrific books that I quote below. And William Pepper's *An Act of State*, published in London, is jaw-dropping. Pepper was the lawyer in a much suppressed case, *King v Jowers,* in which Coretta was awarded a payment. The verdict of the jurors, who had heard 70 witnesses was this:

"YES, Loyd Jowers participated in a conspiracy to do harm to Martin Luther King. And YES, others, including governmental agencies were parties to this conspiracy." (p 147)

So there you go. Case closed. It was a civil action brought by the King family against Loyd Jowers, asking damages of $100. The reason for asking a low amount was that Jowers had already come forward in 1993 to confess. No one would listen to him. For years he had asked the government to grant him immunity from prosecution if he'd identify the other participants.

This request was not granted. The real reason is that the executive branch, which is the law enforcer, never allows its covert operatives to be prosecuted. If a citizen sues, the judicial branch steps in and "does the right thing" -- as Chin did in *Gallop*.

From Jerry Ray's Book, *Memoir of Injustice*

Jerry refers to his brother as Jimmy, as that is what he was always called. Jerry says the media used "James Earl Ray" to make him look more fierce. Brother Jerry has done us a service by insisting that "racism" never came into his family's story. Government needed to develop the death of MLK as a black-white problem.

TIME, on January 26, 1976, quoted a book by George McMillan, purportedly interviewing co-prisoners of Jimmy from an earlier incarceration. They alleged:

> "In 1963 and 1964 Martin Luther King was on TV talking defiantly about how black people were going to get their rights .... Ray watched it avidly on the cellblock TV. He boiled when King came on; he began to call him Martin 'Lucifer' King and Martin Luther 'Coon.' ... "Somebody's gotta get him," Ray would say, his face drawn with tension, his fists clenched, "Somebody's gotta get him."

Jerry tracked down the fact that there were no cell-block TVs before 1970! Shame on Time magazine -- today, too.

Jerry reveals that Charlie Stephens, who reported that he saw Jimmy Ray in the motel hallway right after MLK was shot, was trying to qualify for the $100,000.00 award "for information leading to arrest and conviction." When he was deprived of the award, he changed his story. His wife Grace had declared – even when the money was on offer – that Charlie was inebriated and could not get up off the bed, so he couldn't have seen anyone in the hallway. Tamara Carter writes, in *Memoir of Injustice* (2010): "Grace was then taken to John Gaston Hospital's psychiatric ward. On July 31, 1968, Judge Harry Pierotti … had her committed…. She remained a ward for about ten years."

Jerry also reveals that Ray's first lawyer "who probably worked for the prosecution"-- as often happens -- coerced him into making a guilty plea "to avoid the death sentence." Days later, Jimmy wrote to Judge Preston Battle asking for a trial. The **judge was then found dead** at his desk.

Jerry speaks with sorrow of his brother, John, who was accused of bank robbery. There was no evidence for it, except the testimony of an FBI snitch named Catman. (This suggests it was the FBI that robbed the bank, surely a common occurrence).

From Pepper's *An Act of State: The Execution of MLK*

William Pepper served as lawyer for the plaintiff, Coretta Scott King. He spent decades gathering the pieces of how the government "executed" Martin. An informer, Jack Terrell, told him that a death squad was sent to Memphis to kill King. It had made three earlier forays to get King, but those were cancelled. Pepper identifies the group as an Alpha 184 unit of the American army. On April 4, they again got called off.

They were only a backup plan if Liberto couldn't do it. But Liberto did do it. He had his men, including Jowers, hide in the bushes and wait to shoot King when he came out on the balcony

So who is Frank Liberto? A crime boss. Why wasn't he arrested? Because he helps the FBI. Please read that sentence ten times.

From *Truth at Last*, by John Ray and Lyndon Barsten

You had better have your smelling salts handy. This is the story by John, one of the four brothers (none of whom got married). His book is wonderfully organized by Lyndon Barsten. In 1971, John went to prison for a trumped-up bank robbery.

> "Not only was the trial fixed but the jury room was also bugged – pretty typical of the feds. I know this because the federal marshals saw another judge, a former FBI employee, dancing and celebrating because he had information from electronic surveillance of the jury room that it was not going well for me.... Goldstein the actual bank robber got 13 years while I got 18 years. Goldie's sentence would later be overturned, just as the feds had promised him" (page 149).

I deduce that John's incarceration was meant to keep him away from helping Jimmy, post-1968. Also their brother Frank had been killed in a car crash in 1963. The Ray's were a strong family, and we can't have that, can we?

John tells us that Jimmy's first arrest occurred at age 21 a few months after he got out of the Army. Jimmy said "The army put me on the road to ruin." They had used **mind control** on Jimmy and told him to hurt a fellow soldier named Washington. That man became disabled for life and the Ray brothers tried for years to find him – they finally did – to tell him it what really happened.

Here's how the Justice Department massages the story:

> In March 1969, Ray pled guilty to murdering Dr. King.... he was sentenced to 99 years. Three days after pleading guilty, and for the next 30 years until his death in April 1998, Ray repeatedly attempted to withdraw his plea and obtain a trial. [No mention of the judge's death.] Ray continually filed motions and lawsuits in both state and federal court. [Vexatious?] ... In 1994, Ray filed the last of his several state petitions. The petition was still pending in April 1998, when Ray died in prison. [Wouldn't you know it.] Ray persistently maintained that Raoul orchestrated the assassination plot, framing him. He

nonetheless failed to provide a coherent, consistent description of his own activities with Raoul. [To protect John and Jerry?] Most recently, after Ray's death in 1998, King family members filed a civil complaint charging Loyd Jowers with participating in a conspiracy... with allegations of a government-directed plot involving African American ministers [shock city] closely associated with Dr. King.

Others besides Jowers have accused Liberto of having Mafia connections. Whitlock claims that Liberto disclosed he was acquainted with Carlos Marcello, when the two were children in New Orleans. McFerren alleges that the backroom in Liberto's produce market was used as a Mafia meeting place. [Could be a coincidence]. The HSCA investigated the possibility of Liberto's involvement with organized crime.... neither the FBI nor the New Orleans Police had any record of such involvement. [Surprise!] The HSCA extensively examined each specific claim and found nothing to evidence a conspiracy involving the police. [Ditto!] Our investigation [eagerly] considered the allegations anew. We learned nothing to contradict the HSCA's findings and instead discovered additional evidence supporting them.

The DoJ is unwilling to prosecute even when the acts call for it. I name this AGHB – attorney general holdback. Let me quote again from the book by John Ray and Lyndon Barsten:

"I have no specific information about the CIA, James's handlers, military intelligence, or the FBI. I'll just lump them together and call them the feds. This is also the term my brother James used, because I don't think he knew who he was dealing with most of the time.... The feds were behind James' lawyer Hanes. They are all connected. Most of them are moved into positions like US Attorneys, state's attorney, or other positions of power" (2008: 81).

chapter ten

Martina Correia, supported by nuns in Dublin

Throughout Europe, protests against Troy's execution

10. We Were Troy Davis; We Still Are Troy Davis

Oh well for the fisherman's boy
That he shouts with his sister at play
Oh well for the sailor lad
That he sings in his boat on the bay...

Break, break, break,
At the foot of thy crags, O Sea!
But the tender grace of a day that is dead
Will never come back to me.

   -- Alfred Lord Tennyson, *Break, Break, Break* (1835)

Long story short, a man in Georgia, Troy Davis, was framed at age 20 for a murder. Of the nine "eyewitnesses" – and I use the term loosely -- whose testimony was the only basis for Troy's 1991 conviction, seven later said they had been coerced by police. (How would *you* stand up against police?)

There was no weapon, no motive, etc. So after the recantations there was no case left. That is, unless SCOTUS could think of a way to nevertheless send Troy to the cemetery. This they did, using a creative approach to the English language (see the chapter below on Judicial Treason). In 2011, the year Troy was executed, there had been a final "No" from the US Supreme Court.

Its ruling appears over the signature of a federal district judge in Georgia, William T. Moore, Jr. The Great Nine had tasked him, in effect, with answering the question: Would the jury have voted differently if they knew the witnesses lied?

Please read what the recanters say in the next page. They are to be thanked for their decency. It's good to be reminded that some folks will stand up for what's right. Goodonya, kind souls.

Recantations by Six 'Eyewitnesses' Whose Original 1991 Testimony Had Been Used To Convict Troy Davis

1. Antoine Williams: They asked me to describe the shooter and what he looked like and what he was wearing. I kept telling them that I didn't know. It was dark, my windows were tinted, and I was scared. .... After the officers talked to me, they gave me a statement and told me to sign it. I signed it. I did not read it because I cannot read.

2. Kevin McQueen: The truth is that Troy never confessed to me... I made up the confession from information I had heard on TV.

3. Jeffrey Sapp: I got tired of them harassing me, and they made it clear that the only way they would leave me alone is if I told them what they wanted to hear. I told them that Troy told me he did it, but it wasn't true. ....I didn't want to have any more problems with the cops, so I testified against Troy.

4. Darrell Collins: After a couple of hours of the detectives yelling at me and threatening me, I finally broke down and told them what they wanted to hear. They would tell me things that they said had happened and I would repeat whatever they said. ... the police had me so messed up that I felt that's all I could do or else I would go to jail.

5. Dorothy Ferrell: From the way the officer was talking, he gave me the impression that I should say that Troy Davis was the one who shot the officer like the other witness had .... I also felt like I had to cooperate with the officer because of my being on parole.... The truth was that I didn't see who shot [MacPhail].

6. Larry Young: I couldn't honestly remember what anyone looked like or what different people were wearing. Plus, I had been drinking that day, so I just couldn't tell who did what. The cops didn't want to hear that and kept pressing me to give them answers. They made it clear that we weren't leaving until I told them what they wanted to hear ....

Did Dorothy Ferrell See a Smirky Smile?

Troy Davis was probably set up from Day One. The fact that Judge Moore came out with such a piece of nonsense as the March 25, 2011 ruling (see appendix L), tells us that there is a great vested interest in this case. The purpose of the whole affair has been 'shock and awe.' Executing an innocent prisoner, and thereby giving all Americans 'learned helplessness,' was the goal. Giving African-Americans a jolt (as usual) to make them feel bad, was also a goal. -- That's my theory. And I'll bet Moore is not the real author of the ruling.

Within a day or two of Troy's 'crime,' the police got a lady named Dorothy Ferrell to say that she not only saw Troy shoot Mark MacPhail, but that he gave a 'smirky smile' while doing so. This sort of human-nature data on the accused is read by millions as evidence of his character – as if he were the type who was pleased to have killed someone.

Many of our famous killers, especially assassins, are said to have had revenge as their motive. Thus we often hear the terms 'disgruntled employee' or 'jilted lover.' It's an established idea in pop psychology that humans respond to being treated badly by an employer, or being rejected by a lover, by wanting to harm to that person. In reality it is very rare for the disgruntled and the jilted to act on their feelings by killing someone, but our ability to relate to their hurt makes us fall for this line of reasoning.

Proof that Dorothy's original testimony was nonsense, is as follows: In 2011, a few weeks before the execution of the wrongly- convicted Davis, Jen Marlowe, a video maker who uses the name 'Donkeysaddle,' asked Troy's sister, Martina Correia, to help her make a video re-enactment of the 1989 scene.

Please review the three photos on the next page. They show the famous Burger King parking lot where the fatal shooting of Mark MacPhail took place. The witness Dorothy Ferrell was across the street when it happened. Donkeysaddle stands where Ms Ferrell stood, on the balcony of a hotel across the street, holding the camera.

The Video by Jen Marlowe (a.k.a. 'Donkeysaddle')

In Photo #1, Martina stands in the action spot, so we can see how far away Ferrell's viewing stand really was. We can only make out that Martina is medium height, dark-skinned, and wearing a pale jacket over jeans. The camera is using 'zoom' lens.

Now look at the Photo #2. Donkeysaddle has switched to 'medium zoom.' The model, Martina, can no longer be identified by race or by gender. At most, you could say that the person is wearing a hip-length jacket. It is impossible to see a smirky smile, or any facial expression.

But now for the *pièce de résistance:* Photo #3, with the camera using 'no zoom.' I have reasonably good eyesight, and cannot see a person there at all. Can you? Maybe if there was good lighting that night (it was after midnight), Dorothy Ferrell could have seen that there were people there. If Troy were running, as the prosecution claims, Dorothy may have been able have observed that fact. But no way in the world could a witness on the balcony where she stood discern a "smirky smile."

The person who arranged for Ferrell to lie (as she now claims) can be charged with the crime of "OOJ" - obstruction of justice.

It is very important that we see to this. Furthermore, Ferrell and the others, need, and deserve, our protection, and our thanks.

Note: We are by no means impotent when it comes to giving protection to Dorothy Ferrell. **Everybody knows how to band together against bullies.**

Facts in Troy's Trial (These are not disputed by either side):
-- Troy Anthony Davis was born October 9, 1968, in Savannah, Georgia. At age 20, he attended a party in the Cloverdale district of Savannah, on August 19, 1989. Shortly after Troy exited the Cloverdale party, a young man named Michael Cooper was shot in the face on a nearby street. Michael, the victim of the Cloverdale shooting, has testified that it was NOT Troy Davis who shot him.
-- Later the same night, when Troy Davis was in the parking lot of Burger King, a security guard, Mark MacPhail, was shot to death. Nine people testified that they saw Troy do it. Later, seven of the nine recanted their witness statements.
-- One of the non-recanters is Sylvester Coles, who owns a gun but says he put it in someone's care, an hour before the shooting. Fancy that! Several people have testified that Sylvester was the shooter, including his own cousin. Yet in spite of that testimony, police **have never treated Sylvester as a suspect** in the case, or even called him in to give a statement. Talk about malfeasance!

The Sororal Treasure Trove
Martina told me several interesting things:

1. Back in 1991, the Davis family was prevented from attending Troy's week-long trial. Martina took this as a sign that somebody did not want the judge or jury to see that the accused had a supportive family. (Outrageous!)

2. Troy's defense team tried to call Sylvester Coles as a witness. They sat outside his house for three days and went to his workplace, but were turned away. Martina says Troy's lawyers asked the judge for help but he refused. This is extremely important because of Judge Moore' words:

"Mr. Davis has made clear that he knew both Mr. Coles's work and home address. Had Mr. Davis at any time sought the help of this Court to subpoena Mr. Coles prior to the conclusion of the hearing, the Court would have ordered the United States Marshall Service to serve Mr. Coles. Mr. Davis never made such a request, instead choosing to attempt self-service at the eleventh hour. His half-hearted efforts belie his true intentions: to be able to say that he "attempted" to provide Mr. Coles testimony when, in fact, he never intended to do so." [How was Judge Moore able to know Troy's intentions?]

3. Mark MacPhail, (day job: Savannah policeman) was a private security guard at Burger King. He was wearing a bullet-proof vest! Thus, it seems, that the wound he received in his chest could only have been inflicted if the shooter inserted the gun near the armpit. That is hardly something an assailant could have done while running away, as Troy is said to have done.

4. "Pressure against an acquittal for Troy is constantly coming from the Police Benevolent Association" (Martina's words). One can only guess who is pressuring *them*. By the way, the media invariably referred to the victim as 'Officer MacPhail.' This tends to categorize MacPhail's killer as a cop killer. But why say this? The night he was murdered, MacPhail was not on duty as a cop. He was just a 'guy.'

5. Police did not search Troy's house, at any time, for evidence of guns. Also, it was said that the Cloverdale shooter of Michael Cooper was wearing a 'batman' shirt. It would have been simple to find out if Troy owned such a shirt (But why bother to find out? They already knew the shooter was someone other than Troy.)

6. The police staged a 'capture' of Troy, back at the beginning of the case. At his arraignment, says Martina, loads of cops were filmed outside the courthouse "giving high fives." Note: In doing that, media people commit obstruction of justice, which makes a fair trial impossible – and is a crime. Consider: if the capture event were 'scripted,' the men running the camera would have to have known it was scripted, in order to do their job effectively.

7. Martina said that Troy did indeed run away to Atlanta, from Savannah, when he heard the police were looking for him. His pastor then went to Atlanta to escort Troy back to Savannah where he turned himself in to the police. You can hear the pastor recount this on Youtube. Martina also recalled that her mother had testified, at the original trial, to the fact that for the first 24 hours or so before Troy learned he was a suspect, he stayed at home, not showing any signs of nervousness.

Bits from Judge William Moore's Scandalous 2011 Ruling

- Moore refers to "live, credible testimony" from police and prosecutor, as though it were of the same type as disinterested testimony. This is unheard of. Believe me it's customary for judges to factor-in the **temptation of cops to lie.**

- Moore never says that in the document he is reviewing, some recanters mention being "threatened with guns." And he is silent as to the legal risks taken by recanters. They can be prosecuted for past perjury – **this upgrades the value of their recantations.**

- He misrepresents the defense's effort to subpoena Sylvester Coles, and **fails to say** that some identify Coles as the killer.

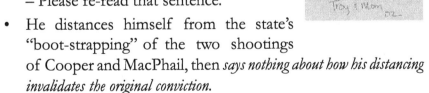
Troy & Mom 02

- Finding no other way to make the police coercion go away he discredits it: "Police would have coerced better than that."[!!!] – Please re-read that sentence.

- He distances himself from the state's "boot-strapping" of the two shootings of Cooper and MacPhail, then *says nothing about how his distancing invalidates the original conviction.*

A Note on Racism. Drives me crazy when I hear this was a race case. Why focus on color? When there is judicial malfeasance, that is the issue, not "who hates whom." The US *has* gone to great lengths to persecute minorities (blacks always, and Muslims lately). But that is a separate complaint. Don't be distracted!

Deaths in the Family

Kimberly Davis lost three members of her family in a nine-month period. Her brother Troy went to God on September 21, 2011. Her Mom had died in April, at age 65. Sister Martina held out till December 1st.

Virgina Davis,
Troy's Mother

Before Troy's execution there was massive community feeling. About *2/3 of a million* people signed a petition for clemency. Recall that the Pardon Board not only had the option of releasing Troy, but of taking a much smaller step, by commuting his sentence to "life."

Monday – September 19, 2011 -- was the day for the Board to meet, at 7 pm, and announce their decision. It caused us to assume that the cliffhanger aspect was being built in to make the "acquittal" more exciting. On three previous occasions Troy had been given last minute stays of execution. But on the Monday night, the Board announced "No pardon." The five members looked pretty distressed at that point. Let's give them credit for that!

On Wednesday, Troy's family and friends set off from Savannah to Jackson, to be with him. Starting at 3pm that day, he had to break away from them all, and go to do whatever one is supposed to do before death. (A man in perfect health and vigor -- can you imagine! Could anything be more macabre? And this in America!) The family was expected to sit in an uncomfortable room all the way till 7pm. Then an announcement was made that the United States Supreme Court was giving the matter one more look.

Everybody was elated! But was this a fake move on SCOTUS' part? Anniliese MacPhail (the mother of "Troy's victim") told a reporter, live on TV, that she had been informed: "Yes there will be a delay tonight, but not a cancellation. The execution will go through." Ahem. Who actually told her that? When Justice Clarence Thomas's decision arrived it simply said "Denied." The murder of Troy then took place at 10.53pm.

MacPhails. The MacPhail family was used all along. Their very existence set up an apparently relevant 'angle' to the case for journalists to chat about, as a distraction. Nonsense, In America, the defendant is answerable to the public, not to a victim's family. It was annoying that the media suddenly started referring to MacPhail's widow by her new surname. Until then, we were always given the impression that she hadn't re-married. Even a day before, she was called Joan MacPhail. Now she was Joan Something-Else. That was the no doubt media's way of rubbing it in. Joke's on us.

When Troy was about to die, the MacPhail family was seated behind the window to watch, and amazingly – as was reported by a UK journalist in the room – Troy struggled from his supine position to lift his head and speak directly to them! His words:

> "I'd like to address the MacPhail family. Let you know, despite the situation you are in, I'm not the one who personally killed your son, your father, your brother. I am innocent. The incident that happened that night is not my fault. I did not have a gun. All I can ask... is that you look deeper into this case so that you really can finally see the truth."

Farewell to the Lovely, Valiant, Lots-of-Fun Martina

Some people prove the possibility of 'higher humanity' just by the way they carry on their daily lives, or the way they go about a special mission. Martina seemed to do both. How terrible for her son Antone Davis-Correia and her sister Kimberly to have lost Martina 70 days after Troy died, all while they were still mourning the death of Virginia, their Grandmother/Mother.

Of course, the Pardon Board knew that Martina had late-stage breast cancer, and that the family was therefore going to be reduced -- this was yet another grounds on which they, or the Governor, should have shown mercy.

How Were the Pardon Board Members Controlled?

The Georgia Pardon Board, 2008

As everyone knows, President Bill Clinton pardoned major drug dealer Marc Rich -- and later had the colossal gall to say that he regretted pardoning him! In 1992, President George Bush pardoned Defense Secretary Caspar Weinberger before Weinberger was even tried – lest a trial reveal the Bush family's crimes. For Troy Davis, it was asking too much for the Georgia Board of Pardons and Parole to respond to massive community urging that they either free him or lower his sentence to "life."

What's going on here? There are five members of the pardon board. That entity came about by an amendment to Georgia's state constitution in 1943. The pay is $100K per year with a guaranteed 7-year tenure. At the crucial time, 2011, the five pardoners included Robert Keller, Gale Buckner, and James Donald, chairman. Donald's website says: "his passion led to more faith-based programming and services." (One might worry about the "programming.")

Two-thirds of a million citizens signed petitions, and 3,000 clergymen did, too. A past governor of Georgia, President Jimmy Carter, spoke up for Troy, as did leaders in the European Parliament. The National Association of Criminal Defense Lawyers made a resolution to ask for clemency for Troy, noting that "the death penalty is a permanent solution and mistakes cannot be undone." They specifically stated that there was another suspect in the case (Sylvester Coles).

In other words, the Pardon Board must have been acting in bad faith. Way back in 2008, when Gale Buckner was chairman, there was an execution date set and a chance for a pardon. At that time Martina blogged:

> "I want to first tell you that something strange has taken place with the Parole Board. As we went in, the Chairperson, Gale Buckner, said they had a lot of information to review and a decision would not be made on Friday. The lawyers presented the additional witnesses who told accounts of police detectives threatening them with guns and the DA **threatening them with perjury if they changed their testimonies** against Troy. Most of these people were teenagers; one guy who testified was 15 years old at the time and admitted that he and his friends were the ones involved in a shooting earlier that night [the one at Cloverdale] and they threw shell casings near the scene that of course did not have Troy's prints on them." [Emphasis added]

Martina listed some other breaches by police, and said:

> "We were so very confident when we left the room. It was 'no way Troy's sentence should not have been commuted.' Then, less than 30 minutes after the DA's side left, the Parole Board held a press conference and denied a pardon for Troy."

OK, Ms Buckner, what happened? Why did you do that? Gale Buckner has a background in Georgia's "FBI" and was a police sergeant. Let us ask: Does it suit the people of Georgia that their Pardon Board consists entirely of persons who have a background in law enforcement? Persons such as Troy have already had the full force of police, courts, and district attorneys arrayed against them. Isn't their need now to see ordinary folks, like you and me, making a humane evaluation of their plea? Wouldn't any sane person in California have spared Tookie Williams from execution? Governor Schwarzenegger said No.

Board member Robert Keller had led, for many years, the Prosecutor's Attorneys Council in Georgia. Without knowing a thing about him, could you guess that he would feel red- faced in front of his colleagues if he intimated "Hey, this chap from Savannah was prosecuted by a villain"?

When he was appointed Pardoner, an official website noted, "Although Keller's absence from Prosecutor's Attorneys Council will be deeply felt throughout the prosecutorial community, he assures us that he will be 'only a phone call away.'" Oh my.

Gale Buckner was – properly – free to turn down Troy's request for a pardon. If she is going to accept a high salary for working on that board, she should make hard decisions, including ones that are painful to announce. But as described above, she walked into the hearing room forearmed with the decision. There was no time in which she could have applied her free mind to the task of analyzing Troy's request for a pardon, incorporating the stuff that was presented that day, such as: "The police went to the home of Mr. and Mrs. Davis and grabbed a photo of their son. Police then showed it to 'witnesses' for identification."

She, being a policeperson, would know that the required method is to have witnesses pick Troy out in a police line-up! It is important to understand that the pardoners were working for higher-ups. Not that this excuses them!

Note: one year after Troy's death, Gale became a judge.

National Trauma. Back in 1963, we, as a nation, saw President Kennedy killed in a well-viewed setting, and that traumatized us. But we had not been told to get ready for his assassination. Re Troy's death, the authorities said "Just watch, Everybody, we really are going to do it.

Years ago, Troy said "They really are going to kill me. But please don't forget me when I'm gone." Let's take his request seriously! Let's invoke the material-witness law and arrest anyone who is likely to escape with information about the crime of the murder of Troy Davis. (This law is at 18 USC 3144.) You can see on the face of it that the ruling by Judge William Moore was very improper. It appears in Appendix L.

The Ease of Disbarment. Here is a case taken straight off the Internet (I changed the name). Licences are, of course, public:

These disciplinary matters are before the Court on the Notices of Discipline filed by the State Bar. As Patrick Bodkin failed to file a Notice of Rejection, he is in default, has waived his right to hearing, and is subject to such discipline and further proceedings. Rule 4-208.1b

The facts show that a client retained Bodkin to represent him in post-trial motions and an appeal in a criminal case. In April 2011 Bodkin filed a motion for new trial on his client's behalf in which he stated that he would submit a supplemental motion and brief after he reviewed the trial transcripts. Over several months, the client paid Bodkin $2,500 to pursue the motion for new trial. After filing [it] however, he did nothing else in the client's case. ... [Another] client retained Bodkin to represent him in efforts to obtain money owed to the client by another individual in a lawsuit The client paid a fee of $500. The trial was conducted in March 2011 and the court entered a judgment in favor of the client Thereafter, the client paid Bodkin a $300 retainer to represent him against another party who owed him.

The client contacted Bodkin a few months later and Bodkin told him everything was going well, but thereafter Bodkin stopped taking or responding to his client's calls, his telephone number was disconnected and his office was closed.

Bodkin failed to take any action to collect the amount of the judgment awarded in the first case or return the documents with the information necessary to locate the judgment debtor, and failed to take any action in the second case, or refund the retainer paid by the client. ...Bodkin did not respond to the Notice of Investigation. We have reviewed the record and agree that disbarment is the appropriate sanction.

Therefore, it hereby is ordered that the name of Patrick Bodkin be removed from the rolls of persons authorized to practice law in the State of Georgia. Disbarred. All the Justices concur.

-- March 4, 2013. Supreme Court of Georgia.

chapter eleven

The Garden of Eden (Jacob Savery, 1600)

And God said, "Let the water teem with living creatures, and let birds fly above the earth across the vault of the sky." And God saw that it was good. And there was evening, and there was morning—the fifth day.   -- Genesis 1: 20,23

And the Lord God said, "Behold, the man is become as one of us, to know good and evil: and now, lest he put forth his hand, and take also of the tree of life, and eat, and live for ever." -- Genesis 3:23

PART III. WHAT LAW CAN AND CANNOT DO

11. Values Must Form the Basis of Law

The World is too much with us; late and soon,
Getting and spending, we lay waste our powers;
Little we see in Nature that is ours...
For this, for everything, we are out of tune.

-- William Wordsworth, *The World Is Too Much with Us* (1802)

Part III's argument is that the law has to be in tune with the biological reality of *Homo sapiens*. Going for higher principles of justice may sound like a noble plan but it will collapse if not based on reality.

The present chapter is about 'values.' The very word conjures up good things. Why wouldn't it? If something strikes the 'good' feeling in us, we label it valuable. We value warm weather, rest and recreation, the beauty of a sunset, a compliment, a hug. We negatively value pain, frustration, and debasement.

This is all thanks to biology. Animals, too, have values. You could list the values of a particular species of bird, fish, mammal, even of insects. They value certain things they like, and they like certain things because these aid survival.

In humans the two genders may have non-identical values. Females value a good gossip session; males don't. Males value intense competition, all the better if done by teams; females don't. These different values evolved "for a reason." Cultures too, develop certain preferences as to how to live. The French are noted for valuing cuisine, the Scots get off on frugality. New Hampshirites proclaim a value of independence. (Their motto is: Live free or die.) But we always borrow from other cultures.

The Judaic Ethic of Community

A culture has to make sense. It has to have internal consistency. Really, it has to be able to identify its values. The following is an excerpt from Meir Tamari's excellent 2014 book.

Meir Tamari, *With All Your Possessions* (page numbers shown):

"It is simply not true that men work only for wages. Work often reflects a person's intellectual, emotional and artistic aspirations... terms of employment influence, consciously and unconsciously, the political, social, and educational structure of any society. (131) The public sanction of resentment is Judaism's weapon against the creation of an ideological and spiritual atmosphere in which obligations can be ignored, or discharged merely by a financial penalty. Peer group pressure and public disapproval would be a powerful factor in achieving honest labor relations. (209)

In any society, there are certain functions and needs that lie beyond the domain of the individual and, therefore, have to be fulfilled by the group. ... (210) Perhaps the most Jewish of the underpinnings of taxation is the now universally accepted concept of society's responsibility for the needs of its members. The Jewish provision of such services, as opposed to relying on personal charity, dates back to antiquity. [And so] tax evasion was tantamount to theft. (212)

Neighbors had the ability to force each other to finance common needs out of a joint fund. (213) The Mishna tells us that the people of a city can force all citizens to participate in the financing of projects needed for the security and wellbeing of the town. Certain types of taxes, and assistance to the poor, were automatically funded on the basis of wealth [per] the greater moral responsibility of the rich for this public need.

In any society, a breakdown in the moral basis for taxation is rapidly translated into widespread tax evasion. (220) The moral teachings of Judaism however, created an ideological climate in which the individuals' obligations to the communal well-being were constantly reiterated, so that they became an integral part of him. Until the Napoleonic Wars, the Jew as an individual had no existence outside of the community. (227)

Good deeds and righteous actions are not developed simply

by intellectual training. (244) It is necessary to have role models in one's home and to acquire cultural and behavioral patterns characteristic of previous generations. The family of Abraham were practitioners of hospitality and the heirs to a tradition of kindness. 'Do not rely upon the broken reed of human support and do not set up gold as your hope, for that is the beginning of idolatry. Rather, distribute your money according to God's will; he is able to cover your deficit... Rejoice in your lot, whether it be large or small.' (251)

Jewish justice insists on symmetry of rights and obligations. So the poor may not glean or harvest before the harvesters have completed their work. (256) Judaism is a communally oriented religion, more interested in creating a holy nation than in developing spiritually mature individuals. Living off charity and welfare never became a legitimate and acceptable way of living in Judaism, as has happened in many modern welfare systems. Maimonides limited recourse to the communal funds to those who did not have fourteen meals for the week." (258)

Law Is Itself a Value

The Hebrews and the Romans were both admired for law. It is among their great gifts to posterity. The books of the Bible that lay down the law, such as Deuteronomy and Leviticus, reflect an earlier law, the Code of Hammurabi. In modern times, the United States became greatly admired for "rule of law."

As stated at the beginning of this chapter, law depends on values, but it is an important notion that we can value the law itself. Indeed to have the "rule of law" means that the law is our ruler, and it's normal for humans to love their rulers.

This year is the 800th anniversary of the Magna Charta. I believe it is accurate to say that by declaring certain ideals about justice, the barons of England of 1215 made our lives different. Note: they did not come to their ideas by inspiration but by custom. Many of the demands the barons specified to King John were about sticking to the old ways of, say, inheritance, or of the obligation of certain men to build roads. Still, they also said:

> "We have also granted to all freemen of our kingdom, for us and our heirs forever, all the underwritten liberties, to be had and held by them and their heirs ... forever.... To no one will we sell, to no one will we refuse or delay, right or justice. ... We will appoint as justices, constables, sheriffs, or bailiffs only such as know the law of the realm and mean to observe it well."

The American founding fathers, using the philosophical breakthroughs of the eighteenth century, decided that they would create a shield against oppressive rulers. They would see to it that the persons who would officially hold authority would be boxed in by limitations on power (see Appendix N).

Most of the chapters of this book are about the breakdown of the system they created. Does it mean the system is ill-conceived? I personally don't think so. I think two things stand in the way of our enjoying the rule of law at the moment. One is that the Constitution gives most attention to the problem of a government wielding power. It neglects a related matter – the ability of the wealthy to buy off, and control the government.

The other issue is that we did not anticipate the extent of the Top Dogs' ability to control our thinking, especially via mass media. Deceit is now so widespread that it is almost impossible to have a sensible discussion. People are living in a fantasy. Wow.

I wonder if the lack of interest in rule of law has been deliberately promoted to young people, clandestinely. Brendan O'Neill, writing in *The Spectator*, 22 November 2014, lamented what he calls Stepford students. He quotes their theme as: **"Free speech is so last century. Today's students want the 'right to be comfortable.'"** That's a recipe for disaster. It simply translates to: let the ruthless take over. "I don't value my freedom enough to want to put effort into it."

Note: the *Oxford Dictionary* defines *Stepford* as "denoting someone who is robotically conformist or obedient."

This needs to be turned around A.S.A.P.

You Can't Make a Silk Purse from a Sow's Ear

Now consider this example of people talking crazy. Can it be that we have strayed so far from an understanding of human nature that we think a culture can be conjured up out of thin air? At a NATO summit in Riga, Latvia in 2006, Allen Sens of Canada was asked to come up with some justification for NATO to act as a polity. NATO is a military organization. It has no ability to teach ethics to anyone and it would not even know how to argue for one set of ethics or another. That's not what warriors do.

> **"Riga and Beyond: The Political Transformation of NATO"**
> By Alan Sens (Comments in square brackets by Mary Maxwell)
>
> "Since the end of the Cold War [which never actually existed] NATO has undertaken a series of extensive reforms designed to adapt the Alliance to new security threats and challenges [most of which it designed in the first place]. NATO has been used to facilitate collective military action [and how!].
>
> An Alliance that was once an instrument of deterrence and containment has become a mechanism for power projection and security consultation. The concept of "transformation" [is] now the driving force behind efforts to make NATO more useful and effective [to the Top Dogs, that is]....
>
> By its nature, however, the transformation agenda is narrowly focused on military affairs. NATO must undergo a political transformation ... This political transformation must include building global partnerships [a very scary word, trust me] developing the ability of the Alliance to respond to the ethical dimension of military action [say what?], and improving the state-building and peace-building capacities of the Alliance.
>
> *The need for a political transformation*
> Meanwhile, authoritarian states continue to threaten regional stability. [I can think of two.] The proliferation of weapons of mass destruction or threat thereof [e.g., hurricanes], raises fears of their use in warfare and provokes crises with countries such as N. Korea and Iran. Organised crime [married to government] breeds corruption and fear, and diverts resources

away from legitimate economic activity. Illegal migration and shortcomings in social integration of immigrant communities can create a racially and religiously defined underclass [as intended], fuelling identity-inspired violence in society.

Energy security is a growing concern as the dependence of NATO countries on foreign sources of energy increases. [Actually all energy is free, from the sun.] Finally, climate change and environmental degradation will precipitate an increase in environmentally-induced conflict [on schedule].

Taken together, these issues present a much more complex security challenge for NATO's member states than that presented by the Soviet Union. [Indeed it would be hard to understate the challenges posed by the Soviets]....

Military force can terminate or establish order in intrastate conflicts or failed states, but cannot create a lasting peace [well, that's true enough]. Energy security cannot be achieved through the use of military power [Go to the head of the class].

The moral clarity that characterised the Cold War in Europe is largely gone. [Ahem, as I said it was a psywar only.] Morality, legality, and ethics now play a much more prominent role in the establishment and maintenance of NATO's international legitimacy. ... [Swearda God, Professor Sens actually said that.]

Building global partnerships
NATO can establish consultative groups combining government officials, academia [already there; they arrivedin the late 1990s]. NATO cannot maximise its performance, influence, or effectiveness without a solid understanding of the impact its activities and missions are having on people, communities, and societies, [so let's tell NATO what that impact is] .... This will enable the Alliance to establish appropriate rules of engagement, and create useful 'quick impact' projects. [You heard it here first.]

Developing NATO's ethical awareness [No! Mommy, help!]
The moral foundation of the Alliance's actions, both in the *justice of its cause* and the means it employs..." (end of Sens' essay).

What about the Value of Honesty?

As individuals, it is in our interest to lie, steal, rape, and kill. But it is in our interest not to let others do likewise So, over time, the solution was arrived at: all members would be told to refrain from those 'sins.' Individuals fear disapproval and loss of reputation, hence they comply.

In my time, the sin of lying was associated with religion and when religion took a beating lying became acceptable. This is a disaster. In the modern world most of our interactions were designed at a tome when lying was a punishable sin. Were the rule to change so that lying is not punishable, you couldn't, say, sue the grocer for selling you something that he said was orange juice but was only colored water. And what about the more intimate understandings between friends? They all assume honesty.

If you categorize typical lies you see their purpose. We lie to present a better view of ourselves, we lie to deny the blame for something we did, we lie to put someone off the track so we can take better advantage of him.

Since the time of Edward Bernays (a nephew of Freud), the advertising industry in US has celebrated any and all skills for fooling people. We have tended to applaud, as it seems to enhance *business*, one of America's stated values.

But PR firms are on the government payroll to influence people to accept what "the government" wants. Hey, I thought we were the government! What's going on? Do we pay people to deceive us? We pay to buy a newpaper that causes us to think the wrong party is the criminal.

An important point is to note that we are hard-wired to believe the leader and to criticize anyone who doubts the leader. Wow, what opportunity that gives to politicians! It seems that any statement they make 'ex cathedra' is fine.

Who is Rupert Murdoch? Is there any reason we should believe the things he tells us, especially as to who is to blame for things? No. He is a sinner in the old-fashioned sense and deserves to be given the heave-ho by society.

Come on, men. *HE-EAVE HO.*

chapter twelve

Protestors in Canada appear to be the enemy.

'Active denial weapon' to deny space to protestors by heating their skin.
Usable for perimiter security, like a cattle prod, and for crowd control.
Los Angeles sheriff says it can be used "to break up fights in prisons."

12. You and I Are the Cops and That's That

We didn't love freedom enough. And even more – we had no awareness of the real situation.... We purely and simply deserved everything that happened afterward.

-- Aleksandr Solzhenitsyn (1918-2008), *The Gulag Archipelago*

Questions about an Emerging Police State in the US

Who is authorized to arrest you these days? Can he enter your home without a warrant? Without knocking?

Must the arrest occur in daylight, or is 3.30 am OK?

Can the cops read your written documents in your home?

Can they order others to exit your home while they are arresting you?

Can they throw you to the floor before announcing the purpose of their visit?

Do the cops answer to the mayor of your town? What's the role of county sheriff?

What does it mean for cops to be 'deputized' by a federal agency such as FBI?   What is a task force?

May they handcuff you behind your back? Can they tear-gas you?

Under what circumstances can they 'Tase you?

Must a cop reveal his name if you ask for it?

Can you be arrested and detained without any charges being laid?

If you are unhappy with police, to whom can you complain? Can you sue policepersons in their personal capacity?

If your property is taken from you, under 'asset forfeiture,' who gets it?

Must you submit to TSA searches at the airport?

Can you be made to hand over any guns that you lawfully possess? Can they seize *any food you own?*

Can a 'contractor' arrest you? In the event of a natural disaster, must you obey an order to leave your home?

Can they hit you with a drone? Can they water-board you?

Note: Answers to all of the above will be found on the next page:

111

The Bill of Rights   **I.** Congress shall make no law respecting an establishment of religion, or prohibiting the free exercise thereof; or abridging the freedom of speech, or of the press; or the right of the people peaceably to assemble, and to petition the government for a redress of grievances.   **II.** A well regulated militia, being necessary to the security of a free state, the right of the people to keep and bear arms, shall not be infringed.   **III.** No soldier shall, in time of peace be quartered in any house, without the consent of the owner, nor in time of war, but in a manner to be prescribed by law.   **IV.** The right of the people to be secure in their persons, houses, papers, and effects, against unreasonable searches and seizures, shall not be violated, and no warrants shall issue, but upon probable cause, supported by oath or affirmation, and particularly describing the place to be searched, and the persons or things to be seized. **V.** No person shall be held to answer for a capital, or otherwise infamous crime, unless on a presentment or indictment of a grand jury, except in cases arising in the land or naval forces, or in the militia, when in actual service in time of war or public danger; nor shall any person be subject for the same offense to be twice put in jeopardy of life or limb; nor shall be compelled in any criminal case to be a witness against himself, nor be deprived of life, liberty, or property, without due process of law; nor shall private property be taken for public use, without just compensation. **VI.** In all criminal prosecutions, the accused shall enjoy the right to a speedy and public trial, by an impartial jury of the state and district wherein the crime shall have been committed, which district shall have been previously ascertained by law, and to be informed of the nature and cause of the accusation; to be confronted with the witnesses against him; to have compulsory process for obtaining witnesses in his favor, and to have the assistance of counsel for his defense.   **VII.** In suits at common law, where the value in controversy shall exceed twenty dollars, the right of trial by jury shall be preserved, and no fact tried by a jury, shall be otherwise reexamined in any court of the United States, than according to the rules of the common law. **VIII.** Excessive bail shall not be required, nor excessive fines imposed, nor cruel and unusual punishments inflicted. **IX.** The enumeration in the Constitution, of certain rights, shall not be construed to deny or disparage others retained by the people. **X.** The powers not delegated to the United States by the Constitution, nor prohibited by it to the states, are reserved to the states respectively, or to the people.   [Came into force in 1789. Still in force!]

Is There Some Reason Why 'Rights' Aren't Honored?

We are in huge trouble right now. There is an amazing Youtube video of Senator Rand Paul bawling out Homeland Security for distributing to police 12,000 bayonets – yes I said b-a-y-o-n-e-t-s. There can never, ever be a legitimate domestic use for such weapons.

And Bill van Auken observed, at Globalresearch.ca:

> "This week's deployment of Blackhawk helicopters in Chicago is only the latest in a series of "urban warfare training. The Army operates a Center in Indiana with over 1,500 'training structures' designed to simulate houses, schools, hospitals and factories... for both foreign and domestic scenarios."

Sorry, there cannot legally be a domestic scenario that would call for urban warfare. Think about it for a minute. What folks in the US are going to start a war on the streets? None. It is a fantasy. Many have started to believe it. Since 1970, the "Arab terrorist" has been displayed worldwide by the media. In many places, they use other symbolic baddies, for example in Ireland the terrorists were the IRA.

Another baddy who has been used to justify (and *"used* to justify" is the correct phrase) an increase in policing is the drug dealer. But where do the drugs come from? Cocaine comes in from South America, and heroin from Asia, both with the full cooperation of the US authorities. Just like the Brits used opium to mess up Chinese society circa 1850, our Secret Government does it to us.

Conspiracy

What ho! A secret government? Is Mary Maxwell a closet conspiracist? No I'm not in the closet; I am fully out. I have a PhD in Politics, which means I studied how power works. It works by such things as just mentioned – Britain brought China to the point of submission by getting people hooked on drugs (imported from India).

Three more ways a few at the top can obtain, and maintain, control of millions of people: 1. Cause fear – when folks are fearful they cannot think; they want to obey. 2. Use lavish visuals to assure people that the men at the top are glorious and strong and invincible (They're not, of course, which is why they rely on trickery), and 3. Destroy the people's power base. This includes their religion, their family stability, talented local leaders, and traditions.

It's been a quarter century since I got my Politics degree; I'd now add a couple of more ways that the 'Party' can run the country. One is simply hypnosis. It is widely used today in commercial contexts, so you can be sure it's being used by officials. (And, importantly it's used **on** officials. Recall the zombified Congressmen and generals at the Tillman hearings?)

They're Trending Tonight
The other way to control the public – I doubt that you'll believe me – is to teach people that there is nothing permanent, no customs to hang onto. Everything's in flux. But not in chaos. Rather, we are shown some trends. For example there is a trend in police violence, a trend of persons living in the parental home till age 30, a trend in prescribing blood-thinning medication, a downward trend of interest in books.

This brings our mimic instinct into play. Doing what the trend is doing was an adaptive trait in evolutionary times. If an individual invented a smart new technique, others could copy it fast. I believe it is almost irresistible to feel respect for whatever is new.

This happens ever more easily as our sense of history gets cancelled out. Why look to the way our grandparents did things? They are old and stupid. Better look to celebs. They must be worthy of imitating since they are, by definition, celebrated. "Only 23 years old but wise!"

It Isn't Sexy but Its Very Good

There really is a way for us to re-establish control over the emerging police state. I know it won't sound sexy. I am referring to the law, and especially the Constitution.

Since John Locke's 1690 *Two Treatises on Government* we've been trying to overcome the destiny of hierarchy. We did in fact create a social contract of the US. Please see Appendix N for Massachusetts' constitution of 1790, written by John Adams. He said all citizens covenant with one another, and:

> Art. V. All power residing originally in the people, and being derived from them, the several magistrates and officers of government vested with authority, whether legislative, executive, or judicial, are the substitutes and agents, and are at all times accountable to them.

I once attended a hearing in New Hampshire at which a citizen said to the legislators with perfect courtesy, "I respectfully remind you that you are my substitutes and agent, and are at all times accountable to me." That man had the baby in hand and was not about to throw it out with the bathwater! We should be taking care of the baby – the constitution right now.

Point of fact, "they" are very worried that we will read the law and chat with each other about it. Consider this:

> "Almost all the governments, which exist at present, have been founded originally, either on usurpation or conquest, or both, without any pretense of a fair consent of the people. When an artful and bold man is placed at the head of an army or faction, it is often easy for him, by employing, sometimes violence, sometimes false pretenses, to establish his dominion. **He allows no such open communication, that his enemies can know, with certainty, their number or force. He gives them no leisure to assemble together in a body to oppose him.** Even all those ...may wish his fall; but their ignorance of each other's intention keeps them in awe, and is the sole cause of his security." David Hume, *Of the Original Contract.* (1752)

UK's Policing Grab - from historyandpolicy.org

Historian Chris Williams shows how town control gave way:

• A Municipal Corporations Act of 1835 had made towns of England and Wales self-governing. Each would select a select a 'watch committee' from their number to run the police force. A town could therefore veto individual prosecutions. (Naturally! The town governs itself.)

• In 1856, Home Office tried to get laws limiting the rights of boroughs to control their own police forces. But these efforts were *defeated* – "the people knew better."

• Bribery then entered. Per an act of parliament in 1857, "central government paid a quarter of the costs of 'efficient' forces for all towns of more than 5,000 people."

• Then World War I. "The cherished independence of the watch committees could be extinguished at will." In 1919, there were police strikes. (Gosh, I wonder who provoked those?) This led the Desborough Committee to say "police wages should be increased, and set centrally for the first time."

• In 1930 the case of *Fisher v Oldham* used intellectual gymnastics to show that a constable was ultimately responsible to the law rather than to his superiors. Oh my.

• There were 'Red scares,' that old chestnut. The security state "saw an unprecedented level of peacetime planning for counter-insurgency."

• Home Office "took increasing responsibility for producing a class of leaders for police forces, and thus intervened in matters of training and promotion, setting up the Hendon Police College in 1933." See? This is how the authority wafts high up into the sky.

• "By the 1950s, Whitehall introduced a policy of refusing to appoint any Chief Constable who had no experience in a *different* force: this was clearly designed to create a more nationally homogenous force." (Also it's reminiscent of Stalin's tactic of *transmigrasie*. A cop from far away won't be chided by his mother for being too harsh on the local homeless people, right?)

The summary on the preceding page of how the UK got its police nationalized is a close prototype of what is going in the US today. Even the color of police cars (black and white) is becoming national. This is not a good sign. Please worry.

It's Not Like They Are Trying to Arrest Bad Citizens

Time now for devotees of the red, white, and blue to face truths that we have been avoiding for 44 years. In the April 1971 issue of Harper's, Frank Donner, reported that a "Citizen's Commission to Investigate the FBI" (yay!) came across an official document that explained why it spies on students:

> "for plenty of reasons, chief of which are it will enhance the paranoia endemic in these circles and will further serve to get the point across that there is an FBI agent behind every mailbox. In addition, some will be overcome by the overwhelming personalities of the contacting agent and will volunteer to tell all -- perhaps on a continuing basis."

Donner made an interesting observation as to how a federal agent may quell his own guilt. Namely, "his bad feelings about snooping into people's lives may be assuaged by exaggerating what he finds!" Hmm. Donner quotes Allen Dulles' *Craft of Intelligence and agents provocateurs*, about the use of agents provocateurs. It is to "provide the pretext for arresting any or all of [the group's] members." Terrific.

It's my guess that the Rodney King beating did not take place. One measuring stick is "the results." The acquittal of the cops who beat King led to a riot (done by agents provocateurs, say I). Thus in 1992 the military was on the streets of Los Angeles. And they were not allowed to intervene. ...

We also have death squads here in the land of the free. William Pepper, a lawyer, was determined to find out who killed Martin Luther King. He clearly established that James Earl Ray was not the one. (See Chapter 9.) Pepper discovered the feds wanted Ray bumped off in 1976. How to do it? They helped him escape prison and then sent 30 SWAT snipers to kill him. A hero, Governor Blanton of Tennessee, took a helicopter to the scene and told the snipers to amscray.

Note: Blanton later lost the governorship in a "cash for clemency" scandal. A heroic deed brings many risks.

NOW FOR THE GOOD NEWS

We don't have to continue on the path we're on. The police state is not inevitable. It would not happen if the culture opposed it. Listen to this pleasant comment from Frenchman Frederic Bastiat writing in 1848. His beautiful book, *The Law*, is free online. (He wrote it to oppose the Paris Commune):

> "It is not true that the legislator has absolute power over our persons and property. The existence of persons and property preceded the existence of the legislator, and his function is only to guarantee their safety.
>
> It is not true that the function of law is to regulate our consciences, our ideas, our wills, our education, our opinions, our work, our trade, our talents, or our pleasures. The function of law is to protect the free exercise of these rights, and to prevent any person from interfering with the free exercise of these same rights by any other person.
>
> Since law necessarily requires the support of force, its lawful domain is only in the areas where the use of force is necessary. This is justice."

What we need to is change our attitude, stop training police to think of the citizenry as a bunch of terrorists, and put some dignity back into the community.

We need to tell the baddies to amscray. They are laughing at us, as well they should, for being such easy pickin's.

118

OPINION – What Is Women's Role?

There is such a thing as a "female role," thank God. In the class Mammalia, that role involves the production and feeding of offspring. In the order Primata, there's much teaching of the young and definitely quite a bit of being sociable and maintaining relationships.

Not too long ago, human females were kind. Maybe they are still kind, but it's not so much talked about as it was, so there's less expectation of it. Expectation is a significant force in making something occur. In private lives we see no shortage of women giving themselves to the nth degree to help family members. Many now do fulltime nursing of aged parents, or raise grandchildren. But where is the woman-based, love-based, estrogen-based, call it what you will, contribution to getting us out of the unbearable political situations that are developing?

Girls, please pump up your estrogen and fix this terrible world. You know you can do it. We were made to do it.

As for women being assigned to the battlefield, this is ridiculous. It is a man's job. Did you know that in 2003 many US women with little babies at home were "deployed" to battle? Is that stupid or what? Did you know that when war took us by surprise in 1990, many women in the army "got themselves pregnant" to get a ticket out? A man with a woman companion in battle will treat her more protectively than he treats other buddies; that's bad for team spirit. Hey, it's OK to say *Vive la différence*. It is OK for men to be admired.

One of the writers of the *All in the Family* sitcom said if he wrote lines making Archie Bunker look strong he was told to rewrite. See? The tone of the two sexes is being designed by bosses who want us not to have strong men. Why would that be?

Attention Grandmothers. Niels Harrit, grandfather of six, says "There's no way our children can expect a future like ours unless we face the unresolved questions of 9-11." So true.

chapter thirteen

Japan 2011. Is this our future?

13. Geo-engineering: Are Hurricanes Legal?

A lobotomy of individual thought, objective reasoning, and resistance to the crimes of power has been largely achieved.

-- Christopher Brooks, *GumshoeNews.com* (2015)

Legibus sumptis desinentibus legibus naturae utendum est. When laws imposed by the State fail, we must use the laws of nature. (Law maxim)

Modern law did not spring full-blown from the brow of Zeus. It developed. Now we must develop 'weather-control' law.

One doesn't have to be a rocket scientist to know that the major tsunamis of our time: Indonesia, 2004; Samoa, 2009; Japan 2011, and other "natural" disasters, were maliciously created.

Have a look at the popular movie *The Sinking of Japan*. It contains scenes, admittedly made by Hollywood special effects persons, in 2006, of a tsunami in Japan that is extremely similar to the one that took place five years later in 2011. What made the author of the movie think of such a thing? How did the movie producer have enough knowledge to get such an accurate presentation?

Look at Hurricane Katrina, which devastated the Gulf coast in 2005 (which, among other things, allowed President GW Bush to upgrade John Roberts' nomination for US Supreme Court from justice to chief justice – a man no one had ever heard of, while everyone was busy with the hurricane). How was FEMA so well prepared?

I realize there's not much awareness of geo-engineering yet, but we can use "circumstantial evidence" defined as:

"Evidence and testimony that permits conclusions…. Many circumstances can **create inferences** about an accused's guilt, including the presence of a motive or opportunity to commit the crime, **any denials, evasions, a contradiction on the part of the accused**." [Emphasis added]   -- Freedictionary.com

Events That Were Conceivably Man-made

Landslides and mudslides: China 2010; Guatemala 2010

Tsunamis: Indian Ocean 2004; Samoa 2009; Japan 2011

Floods: Peru and Chile 2009; Pakistan 2010; Queensland, Australia 2012

Heat Wave: France 2003 (14,000 died, mostly elderly)

Earthquakes: Gujerat, India 2001; Sumatra, Indonesia 2005; Bam, Iran 2003; Pakistan 2005; Christchurch, NZ 2011; Sichuan, China 2008; Haiti 2010

Cyclones: Burma 2009; Philippines 2013

Fires: Victoria, Australia 2009; Greek Islands 2009

Tornados: Joplin, USA 2010; Calcutta, India, 2010

Volcanoes: Iceland 2010; (Alert December 24, 2010 Chile)

Hailstorms: Philippines 2013 [and many more such events]

Hurricanes: Katrina 2005. Perhaps all major hurricanes in USA? For example: Betty, Andrew, Irene, Sandy.

President Obama consoles tornado victim in Joplin, Missouri, 2011

Circumstantial Evidence of Weather Control

Whilst government officials deny the very existence of weather control, ordinary folk can easily see it.

If the matter ever comes to court, circumstantial evidence of naughtiness can be cited. For example:

1. The odd timing of two hailstorms in Australia – both at afternoon rush hour, one in Melbourne, one in Perth

2. The fact that Iceland was threatened by the International Monetary Fund shortly before its volcano erupted

3. The fact that US troops were present in Port-au-Prince just before Haiti's 2010 earthquake and yet they were held back from assisting people

4. The fact that on the previous day the US military had a drill for a hurricane in Haiti

5. The flurry of relevant put options on the stock market, which happened in regard to several disasters

6. The fact that in this terrorism-conscious world, *no official articulates the possibility* that enemies may be blamed!

7. The irresponsible behavior of the Royal Commission that 'investigated' the 2009 bushfire in Victoria, Australia

8. The rather high rate of disasters occuring at Christmas

9. The fact that journalists were prevented from taking photos at the Halliburton Gulf of Mexico oil surge.

Clarifying What HAARP Is

The website of University of Alaska says:

"HAARP [High-Frequency Active Auroral Research Project] is a scientific endeavor aimed at studying the properties and behavior of the ionosphere, with particular emphasis on being able to understand and use it to enhance communications and surveillance systems for both civilian and defense purposes."

On the next page is a photo of HAARP, in Alaska, It is an ionosphere-heater, based on discoveries made by the genius Nikola Tesla. You can read the patents for HAARP's technology, and all patents, at uspto.gov (US Patent and Trade Office).

Amazing technology near Achorage, Alaksa

Note: In 1957, an International Geophysical Year was run by the "International Council of Scientific Unions." The National Academy of Science's website, nas.edu, tells us:

> "Technical panels were formed to pursue work in the following areas: aurora and airglow, cosmic rays, geomagnetism, glaciology, gravity, ionospheric physics, longitude and latitude determination, meteorology, oceanography, rocketry, seismology, and solar activity."

Orwell's Predictions (Written in 1949) for the Year "1984"

George Orwell's 'novel,' *1984*, makes you hate the idea of living under Socialism. But in other ways it conditions you to changes that do come about. I think Orwell was informed by insiders that the production of artificial earthquakes and tsunamis ("tidal waves") was on the drawing board. He said:

> "Teams of experts are indefatigably at work. Some are concerned simply with planning the logistics of future wars; others explore even remoter possibilities such as focusing the sun's rays through lenses suspended thousands of kilometers away in space, or producing artificial earthquakes and tidal waves by tapping the heat at the earth's centre."

Note: The main character in *1984*, Winston, works at the "Ministry of Truth" where his job is to suppress history. That's because if people knew the past, they would be empowered! Ahem.

Quotes from Insiders and Authorities

1. On the website juscogens.com, there is a pertinent article written by Avraham Zuroff in the Israel National News on August 25, 2009. He says that **simulations of earthquakes** being carried out in Israel are financed by the US Department of Defense, in a joint project with the University of Hawaii. He goes along with the idea that the purpose of the explosion is "to calibrate its equipment":

> "In the last few years, the Geophysical Institute has created several earthquake simulations in order to calibrate its equipment. In June 2004, the institute detonated 32 tons of explosives in the southern Negev. In June, 2005, the institute detonated 20 tons in the Beit Alfa quarries in the Jezreel Valley south of the Galilee." -- Zuroff

2. On July 27, 1972, Rep G. Gude, after returning from the Stockholm Conference on the environment, said this to a Senate committee:

> "It may be possible to **initiate military weather modification** projects without being detected. In other words, the military results may not be visibly tied to the initiating party. This raises the possibility of clandestine use of geophysical warfare **where a country does not know if it has been attacked.** The uncertainty of this situation, the fear of not knowing how another country might be altering your climate is highly **destabilizing.**"
>
> "Suppose, for example, that a US plane flies a routine, non military mission near Chile, Egypt, or Tanzania and by some quirk of fate a major earthquake, flood, or forest fire occurs in one of these countries. Because **we have been tinkering with geophysical** warfare, we could be charged with creating that environmental calamity due to **the mere proximity of the U.S. aircraft.**" [Emphasis added]

Mary Gregory's Observations and Speculations

There are many dissidents today who are writing about the new weaponry. Wait! Why call them 'dissidents?' Are they being naughty? Is it a sin to tell their fellow humans what is being done to them? One is Mary Efrosini Gregory of the Queens borough of New York. She has written three books about the new technology of EM – electro-magnetism. She learns a lot from the websites of defense contractors who, naturally, boast about the capabilities of their latest products.

Often she goes beyond reporting, into speculation. I list three of her ideas below. They could well be wrong, but give a taste of how she observes carefully, and then tries to figure what the motive of the powerful may be.

Mary Efrosini Gregory, in *Microwave War* (2012), opines:

---

1. On May 12, 2008 in Sichuan, China – near Tibet -- a 7.9 earthquake **killed 70,000 people**. Its purpose may have been to give Western aid workers an excuse to **enter Tibet**. Once inside, they could augment local protests against China.

2. A huge glacier in the Andes, 200 miles north of Lima, Peru, breaks and falls into a lake. This glacier would have been the people's supply of drinking water for centuries to come. Now the **people will soon be without water**. "I am wondering whether the US heated it up aerially to take a step forward in reducing the world's population."

3. The timing of the volcano in Iceland that spewed ash, which was hazardous to planes, was intended to **exempt all heads of government** from attending the 2011 funeral of the Polish leaders -- who were killed en masse on the anniversary of the Katyn massacre. In other words, their recent "accidental death" was a punishment to Poland for standing up to the EU, the IMF, or some arm of the cabal. World leaders were required to boycott the funeral -- M.E.G. [Emphasis added by M Maxwell]

Environmental Modification Treaty, 1977: "En-Mod"

> "Each State Party to this Convention undertakes not to engage in military or any other hostile use of environmental modification techniques having widespread, long-lasting or severe effects as the means of destruction, damage or injury ... [This refers to] the deliberate manipulation of natural processes -- the dynamics, composition or structure of the Earth, including its biota, lithosphere, hydrosphere and atmosphere, or of outer space...." [Signed by US in 1982]

The point of quoting a multilateral treaty, sprung from a UN General Assembly resolution, is not to suggest that international law can be effective. (Recall Chapter 5) Two treaties that have a lot of sensible provisions -- the Law of the Seas and the Convention on Biodiversity -- are toothless.

The main purpose of the above quote is to indicate that "environmental **modification**" does in fact exist (else why the efforts to oppose it?). There is also a declassified Senate hearing in which the US military revealed the extent to which it had used weather control ("Operation Popeye").

Here's a word from EO Wilson's 2014 book, *The Meaning of Hunan Exisence,* (pages 131-132):

> "The remainder of the century will be a bottleneck of growing human impact on the environment and diminishing biodiversity. We bear all of the responsibility of bringing ourselves and as much as possible of the rest of life through this into a sustainable Edenic existence. Our choice will be a profoundly moral one. Its fulfillment depends on knowledge still lacking and a sense of common decency still not felt. We alone among all species have grasped the reality of the living world, seen the beauty of nature and given value to the individual. We alone have measured the quality of mercy among our own kind. Might we now extend the same concern to the living world that gave us birth?"

chapter fourteen

Martina Correia (1968-2011)

When maidens such as Hester die
Their place ye may not well supply...
A springy motion in her gate, a rising step did indicate
Of pride and joy no common rate...
A waking eye, a prying mind,
A heart that stirs is hard to bind;
A hawk's keen sight ye cannot blind,
You could not Hester.

-- Charles Lamb, *Hester*

14. Type-2 Judicial Treason

Judex est lex loquens. The judge is the law speaking. (Law maxim)

An enemy at the gates is less formidable, for he carries his banner openly. But the traitor moves amongst those within the gate ... in the very halls of government itself. For the traitor appears not a traitor; he speaks in accents familiar to his victims.... He rots the soul of a nation, he works secretly and unknown in the night to undermine the pillars of the city, **he infects the body politic so that it can no longer resist.** [Emphasis added] -- Marcus Tullius Cicero (43BC)

We are in a race against time. You know the stage is set for martial law. You know that more natural disasters are being planned. We ought to get off the mild tack of talking about 'prosecutorial misconduct' and 'judges who commit ethics violations,' and face up to what is really happening. Treason is happening. Make some arrests now. Start with the judges.

'Never Call Any American a Traitor, No Matter What'

There seems to be an odd taboo on calling a spade a spade. In 1966 John A Walker, a Navy man, photocopied umpteen documents and sold them to the Russians. His aid to the enemy matched perfectly the definition of treason in the Constitution:

> Article III, Section 3: Treason against the United States, shall consist only in levying War against them, or in adhering to their Enemies, giving them Aid and Comfort.

Yet the word 'treason' never appeared on John A Walker's charge sheet. Probably the Top Dogs want to prevent our learning much about it. Needless to say, Brian Nichols was not charged with treason, although killing a judge in the courtroom would qualify.

The Whiskey Rebellion

The major precedent for treason is a 1793 case. Some farmers refused to pay tax on whiskey they distilled. They tarred and feathered the tax collectors! President Washington called out the troops. (In fact he led them part way to Pennsylvania, on horseback, while president. Fancy that.) Men fired on the troops and were later convicted of treason.

That seems logical. We can't have people killing our law enforcers; such traitors would be wrecking the nation's rule of law, which is our main protection. As for the murder of Pat Tillman while he was in uniform, there can be no doubt that it was an act of treason. Some persons (reportedly the men in the GMV) levied war on the US. No question. Interrogate all those men posthaste.

Do Judges Commit Treason? Let Me Count the Types

When Napoleon cast aside the rule of the French constitution, Sir Walter Scott accused him of parricide, parent-killing, the constitution being the parent. This is apposite for the US, too. In fact it is probably the greatest type of treason occurring. Members of Congress do it with gay abandon, allowing the Pentagon to make war without the requisite permission of the legislature.

Some folks call that malfeasance, but it's worse. As stated above, we need rule of law for protection, especially the rule of the Constitution whose job it is to prevent power concentration. If Congress passes laws that violate the Constitution, the Third Branch of government should step in and find such laws null and void. But we rarely hear of successful challenges to the mightily unconstitutional Homeland Security Act. Judges take orders from above. See, in Appendix M, a SCOTUS ruling on strip searches that is the very antithesis of the Fourth Amendment.

We can divide judges' treason into two types. Let's use the name Type-1 Judicial Treason for the parricide type, in which the people become deprived of their parent, the Constitution. Next, we can identify a type in which the judge "wages war on the United States." This Type-2 Judicial Treason can be called active-violence treason, as the rulings made by the judge cause physical harm to citizens. (Of course I don't mean when a judge metes out a lawful sentence that is harmful legitimately.)

Active-Violence Treason by a Judge (Type 2)

For all intents and purposes, every judge holds in her hand a whip, a gun, a cage, and some sort of weapon to impoverish a person. (Picture a muzzle that would prevent the person from eating, for example). In short, she can do violence, and if she is a top judge she is answerable to no one for what she does. (Actually, she is answerable to Congress or state legislatures, thanks to impeachment.)

Charging the Judge with Theft Is Just a Distraction

Often when bad behavior of a judge is investigated, we find that there was a payout for the bad behavior. When you think of it, every time there is a financial disparity between two parties in a case, there is temptation for the wealthy party to bribe the court for a favorable solution to the case. For example, CBS News carried this Associated Press story on February 18, 2011:

> "A former juvenile court judge [Mark Ciavarella of Scranton, Pennsylvania] was convicted Friday of racketeering in a case that accused him of sending youth offenders to for-profit detention centers in exchange for millions of dollars in illicit payments from the builder and owner of the lockups."

Don't rule out that the entire affair was a set-up to make us concentrate on the factor of greed. It left people feeling helpless. "Well, you know, that's human nature; even our judges are corrupt. Not much we can do...."

But of course there is plenty we can do. That judge committed, first and foremost, the active-violence of putting children in a cell. He caged them, which is violent, and left them to suffer many other violent assaults in prison, not to mention the assault on the child's brain that accompanies separation from family (and which harms him or her permanently).

Ciavarella waged war on the United States. He committed Type 2 Judicial Treason. At the same moment he may have committed Type I (parricide), having not furnished the child with one of the protections of the Bill of Rights, the right to a fair trial. But where a judge commits Type 2, we can afford to ignore Type 1. The public needs to get acquainted with Type 2 Treason.

Treason in the Troy Davis Case

There they sat, in the large meeting room in Jackson prison, Troy's siblings, nephew, and friends, waiting for him in the execution room to be injected with a poison that would kill him, at age 43 while he was in good health. The mind boggles.

This awaited killing was despite the community having asked for his sentence to be commuted to life, despite there being a petition for coram nobis having been received in Chatham County Court regarding fraud-upon-the-court, and despite the fact, as everyone knew, that Kimberly Davis had just lost her mother and was scheduled to lose her sister any day. Not to mention the fact that Sylvester Coles had been accused of the crime but police wouldn't question him.

Treason was committed. War was waged on a citizen. This outrageous crime must not go unpunished. And what is the punishment for treason? It's codified in the United States Code (at 18 USC 2381). The punishment is death.

A Plea for the Revival of Constitutionalism

The American constitution is one of the wonders of the world. It solves the main problem that is killing us today: that of the concentration of power. It showed us, in 1787 -- and still shows us now if we'd only pay attention -- the way to **use the goodwill** of the whole society. Biologically there is no other way to overcome the problem of power; *you have to get people to support the nicer arrangement.* It takes education. It takes social trust -- all must **feel assured that the authorities will pounce** appropriately on anyone who tries to wreck our system.

Sweardagod this used to be understood, and can be again.

*Troy Anthony Davis, honors graduate... was
not expecting, on that occasion, that for 7,300
mornings of his life he would be waking up in a prison cell*

CONTORTIONIST'S DELIGHT"

This excerpts Judge Moore's analysis of one of the recantations, that of Darrell Collins who was 16 when he testified. [Comments in brackets are by Mary W Maxwell]

"At the trial, Mr. Collins reaffirmed [!] that Mr. Davis was wearing the white shirt and assaulted Mr. Young. His present recantation is a second attempt at recantation in which he goes further than he did at trial [At trial, he had to 'recant' when the cross-examiner found inconsistencies.]; it is new only in its breadth and rationale, not in its existence. [I want Judge Moore disbarred right now. There has to be respect for our intelligence.]

Mr. Collins also told the police that Mr. Davis was responsible for the Cloverdale shooting, but recanted this testimony at trial. [Judge knows that Cooper the victim said Troy didn't shoot him.]

(Mr Collins) also testified at trial that he included this in his police statement due to police coercion. However [he had testified at trial that he lied about Mr. Davis's involvement in the Cloverdale shooting due to police intimidation. [So what?]

In his recantation affidavit, Mr. Collins claimed a second lie -- that he never saw Mr. Davis strike Larry Young. He averred that he was comfortable revealing the first lie at trial but not the second because he felt the police cared more about whether Mr. Davis assaulted Mr. Young than Mr. Davis's responsibility for the Cloverdale shooting. [Naturally. MacPhail died, Cooper lived.]

At the hearing, Mr. Collins again claimed that he lied about both the assault on Larry Young and the Cloverdale incident due to police coercion. Specifically, he claims that he simply parroted what the police told him to say. [Indeed.] However, he did not recant his earlier testimony that Mr. Davis was wearing the white shirt on the night of the shootings. [Note: SCOTUS could allow Moore to have Collins clarify this matter now.]

At the hearing, Mr. Collins did not recant his testimony regarding the white shirt. Instead, he testified that he presently had no memory of what color shirt Mr. Davis was wearing that night [I call that a recantation!], but would assume that whatever he told the police about the color of Mr. Davis's shirt would have been a lie because all inculpatory testimony he provided is presumptively false in hismind. Of course, that statement is very different [No, it isn't] from stating that, as a matter of his own knowledge, he is sure that he was lying. Mr. Collins' testimony is neither credible [To me it's credible in light of "After a couple of hours of the detectives yelling at me and threatening me."] nor a full recantation. [Shame on you, Judge] First, regardless of the recantation, Mr. Collins's previous testimony, that has never been unequivocally recanted [I would say it has been "comprehensively recanted", wouldn't you?] still provides significant evidence of Mr. Davis's guilt by placing him in the white shirt. [Excuse me, "significant?"? He said he lied.]

Second, if Mr. Collins's claim that he simply parroted false statements fed to him by police is truthful, query why Mr. Collins never directly identified Mr. Davis as Officer MacPhail's murderer. Surely, this would have been the best available false testimony [Mother of God!], and given Mr. Collins's proximity to the murder it would have been as reasonable as any other false testimony [Reasonable in what sense? If he had not been threatened by police, should he have made it up for the sake of reasonableness?] Third, there was credible testimony from Officer [!!] Sweeney and Mr. Lock [say] that Mr. Collins's testimony was not coerced. Further, even if Mr. Collins's allegations regarding coercion and false testimony are true [what? Is the judge now entertaining the possibility that the police are coercive?]] they are not new. Mr. Collins testified at trial that he was coerced and that his statements regarding Mr. Davis's involvement in the Cloverdale shooting were fabricated. Moreover, his explanation as to why he revealed only the lie regarding the Cloverdale shooting at trial is not believable (explaining that Mr. Collins believed the police cared more about his false testimony regarding Mr. Young than the Cloverdale incident). [Excuse me, am I in the Soviet Union?]

Indeed, it would be puzzling to think that the police would not find Mr. Collins's accusations of harassment in the context of the Cloverdale shooting offensive but would be bothered by the exact same allegations with respect to the assault on Young.

[Note: this ruling has put Troy in the cemetery.]

See my petition for a writ of error coram nobis, sent the day before Troy's execution, in Appendix K.

chapter fifteen

Janis Joplin
died 1970, age 27

Freddie Prinze
died 1977, age 23

Harry Chapin
died 1981, age 38

Whitney Houston,
died 2012, age 48

Mae Brussell (1922-1988),
researcher of suspicious deaths

15. Mae Brussell Protected Us, Warned Us

"After they see me, when their mothers are feeding them all that cashmere sweater and girdle _____ [expletive deleted by *New York Times*], maybe they'll have a second thought -- that they can be themselves and win.

-- Janis Joplin (1943-1970)

In 1973, one year after Watergate, Mae Brussell (1922-1988) wrote an article, "Why Is the Senate Watergate Committee functioning as part of the Cover-up?" In it, she identified intelligence and law enforcement baddies:

L Patrick Gray, Acting Director of the FBI,
William Sullivan, of FBI's Division V, Domestic Security,
Robert Mardian, Assistant Attorney General,
Richard Helms, Director of the CIA,
Lt Gen Robert Cushman, Deputy Director of the CIA,
Vernon Walters, Deputy Director of the CIA,
General Alexander Haig, National Security Council,
William Bore, Inspector General [!!!] of the CIA, and
Henry A. Peterson, Assistant Attorney General,
Henry Kissinger, National Security Council [and KGB].

That is, 2 FBI's, 4 CIA's, 2 DOJ', and 2 NSC's. (I couldn't resist adding Kissinger's other affiliation, in hopes that readers will peruse the relevant Appendices – I and R – in this book.)

Just fathom it. Agencies whose job the public think of as a sacred trust for fighting crime, defending our democracy, and pursuing justice, twisted around to do the very opposite! As will be seen in Chapter 22, the British Secret Elite committed extreme crimes while wearing the costume of nobility. Hadn't we better get over our automatic deference to persons in high-up roles?

Mae Brussell. Mae was a wealthy Jewish housewife, and mother of four. She had got a head start on Watergate, by having noticed false bits in the official story of JFK's assassination. Like another housewife, Sylvia Meagher, Mae studied all 26 volumes of the Warren Commission, cross-indexing and discovering the existence of heretofore unknown groups and incriminating connections among "law" enforcers.

After Watergate she listed the hard-to-explain deaths of 30 people who may have known too much about that business. Mrs E Howard Hunt, who died in a plane crash, is one. Another is Martha Mitchell, wife of the Attorney General, whom every comedian had a heyday with.

Mae Brussell was also an investigator of the kidnapping of Patty Hearst and the Manson murders. She understood that the same party was behind all of this, and that it was connected to both the distributing of LSD and the mental experiments done on prisoners at Vacaville, California.

Mae was particularly concerned that so many young singers were dying. her list includes Otis Redding, age 26; Jimi Hendrix, 26; Jim Morrison, 27; Mama Cass Elliot, 33; Jim Croce, 30; Janis Joplin 27. She recorded the fact that those persons was doing well and there is no reason to believe a suicide story (and Mama Cass did not "choke on her food"). Brussell notes:

> "Persons around the musicians had strange backgrounds and were often suspect. All of these musicians were at the peak of a creative period and success at the time they were offered LSD. Their personalities altered. Optimism and gratification were replaced with doubt and misery."

One of Mae's theories is that the singers were able to attract followers, which is a no-no for the Powers That Be. I agree but I also think that often "they" give the singer training and promotion and then cause his/her death as part of the aim to break hearts. This sort of thing is known in Tavistockese as policy of "turbulence." Mae Brussell's meticulous research is recorded in a 2013 biography by Alex Constantine who was her student.

Brussell saw patterns of murders identical to those in Germany (which she learned about from E Gumbrel's 1922 book, *Four Years of Political Murders*, most of which were later admitted to!) Listen to her, quoted in Paul Krassner's 1978 "The Mind of Mae Brussell" (online)

> "How much violence was there in Nazi Germany, before the old Germany, the center of theater, opera, philosophy, poetry, psychology and medicine, was destroyed? How many incidents took place that were not coincidental? Was it when the first tailor disappeared? Or librarian? Or when the first press was closed or the first song eliminated? Or when the first political science teacher was killed coming home on his bike? How many incidents happened that were perfectly normal until people woke up?

Eine Kleine Recap of Terms

So far in this book I've been forced to concoct new terms:

1. **The Harrit rule**. Professor Niels Harrit can prove that WTC Building 7 came down by controlled demolition. Thus we know that courts won't allow his case to be heard. *Courts mustn't bring forth the truth*. I call this "the Harrit rule."

2. **Attorney general holdback – AGHB**. The Framers of the Constitution did not really provide for this. Article II gives the executive the job of law enforcement -- so if it happens to be government that is acting criminally, officials are protected from exposure or punishment!

3. **Type-2 Judicial Treason**. A judge who wreaks violence on a person, commits the treason of "waging war on the people" -- unless the ruling was called for.

I've only just noticed that these concepts are all of a piece! Folks may call it 'corruption.' but I see it as the normal activity of the powerful. They HAVE to prevent courts from pursuing justice. God help them if people catch on!

Who Is Causing the Trouble? Could It Be 'the Jews?'

Please allow me to state my thesis again. I hold what is often called a conspiratorial view. I think it is perfectly within the job description of a political scientist to inspect open power in human affairs and to infer the presence of secret power. Any man and his dog and cat can see that 9-11 did not take place by dint of 19 men stealing four airplanes. It was a marvelous staged drama.

Many officials of the US government were participants, and many employees of the media took an active part in spreading the untruths. (That makes them criminal, per the crime of being an accessory after the fact of murder, or, of being an accomplice if they planned it.)

There is a concentration of Jewish men in the highest ranks of the American media. Accordingly, many commentators hold forth on the role of either Jews or "Zionists" in causing 9-11. This, however, is a sign of our usual sloppy thinking. We are hard-wired to believe that our enemy, or rival, is a tribe, since it naturally was always a tribe, in bygone days.

This does not hold now. As we will see in Chapter 22, even when an identifiable nation such as England or the US is openly making war, with thousands of troops in the nation's uniform, the party causing the war can be as small (and as hidden) as a roundtable of men at Oxford. Thus if Germany has a grievance about World War I, there's not much point in their trying to get "England" to apologize for having pulled a trick on them. "England" – the English folk – did not do it.

Our penchant for thinking that an ethnic group is the baddy is seen in our quick acceptance of the utterly daft idea that Muslims working for "Osama Bin Laden" attacked the WTC. No doubt we may also fall prey to believing it's Jews. Please don't succumb to this; it is a snare. And it prevents a deeper search.

Is Israel a Big Power?

Israel is small beer. But picture how the "offices" of Israel can, and do, use our governmental "offices" to get things. Dov Zakheim, a dual citizen US-Israel (and a VP of Booz Allen) was the Comptroller of the much-robbed-from Defense Department in the Bush Administration starting in 2001. I learned from a Youtube video (it may be accurate or not) that Zakheim arranged to sell US-owned F-16 fighter jets to Israel at a fantastic bargain.

Well, if true, that's normal corruption (if Zakheim got some huge kickback). Or, maybe it's treason. If he helped his other nation at our expense, you could say he acted nobly as an Israeli and treacherously as an American.

Note: the definition of treason in the Constitution is quite narrow. A person has to levy war against the United States (or give aid and comfort to the enemy) to qualify. Probably the definition is *too* narrow, as we all know instinctively when someone has been disloyal to his or her group. It does not require engagement in war.

Anyway, if a member of the Defense Department plays a dirty game he or she should be indicted, tried, jailed, whatever the normal procedure is. Dual citizenship is not the crime and being Jewish is not the crime. It would be a crime no matter who committed it. In fact it would be good to bring to trial very publicly someone who is being accused, in whispers, of acting against America for Israel. Let everyone bring emotions into it. Clear the air.

Who, Then, Runs World Government?

In 2008 Henry Kissinger, slave to World Governors, said:

> "The most important challenge is: how to distill a new international order from three simultaneous revolutions:
> (a) the transformation of the traditional state system of Europe; (b) the radical Islamist challenge to historic notions of sovereignty; and (c) the drift of the center of gravity of international affairs from the Atlantic to the Pacific and Indian Oceans." -- International Tribune, April 8, 2008.

Of course that's nonsense. The European mergers were cannily directed by the people Kissinger works for, and so was the "radical Islamist challenge" (as Brzezinski clearly admitted in a 1998 interview). These guys never talk real. I mean could they ever say "Yes we ran MK-Ultra to find out how to destroy children's minds, and yes we kill any doctor who may find the cure for autism? And sure, we did 9-11?" No, they have to speak nonsense. Gibberish.

My Sociobiological Theory of World Government

Since becoming a pupil of EO Wilson in 1978, I have viewed humans as a biological species more than as a historic entity. To me it makes perfect sense to imagine that a few men climbed to the top – World Government – and are now in trouble as it is hard to stay at the top. When one man acquires formidable power he has to worry daily about being overthrown by a rival, or as an act of vengeance. Hierarchy is normal in some mammal species. A fur seal takes such complete control that he exclusively does all the mating. (Must be exhausting.)

Now picture what happened to our poor old human overlords when 20th century technology arose. They had to jockey every which way to keep from being clobbered.

What Is the Likely Genealogy of These Bozos?

When did the baddies begin their murderous course? John Dee (1527-1609), in the reign of Queen Elizabeth I, seems to have been a world planner. He was a friend of Grey, ancestor of the Grey we met in Chapter 21, and the Cecil family of spies. Many writers chalk everything up to the Rothschilds, as that family was able to buy

A Fur Seal

governments and initiate wars. I doubt if anyone can compete with Rothschild so they collude. The Church is involved, too!

John Coleman wrote *The Conspirators' Hierarchy* in 1996 from his experience in British Intelligence. I can't find anything to quarrel with in his book. He says a Committee of 300 runs all big businesses and all governments. I also trust the late Antony Sutton's claim that there never was a Cold War between communism and capitalism. Rather, Wall Street ran both. Nesta Webster's scholarly history, *Secret Societies* (1924), shows the French and Russian 'revolutions' to be identical, top-down coups. Anton Chaitkin's *Treason in America* (1999) lays out the real conspirators of the US Civil War of 1863. Big surprises!

Let My Bozos Go!

I feel sure my "sociobiological" view is right. For ten years I have been applying it and I've never noticed anything that refutes it. Granted, there should be alpha wannabees out there causing trouble for the Bozos. But perhaps no individual can strike at them with any prospect of surviving.

The thing we should concentrate on is finding ways for the poor fools at the top to "retire." I suppose the dismantling of their empire will come with great tragedy, but if we find better ways to run the earth, folks might be attracted to it. Presently each of us is locked in to the system. Leaving it would mean not having access to food. We tend to say "Let it ride for another month or so." Look at how eager we are to dismiss anyone who has real evidence of what is going on.

Anyway, as trapped as we are, we're not as trapped as they are! Poor buggers. And talk about mind control, they can't even think! There can never even have a moment of emotional balance, much less joy or dreams of the future.

Let my Bozos go!

chapter sixteen

The swan boats in the Boston Public Garden

Boston Public Library in Copley Square near the
Marathon finish line

PART IV. GET YOUR HANDS MUDDY

16. Boston Marathon: Enough is Enough

Lacrimosa dies illa/Qua resurget in favilla/ Judicandus homo reus.
On that sad day, the accused will rise from the burning coals
and face judgment. – *Dies Irae*, Holy Office (circa 1260)

For here men are men and their hearts are true.
(Boston College song) -- TH Hurley, *For Boston* (1885)

The Boston case says Tamerlan, and brother Dzhokhar (whose
nickname is Jahar), immigrated to the US as refugees, with
their parents and sisters, 12 years ago. In 2015 they were at the
Marathon finish line when two bombs went off. At that point the
authorities allegedly did not notice them.

Tamerlan, age 24, and Jahar, 19, weren't "found" until late
night April 18th. In the meantime, it is said, they killed a security
guard at MIT, perhaps in an attempt to get his gun. Then they
carjacked the car of student Dun Meng. Dun escaped when the
brothers stopped at a gas station. Later, police located the boys
and "exchanged gunfire." Tamerlan died, (although there is a
Youtube of alive, stripped, being pushed into a paddy wagon.)
Jahar miraculously escaped and hid in a boat.

The next thing you know, he's in hospital. Two years later his
trial begins. His public defender turns out to be Judy Clarke, who
defended Eric Rudolph after he allegedly bombed the Atlanta
Olympics in 1996, and also bombed an abortion clinic and a
lesbian bar. She also defended the Unabomber Ted Kaczynski
who had been an MK-Ultra victim at Harvard in 1959 at age 17.

Judy doesn't engage in cross-examining the prosecutor's
witnesses, such as the one person who saw the Tsarnaevs do the
MIT murder. She does not show skepticism about Dun Meng's
claim that the boys boasted to him that they were the bombers!

Proper Procedure Was Not Followed

The defense attorney, as mentioned, proffered a not-guilty plea, but then said "My client did it." The trial was not conducted properly as she did not beat the dirt out of the opposite side, as is normal in our adversarial system. I'd have **broken down Meng's story**.

Clarke did not beef up Jahar's confidence by having family members visit him. If we are to trust a Youtube clip of the two sisters, they were intimidated out of the picture by accusations that they had committed a crime. Similarly, the mother fled to Russia when accused of shop-lifting. If no family members were available, how about the coach who was featured in the *Rolling Stone* article. Does not a school **sports coach traditionally befriend a student** who is in trouble?

Many people attended the Marathon, many wore backpacks. The brothers were accused based on a video. The video does not show them causing explosions. I believe the Constitution's Fifth Amendment applies: "No person shall be held to answer for a capital, or otherwise infamous crime, unless on a **presentment** or indictment of a **grand jury**...." Members of a grand jury look to see how much evidence there is, and decide if a trial is warranted. Tsarnaev was charged with "use of a weapon of mass destruction," per 18 USC 2332.

Policeman Daniel Genck charged in federal district court:

> "I have reviewed videotape footage taken from a security camera ... At approximately 2:38 p.m. (11 minutes before the first explosion) -- two young men can be seen turning left (eastward) onto Boylston from Gloucester Street.... Both men are carrying large knapsacks. At approximately 2:45 p.m., Bomber Two [Genck has already designated the brothers as Bomber One and Two!] can be seen detaching himself from the crowd and walking east toward the Marathon finishing line. He appears to have the thumb of his right hand hooked under the strap of his knapsack and a cell phone in his left hand. He then can be seen apparently [how?] slipping his knapsack onto

the ground.... 30 seconds before the first explosion, he lifts his phone to his ear and keeps it there for approximately 18 seconds. A few seconds after he finishes the call, the large crowd of people around him can be seen reacting to the explosion...." That remark by Genck seems to have sealed Jahar's fate -- as though the boy was receiving a call from a baddy. But the call can be traced. I'll bet it came from his handler. It may have come from the persons who set Jahar up, no?

Officer Genck continues, in his 2013 filing with the Court:

"I have reviewed images of two men taken at approximately 12:17 a.m. by a security camera at the ATM and the gas station/ convenience store where the two carjackers drove with the victim in his car. Based on the men's close physical resemblance to [Massachusetts Vehicle Registry] photos of Tamerlan and Dhokhar, I believe the two men who carjacked, kidnapped, and robbed the victim are Tamerlan and Dzhokhar Tsarnaev...."

That is an **astonishing** *non sequitur*. All Genck is entitled to say is: "I looked at who was on the security camera at the ATM. I compared it with the driver's-licence photos of the brothers and found a good match." He can't claim to have 'witnessed' that they did any carjacking or robbing of the victim!

Further down the page, Genck reports second-hand:

"A gunfight ensued between the car's occupants and law enforcement officers in which numerous shots were fired. [By whom?] One of the men was severely injured and remained at the scene the other managed to escape in the car.... That car was later found abandoned a short distance away, and an intact low-grade explosive device was discovered inside it. In addition, from the scene of the shootout in Watertown, the FBI has recovered two unexploded IEDs."

Next, Genck offers connecting evidence as follows:

147

> "On April 21, 2013, the FBI searched [Jahar's] dormitory room... They seized among other things, a large pyrotechnic, a black jacket and a white hat of the same general appearance as those worn by Bomber Two at the Boston Marathon on April 15, 2013, and BBs."

Seriously. They found a baseball cap in a dorm room!

Instructions to the Jury

If I had been Judge George O'Toole at the trial of Jahar, I'd have instructed the jurors to consider all the times when media deluged the public with analysis of the killers, and it later proved to be garbage. Come to think of it, I'd remind them that a passport of one of the 9-11 hijackers was 'found' on the ground near the WTC -- an absurdity, an insult to us all.

I would also give the jury a lesson in the separation of powers that is the **bedrock of the Constitution**. I would say that the very branch that wants us to see Muslims as a threat to the US is the same executive branch that is gung-ho war in the Middle East. This is a **'conflict of interest.'**

Note: Judges in federal court of the Northern District of Georgia regularly use these Instructions to the Jury.

> "The law presumes that every defendant is innocent. The Defendant does not have to prove [his][her] innocence or produce any evidence at all. The Government must prove guilt beyond a reasonable doubt, and if it fails to do so you must find the Defendant not guilty. // **You must never consider punishment in any way in deciding whether the Defendant is guilty or not guilty.** // You must discuss the case with one another to try to reach agreement. While you are discussing the case, do not hesitate to reexamine your own opinions and change your mind if you become convinced that you were wrong. But do not give up your honest beliefs just because the others think differently.... // **Remember that in a very real way you are judges** – judges of the facts. Your only interest is to seek the truth from the evidence in this case. [Emphasis added]" – gand.uscourts.gov

Dramatis Personae – A Very Partial List

Richard Donohue, cop, wounded in "Watertown gun battle"

Ib Todashev, friend of Tamerlan, killed at home by FBI man

Ruslan Tsarni, Jahar's uncle, was son-in-law of a CIA biggie

Maret Tsarnaeva, in Toronto, disagrees with Officer Genck

Police Commissioner Ed Davis, for Boston Mayor Merino

Henry Nields, MD, PhD, state's Chief Medical Examiner

R. Serino, Emergency mgr, ran marathon bomb drill in 2008

David Heneberry, got ladder, looked into boat, "saw blood"

Bryan McGrory, editor of the Boston Globe, God help us

Deval Patrick, Massachusetts governor, formerly with DoJ

Federal Judge George O'Toole, graduate of BC and Harvard

Judy Clarke, lawyer for mind controlled killers and patsies

Dun Meng, student immigrant from China, Mercedes owner

Law deans: O'Rourke, BU; Minow, Harvard, raise no query

K Feinberg handed $60 million to victims from private fund

> FBI agent Richard Deslauriers: "Today, we are enlisting the public's help to identify the two suspects For clarity, **these images should be the only ones, and I emphasize the only ones, that the public should view to assist us.** Other photos should not be deemed credible, and they unnecessarily **divert the public's attention in the wrong direction** and *create undue work for vital law enforcement resources...* No bit of information, no matter how small, is too small for us to see. Each piece moves us forward towards justice.... If you know anything about the bombings or the men pictured here, please call 1-800-CALL- FBI. [Emphasis added]. OBSTRUCTION OF JUSTICE! HELLO?

To My Knowledge and Belief

Jahar looks like a patsy in the tradition of Albert DeSalvo and James Earl Ray. The 'facts' kept changing e.g., police said he ran over his brother and that he was en route to Manhattan for more killings. Jahar's unavailability for interviews for 2 years suggests his brain was being altered. But the giveaway is always the lack of **proper court procedure**. (Martin Bryant, in Australia got no trial at all – See Appendix Y.) If he disobeys them, raise the alarm. Is the Harrit rule pressuring him?.

Dear Boston

Dear Boston, you raised me up. I lived in Dorchester from age zero to 22, never going further away than Nantasket by boat. I was home when the Sox won the pennant in 1967. I went to Girl Scout Camp in Waltham. I can name every station on the Ashmont line, backwards. I'm a Boston ex-pat in Oz and now I'm 'giving back.' Got to tell you what to do re the Marathon. So pull up a bowl of clam chowder and listen to me. You need my help.

You can start by taking those silly "Boston strong" tee shirts off the market and replace with "Boston weak." Is there anything weaker than a city that goes into voluntary lockdown over a police request to hunt for a 19-year old? Good God. Is there anything weaker (or stupider) than a city that lets a judge run a blatantly fraudulent trial and utters not a word of condemnation? And you call Boston "the Athens of the North"? Socrates would barf.

Come on, get with it. Richard Serino, "assistant Medical director," ran a Emergency Management seminar in 2008 in which he showed how to create a "planned disaster." Yes, they get away with using that phrase, on the grounds that it's necessary to train personnel for the real thing. His slide show, five years before "the real thing" is set at the Marathon finish line. Therefore, please deduce: the 2013 event was planned by these quasi-government personnel.

It's illogical to say "Some boys from Chechnya did it and it had nothing to do with the Emergency Services." You should say "If it walks like a duck and quacks like a duck we know that it is a duck." In law, this is known as a rebuttable presumption. We should PRESUME that Serino's pre-planning got used. But he, under questioning, could rebut it, and show that there was no involvement of any of his men on April 15, 2013.

Indeed you need to call Serino in for questioning on this very matter. BTW, if he says "It's secret, owing to national security," you must arrest him on the spot. Got that? OK.

Now then, O Boson weak ones, find out more about this Judy

Clarke person. Have you ever seen such nonsense in your life as her blaming her own client "so as to prepare a sympathetic jury on sentencing day"? If Judy were a victim of CIA mind-control, we need to reopen her three cases: the Unabomber, the Atlanta Olympic bomber, and Tsarnaev. Not that we have time to run another case, with the judiciary in its perfidious condition, but I'm just sayin.'

Remember when we loved our cops? Yes, we did. Well here's the chance to be good to them. Find out who is pushing them around. Why are there so many privatized "security" companies acting like they are in charge? Recall that the principle excuse for all this is the 9-11 event -- which also was planned and did not require "Muslims."

Now let's deal with O'Toole. He calls himself a judge and draws $199k per year for his "hard work." My grades in law school were lousy. I flunked 8 of 25 courses and had to repeat them, but I would be a better judge than he. I'd have whipped out bench warrants by the cartload.

Actually, O'Toole should have arrested himself for treason. Look, there was a war being waged on the people in Copley Square, for Pete's sake. Never mind federal treason, it was state treason under common law. (No statute of lim, either!) Gee, law thinks of everything.

Of course I'd also seek extradition of the FBI guy in Florida who killed a potential witness, Ibgrahim Todashev (see Appendix O). Naturally, I'd put Aunt Maret under the Witness Protection program, even if it means she has to get a nose job. All these things are doable. Law is great.

Boston should hold a memorial for the dead brother, Tamerlan (what a name!). It should give a creative writing award to the girl who composed the boat-wall confession.

Maybe you Beantowners consider that *The Boston Globe*, and local law schools (Suffolk, N'eastern, BU, BC – Jebby country, NE Law, or HQ) are your friends. Think again. If they are playing the Jahar-is-guilty story, they are your oppressors. They are right now putting your life in danger.

chapter seventeen

Porter Goss (second from left) and colleagues at a dinner. He was simultaneously an elected representative and a member of the CIA, never mind that that violates the Constitutional separation of powers.

America's biggest whistleblower, Gary Webb, journalist for the San José Mercury News, discovered the CIA importation of cocaine for use in the ghetto.

17. A Hall of Fame for Whistleblowers and Law Heroes

The memory of the just is blessed but the memory of the wicked shall rot. -- King Solomon, *Proverbs, 10:7* (circa 930 BC)

Conscience is instinct bred in the house.
-- Henry David Thoreau (1817-1862), *Conscience*

Just think, if a group of laypersons had made a noisy celebration of the accomplishments of the late whistle-blower Gary Webb, back in 1989 when he *effectively solved the drug problem,* we'd have a much happier nation now. Webb learned that the CIA, allegedly to help the Contras in Nicaragua (oh, please), had imported cocaine to the US, and developed crack, a very harmful variation.

Representative Maxine Waters, helped him get a hearing in the House, and who should happen to be chairman of the relevant committee? None other than Porter Goss. He had been one of the, shall we say, principals. Later he became head of CIA. As for Gary Webb, he "shot himself to death" (two bullets) at age 49.

Let's have a Hall of Fame for persons, **especially judges**, who use the law wisely and well. Granted they should do that, it's their job. But 'judicial culture' can change, and persons connected to the court begin to accept a cynical view that it's OK for judges to protect the powerful, and to falsify reality.

Recently a circuit judge (federal appeals court) uttered a remarkable statement. Judge Edith Clement, in a case related to an oil spill by BP (British Petroleum), saw that the way the ruling of the lower sourt had gone, many people, whose business injury was unrelated to the oil spill were getting compensated. She said that if the court failed to correct this "We are party to the fraud." Yay! Into the Hall of Fame she goes.

A List of Whistleblowers Who Died in Just One Decade, 2001-2010 (and these are only the ones I'm aware of!)

Liz Birt 1956-2005 *car crash.* She connects vaccines to autism.

Nicola Calipari 1953-2005 *shot.* Saw US war crimes in Iraq.

Iris Chang 1968-2004 *shot.* Historian of 1934 China/Japan.

Robin Cook 1946-2005 *heart attack.* UK's FM: *al quaeda* hoax!

Rachel Corrie 1979-2003 *bulldozed.* Israel in the West Bank.

Anne Johnson Davis 1953-2010 *suicide.* Satanic ritual abuse.

Bev Eckert 1951-2009 *plane crash.* Widow of 9/11: inside job.

Carla Emery DeLong 1939-2005 *illness.* Protested hypnosis.

Robert Friedman d. 2008 *blood disease.* Exposed Red mafia.

Charlie Gittings 1953-2010 *cancer.* Published US war crimes.

James Hatfield 1958-2001 *overdose.* Bush's A.W.O.L. record.

Gerard Holmgren 1959-2010 *unknown.* No-planes on 9/11.

Molly Ivins 1944-2007 *cancer.* Spoke her mind, in *NY Times.*

David Kelly 1944-2003 *wrist slashed.* Bioweapons of Saddam.

Leola McConnell d. 2007 *disappeared.* Dominatrix of VIPs.

John Murtha 1932-2010 *gall bladder,* in Bethesda. Army woes.

Deborah Palfrey 1956-2008 *hanged.* 'DC madam,' had a list.

Alyssa Peterson 1976-2003 *shot.* Reported US torture in Iraq.

Gunther Russbacher 1942-2005 *illness.* Waco, mind control.

Tim Russert 1950-2008 *heart attack.* Queried Cheney on TV.

Aaron Russo 1943-2007 *cancer.* Income tax law is unproven.

Edward Said 1935-2003 *cancer.* Palestine historical record.

Margie Schoedinger 1960-2005*shot.* Sued GW Bush for rape.

Sherman Skolnick 1930-2006 *unknown.* Jailed bad judges.

Jerry E. Smith 1950-2010 *cancer.* Books on HAARP, weather.

Antony Sutton 1925-2002 *unknown.* Cold War was a fake.

Stephanie Tubbs-Jones 1949-2008 *car crash.* House Ethics.

Gary Webb 1955-2004 *shot.* CIA imports drugs, Iran-Contra.

Paul Wellstone 1944-2002 *small plane crash.* Anti-war senator.

Ted Westhusing 1960-2005 *shot in Iraq.* Queried contractors.

David Wilhelm 1962-2005 *shot.* Customs official in Atlanta.

Tookie Williams 1953-2005 *execution.* CIA drugs to gangs.

Valerie Wolf 1948-2002 *cancer.* MK-ULTRA mind control.

Average age of decedent: 55.

Peterson, Birt, Said/ Sutton, Russbacher, Smith/ Ivins, Westunghus, Eckert/
Russert, Skolnick, Russo. It takes all kinds to make a world. Heroes abound!

The Power Structure Is Revealed by These Heroes

Textbooks inaccurately teach us what's going on. Political reality can be neatly deduced from the type of reaction that a whistleblower gets! In many cases, such as the first 7 here, the revelations contain information about the way **the public is being secretly controlled and weakened.**

1. The US government uses mind control (Wolf, Davis, Emery).
2. Drugs were distributed by CIA (Webb, Tookie Williams, possibly Wilhelm). (Granted, Tookie Williams died legally; he was on Death Row. But he had turned over a new leaf and was teaching ghetto kids to avoid drugs. Governor Schwarzenegger could have pardoned him but didn't. I assume Tookie knew too much.)
3. Autism is connected to vaccines (Birt).
4. 9/11 was an inside job (Eckert, Cooke, Holmgren).
5. Weather disasters are engineered by HAARP (Smith).
6. Russian criminals, "the Red Mafya," were brought to New York in order to cause chaos (Friedman).
7. The Cold War was fake. We helped the USSR. (Sutton).
8. The US commits war crimes (Gittings, Calipari, Peterson).
9. IRS is not authorized under the Constitution (Russo).
10. WACO was a chemical-weapons event (Russbacher).

A few of the whistleblowers listed above discovered *ordinary* naughties, e.g., Schroedinger, Palfrey, and O'Connell revealed sexual activities of Washington personnel, and Hatfield found out that young Bush went AWOL from the National Guard.

Most whistleblowers fell into the job unplanned. They saw something that the nation needed to know about and could not rest until the information was communicated. (Are you like that?) There are also plenty of whistleblowers who, happily, ain't dead. The indefatigable (nonogenarian) Rodney Stich, is one. Bill Windsor is another. We have a further need for brainiacs who will say "OK, now how to turn the situation around?"

Whistleblower Laws. The deceased persons on our list did not get to enjoy laws that protect whistleblowers! These usually forbid employers to retaliate. Note: there is also a False Claims Act, federally and in many states, that actually pays you to bring to book any party that is cheating the government. You can get up to 25% of the damages that company pays – millions! You play the role of a 'relator' by filing a "qui tam" suit. This means you are acting for the nation. *Qui tam de rege* means "on behalf of the king." Per 31 USC 3729, a case can be made against a party that:

"(A) knowingly presents, or causes to be presented, a false or fraudulent claim for payment or approval;... (D) has possession, custody, or control of property or money used, or to be used, by the Government and knowingly delivers ... less than all of that money or property; [etc]."

At present, some former employees of Merck are suing as relators in a complaint that this vaccine manufacturer wrongly stated the effectiveness of the MMR-2 vaccine (thereby cheating the government, which is the main purchaser of vaccines!). It is also possible to file private prosecutions against miscreants when the Attorney General refuses to do so.

Go for It: Be a Leader!

Every society needs the leaders that spontaneously arise. This is quite different from arranging for persons to step into an official role. Modern democracy creates a wrong notion -- that leadership will be found in elected politicians. Today's campaigns are tightly controlled by media. Not only does the press tell us what it wants to tell us about the candidate that it favors, it can stay entirely silent about others (e.g., *moi*, in 2006).

If you are 25 and have been a US citizen for 7 years you can easily run for Congress. You can run on a single issue that you care about. No need to wait for a political party to invite you! Just declare! And there are state offices that you can seek as early as age 18. I'd like to help you.

chapter eighteen

White Houses personages allegedly watching the capture of Bin Laden

Speech by US President Barack Obama, May 1, 2011:

"It was nearly 10 years ago … Hijacked planes cutting through a cloudless September sky. The Twin Towers collapsing to the ground…. The wreckage of Flight 93 in Shanksville where the actions of heroic citizens saved even more heartbreak and destruction…. We reaffirmed our ties to each other and our love of community and country. … We quickly learned that the 9/11 attacks were carried out by Al Qaeda, an organization headed by Osama Bin Laden…. And so we went to war against al Qaeda, to protect our citizens, our friends, and our allies….
And finally, last week, I …authorized an operation to get Osama bin Laden and bring him to justice."

18. Media and Control of the Mind

Mentiri est contra mentum ire. Lying goes against the mind.

Lex punit medacium. The law punishes falsehood. (Law maxims)

Censorship means a loss in the emotional, philosophical, and artistic wealth of a society. -- Andre Sakharov (1970s)

Is there any law that can limit the amount of lying that the media do every day? Can media be stopped from secretly designing our culture? What about the flickering screens, that cause the human brain to switch to alpha waves, increasing the person's suggestibility?

Thanks to the First Amendment's guarantee of freedom of speech, we tend to think "anything goes." There are legal restraints, however. Congress created, by statute, the Federal Communications Commission (which is thus a 'statutory body'). It licenses the use of broadcasting, as the bands are limited. The phone line for complaints is 1-888-CALL-FCC. Why not dial it soon?

The FCC also claims to promote competition. I don't think it does, not does the Department of Justice enforce anti-trust law. The Sherman anti-trust law of 1890 says:

> Section 1: Every contract, combination in the form of trust or otherwise, or conspiracy, in restraint of trade or commerce among the several States, or with foreign nations, is declared to be illegal.
>
> Section 2: Every person who shall monopolize, ... or conspire with any other person or persons, to monopolize any part of the trade or commerce among the several States, or with foreign nations, shall be deemed guilty of a felony.

How Do the Media Handle 9-11?

The 9-11 event had to have been planned far in advance with mainstream media very much involved. Indeed 9-11 was basically a media event, a false flag in which we were told that foreigners had attacked the World Trade Center in New York when in fact the all of that was made up.

Ten years later, Steve Hendrix wrote an article in the *Washington Post* entitled "After 9-11, woman who was at the Pentagon remains skeptical." He's referring to April Gallop as *skeptical!*

"You want to play in the back yard, son?" April Gallop says to the lanky 10-year-old tailing her on the front walk of a neat frame house in a Richmond suburb. "You go around; I'll be right there."

"I won't let him outside by himself," Gallop says in a low voice, looking down the street. A woman walks her dog across the way, not glancing over, not giving a neighborly wave. Gallop leans against her car, a cherry-red BMW with a license plate that reads "A OVRCMER" and a fuel door that is slightly ajar. "Now who's been messing with this?" she murmurs, pushing it closed. A "No Trespassing" sign is tucked into a trellis. Another is planted by the door. Gallop leans against the car and pulls papers from an envelope that a County deputy sheriff hand-delivered a few hours earlier. It's another threat from the landlord. "Why is this happening?" she asks.

The lease payments are up to date, paid during the past six years by a Pentagon Sept. 11 survivors' fund. She thought she was renting to own, but now the property owner wants the house back. Gallop has an appointment with a lawyer the next morning. A new one. Is this the sixth or the seventh? It's hard to remember all the lawsuits filed, the claims denied, the appeals that go 'round and 'round. "Evidently he has formed some kind of opinion about me," she says of the owner.

...Ten years ago, there was no contrail of derision attached to her name. That was before she had fought with government agencies and private charities... Before she had formally accused her government of making up that story about an airliner crashing into her Pentagon office.

She doesn't know how long she was out. "Oh my God, am I in hell?" she wondered as her eyes strained to decipher the jagged heaps of wallboard and office furniture, the computers spitting sparks, the legs and arms sprouting bizarrely from the debris, some waving for help, others crazy-broken and still. And then beneath that, muffled and weak, she heard . . . what? a baby?

Elisha with mom, April Gallop

"Oh my God, is there a baby in hell?" she asked.

A baby. Elisha. On her first day back from maternity leave, her boss had asked the new single mother to come straight to the office, newborn and all. Just handle a bit of urgent paper-work He had been sleeping in his stroller next to her desk.

She pushed through the crust of chairs and cabinets and the pain that felt like hammers pounding her skull and spine. Others were upright now, shouting, shoving rubble away from the loudest screams. She tried to help. The only light was a flare of gritty sun from a hole high above the mountains of debris. Finally she found the place where the feeble cry was the clearest. She reached into the rubble, shouldered aside rocks of concrete and felt cotton on her fingertips. She pulled out her 10-week-old son by his onesie.

"Elisha," she calls into the back yard. His hat pops over the edge of the playground set that the VFW volunteers brought a few years ago. She calls them "my angels," folks who still think of her simply as a hallowed Sept. 11 survivor, her son as a miracle baby. The boy comes up. "Yes, ma'am?" "Let's go see if they've picked the squash. Lock the gates now."

Keeping the Story Going. Even after the public more or less knows the truth about something, the media doggedly keeps up its old position. This year, 2015, for MLK's birthday, the old story about James Earl Ray was rolled out again, never mentioning that Coretta had won the case against Jowers, proving a conspiracy. I call this *journalistic recidivism*.

An amazing aspect of media's control of the public mind is the use of blogs to create falsely the idea that we are listing to the public voice of society. Most often we are listening to paid disinformation artists. Below the *WaPo* article on the skeptical Gallop we see comments that I suspect are planted:

"This woman is really disgusting, she's been receiving endless generosity from the government and private individuals and her response is to slander this country with dishonest and stupid conspiracy theories. -- posted by RealChoices.

"The simple truth is that Ms. Gallop is "questioning" without even trying to find the answers. The truth is at the answer can be found by studying science, understanding Islamic Fundamentalism, and history. Why do they ignore history that shows that Muslim terrorists like targeting planes and the WTC? Why do they ignore
… the videos which clearly show Atta getting on a plane?" -- posted by Abruzzi4.\

"The Post has dipped to its lowest point with this article.. There must be something worthwhile this lady can do without being a drag on society, a pawn of her attorneys and her pathetic, ludicrus cases." -- posted by Cemay1.

Let's start a new truther rumor that this April Gallop was never there. Could she prove otherwise?" — posted by tourist011.

As there are now millions of people who think the towers fell by controlled demolition, not by fire damage, it is fantastic that newspaper editors and TV hosts manage to postpone the reckoning indefinitely. Maybe they've got a Plan B to demolish critics?

Controlling the Human Mind for Power Reasons

In the last 30 years I have seen the American population change from being sophisticated to being something close to stupid. I think it has mainly to do with media. No doubt education is also part of the plan for dumbing people down. Video games are involved. Possibly there is even a "chemical" change being instilled, by fluoridating the water.

Psy-war is good plan, pardon my saying that! I mean: it's a clever new weapon. Sure, the conquerors of the past may have indoctrinated the conquered with selected ideas and may have tried to prevent them from learning much. (African slaves in the American south were punished if they became literate.) But the 20th century saw amazing developments in the way to control minds. Here are some aspects of it that stand out, in the year 2015:

1. We are told stories by the media that did not happen at all (these are called Killer Bee stories after a famous case).
2. Children are not given the basic discipline of learning, such as writing letters or memorizing multiplication tables
3. Everything keeps changing fast, so you can't look forward to a foreseeable future "like your parents' life."
4. Political correctness demands that you not remark on a standard trait of one ethnic group or even of one gender.
5. Celebrities, who appear from nowhere, are plastered on the magazine covers and youth are expected to love them.
6. Billions of dollars are voted by Congress for psy-war (as the law against propagandizing Americans was repealed).
7. Thousands of military personnel are tasked, free of charge to the media, to respond anonymously to blogs.
8. Public relations firms advertise products they've never seen.
9. The role of hero in boys' storybooks has disappeared.
10. Candidates with no charisma are 'trained' for elections.
11. Messages are passed to kids surreptitiously, via songs.
12. Adults who question the laws are subjected to ridicule.
13. Books are being removed from libraries as a policy.
14. Any photo is suspect; it may have been photoshopped.

Time for Teachers To Teach Healthy Skepticism

The major responsibility for the education of children lies with the parents of course. But what about teachers? They have a duty to show kids how to think. I can see that it is asking too much at the moment for a teacher to say "Let's debunk 9-11." But each day's news headlines could be explored with an eye to asking what is the source of the information and whether the tale told makes sense. The class would not have to come to a decision, just analyze.

In Chapter 23 below, I discuss the allegation that Brian Nichols, in a 2005 case where he was accused of date rape, shot the judge in the courtroom and then killed a security guard and hijacked 5 cars. *The Atlanta Constitution Journal* changed the details many times, almost goading the public to complain. The 'hot' part was that he tied her to a toilet while he took a shower. I proffer the denouement:

Bill Hewitt, **"Seven Hours of Terror,"** *People*, March 28, 2005
Around 6 a.m. Nichols told her [Ashley Smith] he was going to have to move the truck, which he admitted he had stolen from the federal agent, David Wilhelm, so that it wouldn't be spotted. He also told her he was going to need her to drive him back in her car once he had ditched the vehicle. "Can I take my cell phone?" she asked. He had no objection and even left the guns behind.

As she drove behind him, she thought about calling the police, but she feared that she might get caught in cross fire when they moved in. ... [i.e., THE EXPLANATION]

After Nichols got rid of the truck about two miles from Smith's apartment complex, he was almost shocked when she swung by to pick him up. "Wow, you didn't drive off ?" he asked. "I thought you were going to." Instead she took him back to the apartment and served him a breakfast of pancakes and juice. "He was overwhelmed," she recalled. "He said, 'Real butter pancakes?'"

Extremes: MK-Ultra and Manchurian Candidates

A lawsuit, filed by Frank Rochelle on behalf of veterans who were given LSD in the Fifties, uses declassified CIA documents. One CIA subproject (admitted to) was to alter the person's mind and character so that he or she would kill on command, and not remember it afterward. Many mind-controlled persons did just that. I believe it explains many unsolved murders. These trained assassins are called 'Manchurian candidates.' I apologize for shocking you if you never knew about this.

In 2005 I came to know several women who underwent MK-Utra programming. It involved torture and even bestiality. I attended their conferences. The credibility of their stories is a famous issue. Occasionally I have heard them state a detail that I know is untrue, but mostly I vigorously vouch for them. (Memories can be planted, but that's no reason to reject all their claims.)

In Canada, one victim named Orlikow won a payment for having been subjected to the sleep treatment invented by Dr Cameron. It wiped out all of a person's memories, even the knowledge of how to control one's bladder. The effrontery of such doctors is remarkable. In Australia Dr Dax and Dr Bailey plied their trade. One of Dr Dax's "patients" was Martin Bryant.

Many Nazi doctors came into America, often by a passport given to them by the Vatican! The ringleader of mind control appears to be Tavistock. You can check the histories of such men as Sidney Gottlieb and Martin Orne. Splitting a child's mind was important. Fathom it.

What Is the Legal Position on Mind Control Stuff?

Is there some way to punish those who pushed this business on us? One punishment that springs to mind is self-flagellation: we really ought to hit ourselves for being so weak. As to real laws, let me list first the most extreme. You can kill someone, and not be punished, if that person is an **outlaw**, that is, beyond the reach of the law. Funnily enough all the biggies seem to beyond the law, judging by AGHB -- attorney general holdback.

The next biggest punishment is for **treason**. This law applies to any American who "wages war against the United States." Surely this encompasses those who routinely tortured children with MK-Ultra (and for no better purpose other than to learn how to control us all).

The next most extreme crime of which the mind controllers may be guilty is **genocide**. Per 18 USC 1091:

> "(a) Basic Offense. Whoever, ...with the specific intent to destroy, in whole or in substantial part, a national, ethnic, racial, or religious group as such (3) causes the permanent impairment of the mental faculties of members of the group through drugs, torture, or similar ...shall be punished....as provided in (b), without [time] limitation."

I believe Charlotte Iserbyt's *Deliberate Dumbing Down of America* shows intentional "**impairment of the mental faculties of a whole generation of children ...**" Granted, the genocide law says "by drugs, torture or similar techniques." How broad is "similar techniques"? Very broad, I'd say, as the two named categories are not similar to one another – drugs and torture.

Note: psychiatrist Joost Merloo gave the name 'menticide' to the crime of killing a mind. He also spoke of "rape of the mind." There are extant laws against rape (penetration of an orifice non-consensually), but I think we don't need to make new law. The plain crime of assault may suffice. Consider, too, the 13th Amendment to the Constitution: "Slavery...shall not exist in the United States."

I have argued in *Truth in Journalism* (2015) that we let doctors get away with crime, as though suing them for malpractice was the only option. This is our fault; we have assumed that disciplinary boards of medical associations would take care of truly bad behavior. Not so. (Be sure to see Appendices J and W).

Consider, too, how the pedophile priests, all those years, were never arrested. My guess is that they themselves were "given" their addiction. I'm pretty sure it was an organized crime, with the same goal as MK-Ultra, to break minds. But also to **turn folks away from religion once the scandal was revealed.**

Watching the show in real time, September 11, 2001 (from official archives)

In July 2015, Coretta Hanna obtained, via FOIA, a photo of Dick Cheney watching the twin towers burn. I hope it will be able to get through the psychological barrier that prevents many people from seeing his guilt. No man, in charge of a nation, during an attack by foreigners, could possibly be so relaxed.

We need to confront the Harrit rule, and stop believing it's inevitable that no official ever gets punished.

As we saw in this chapter, the media is controllable by the FCC and anti-trust law, and the messing up of minds of a whole group violates the law of genocide. Members of the media can also be charged as accessories-after-the-fact of crime. They perform cover-up like mad. (Note: if the crime involved is murder, there is no time limit.)

Can we get journalists to stop obeying the Top Dogs? It is well known that many journalists are committed to telling the truth and many die every year for their trouble. How do the committed ones feel about their colleagues who seem to be in a trance? I assume every anchorperson on TV is given a kind of training that prevents them putting their own thoughts or reactions to the audience.

This is quite a feat. The TV person "in our living room" talks to us like a friend but their brain is not their own. Also the commenters on blogs, who seem to be our neighbors, are likewise spouting the thoughts of of others, their paymasters.

I suggest we not put up with this. It is so insulting.

chapter nineteen

A Maryland general and an Estonian General celebrate 20 years of unconstitutional Bureau's NATO-run Partnerships for Peace.

A protester outside the Syrian embassy in London in 2012

19. 'Constitution Mary' to NATO: Drop Dead

Cry 'havoc' and let slip the dogs of war.
--William Shakespeare, *The Tragedy of Julius Caesar* (1599)

Inter arma, leges silent. In war, laws are silent. (Law maxim)

We moderns may have invented advanced technology, but we are way behind in the mental processes related to 'not being tricked.' Really, it's sensational how we go along with the self-serving gimmicks of the powerful. Take NATO. Do any Americans even know what that entity is? The acronym stands for North Atlantic Treaty Organization – that name tells us nothing. So right away there is a hint that the doings of NATO are not for public discussion. In 1949, when it was formed, we assumed it was "to fight the Communist menace."

Another example of our ability to be tricked is the fact that since the 1990s, foreign troops have been stationed in each of the 50 states of the US. This is almost incredible.

I first read of it in a book by Jim Keith in which he admitted he did not have proof. Upon goolging, I found one British military writer talking about it. After a few more years I noticed Michigan's website boasting about it. They said the "visiting' troops, from Latvia were being taught by Michiganders to understand democracy! And Michigan sent Latvia a gift: a bus for disabled children.

I will show below that US participation in NATO is unconstitutional. In Appendix H, I elaborate on that theme. But first just gaze at this list below of states and their foreign partners who, as I said, have put troops on the ground right here in the US for over twenty years, quietly. Please be shocked into action:

List of 50 States and Their NATO 'Partners' as of 2013

Alabama/Romania
Alaska/Mongolia
Arizona/Kazakhstan
Arkansas/Azerbaijan
California/Ukraine
Colorado/Jordan
Connecticut/Uruguay
Delaware/Trinidad-Tobago
Florida/Venezuela
Georgia/Georgia (cute, eh?)
Hawaii/Indonesia
Idaho/Cambodia
Illinois/Poland
Indiana/Colombia
Iowa/Kosovo
Kansas /Armenia
Kentucky/Ecuador
Louisiana/Bolivia
Maine/ Montenegro
Maryland/Estonia
Massachusetts/Paraguay
Michigan/Latvia
Minnesota/Croatia
Mississippi/Belize
Missouri/Panama

Montana/Kyrgyzstan
Nebraska/Czech Republic
Nevada/Turkmenistan
New Hampshire/El Salvador
New Jersey/Albania
New Mexico/Costa Rica
New York/So Africa
North Carolina/Moldova
North Dakota/Ghana
Ohio/Hungary
Oklahoma/Azerbaijan
Oregon/Bangladesh
Pennsylvania/Lithuania
Rhode Island/Bahamas
South Carolina/Slovakia
South Dakota/Surinam
Tennessee/Bulgaria
Texas/Chile
Utah/Morocco
Vermont/Senegal
Virginia/Tajikistan
Washington/Thailand
West Virginia/Peru
Wisconsin/Nicaragua
Wyoming/Tunisia

…'The State Partnership Program is one of the most important tools that we have in our collective kit bag,' said Commander Ham of the US Africa Command. 'And we see that certainly here between North Carolina and Botswana, where it is hugely powerful.' [??] The Program has grown dramatically since it was formed to support former Soviet bloc countries. Today, it includes 63 countries."
-- Donna Miles, American Press Service. August 20, 2012.

World Government

Who is your enemy? My enemy is World Government. I think we can see from the very existence of NATO that there's a world government. At least there has to be someone running NATO and it clearly is not the US president. Who, then would make the decisions? As we saw in the chapter on Values, Alan Sens was tasked by *someone* with converting NATO into a nation-builder.

I cannot imagine who that person is. I do know there are global entities such as Coca Cola, Google, Merck, and Monsanto. My brain can get around the idea that a group is coordinated enough to trade merchandise or property. But what kind of group would be caring about 'the people' and yet the people not see them or read their statements? It's got to be a secret organization.

I won't take your time describing the legal niceties of NATO; I have put that in a Q&A in Appendix H. It's my guess that whatever the bosses would put on paper is unlikely to reveal the facts. Isn't it better to look at their deeds than their words? One of their deeds mentioned in Chapter 8 above was the Brabant supermarket massacres, done in the interests of a "strategy of tension."

At the moment there is a reported build-up by NATO aimed at Russia. The pretext for action could be the crash of the Malaysian Flight MH17 in the Ukraine in July 2014.

(Was does that tell you about that crash?)

The Brabant massacres are reported in *NATO's Secret Armies*, by Daniele Ganser. He implicates Gladio, a sort of club of men from many European nations, including "Vatican City." One of Gladio's alleged missions after World War II was to stop the march of Communism. But we now know that "we" were sponsoring that march! So all the activities NATO's secret armies did for anti-communism need to be re-evaluated. What were they really for?

Raising Stanley McChrystal to a General Per *Wikipedia*: Stanley McChrystal, born 1953, the son of a Major General. He graduated from the US Military Academy in 1976, was commissioned a second lieutenant, Army. His initial assignment was to 82nd Airborne Division. In 1978, took the Special Forces Officer Course. Upon completion, went to Fort Bragg as commander of an "A-team." In 1981, moved to South Korea as intelligence and operations officer.

He went to the Naval War College in 1989. Was Army Special Operations action officer, J-3, Joint Special Operations Command in which capacity he deployed to Saudi Arabia for Operation Desert Storm. In 1994, McChrystal commanded the 2nd Battalion, 504th Parachute, revamped hand-to-hand combat curricula. After a year as a fellow at Harvard's Kennedy School of Government at Harvard University, he moved up to command the entire 75th Ranger Regiment to August 1999, then spent a year at Council on Foreign Relations. *[unethical!!]*

Promoted to brigadier general on January 1, 2001. He directed all Operation Enduring Freedom operations in Afghanistan. At the beginning of the Iraq War in March 2003, he delivered nationally televised Pentagon briefings. Shortly after the fall of Baghdad he announced, "I would anticipate that the major combat engagements are over." [Was] head of what Newsweek termed "the most secretive force in the U.S. military."

McChrystal's Zarqawi unit was accused of abusing detainees. His Senate confirmation was stalled by members of the Senate Armed Services Committee who sought more information. After meeting with McChrystal in private, they confirmed him. He [took] command of NATO operations.

McChrystal's "strategic assessment team" included Fred Kagan, of the Institute for the Study of War, Stephen Biddle of CFR, Anthony Cordesman, Center for Strategic and International Studies, and Jeremy Shapiro, Brookings.

Note: McChrystal is now privatized and sells his leadership skills.

What about the Dick Act?

In 1903 the US Secretary of State, Elihu Root, arranged for Congress to come up with legislation called the Militia Act. It is also known as the Dick Act, perhaps after someone in the House. It provided federal funding to th states (yes, a hundred years ago) making the militias of the states available for use by the War Department. (The euphemistic name Defense Department came much later.) Of course the militias, which are under the control of each state, were always able to be called up, by Congress, per Article I, section 8 of the Constitution.

The state militias became known as "the National Guard." How's that for a trick? And as said earlier, we now have a "National Guard Bureau" that is unconstitutionally run by the Pentagon, thanks to the National Defense Authorization Act of 2008. (The Pentagon campus is itself peopled by private corporations more than by our military. See Thomas Barnett's *The Pentagon's New Map*).

Let's glance at the *Wikipedia* entry for Elihu Root. (These are usually taken from CIA's National Estimates.):

"By 1916–17, Root was a leading proponent of preparedness, with the expectation the United States would enter World War I. President Woodrow Wilson sent him to Russia in 1917, in a mission that accomplished nothing. Root was a strong advocate of using international law to prevent war, and helped design the International Court of Justice."

See what I meant about the ICJ, in Chapter 5? And to go to Russia in 1917 is highly significant. As for being a "proponent of preparedness" that means he wanted to push the US into the Great War. We will see in Chapter 22 below that a band of men at Oxford was arranging for that war to happen. (Please be angry. This is not funny.)

My Daddy (the Constitution) Can Beat NATO Up

If citizens want to "get rid of" NATO, the way to do it is by hugging the Constitution. That means punishing anyone who is acting illegally, right?

Our beloved Constitution makes clear that submitting to World Government is taboo. So now let's cozy up to the parchment and use it. The reason our country is called the United States is that some *states* decided to *unite*. Those 13 states (British colonies until Independence in 1776) united and sent 55 delegates to Philadelphia in 1787 to "form a more perfect union." The players in the Constitution are thus the states, the people (as we can amend it any time, per Article V), and the three branches of government. Each state retains its sovereignty but agrees that coinage, importation, immigration, etc, will be solely federal. Article I, Section 10 expressly says:

> **"No state shall enter into any Treaty, Alliance or Confederation."**

Possibly Section 10 is a mechanism for us to oust the Pentagon-led National Guard Bureau. However Michigan isn't claiming a treaty with Latvia. Rather, it claims merely to put its guardsmen, its militia, in Pentagon's care. So we look at who is in charge of the guard. Per Article I, sec 8:

> The Congress shall have the Power... To declare war... To raise and support Armies...To provide for calling forth the Militia to execute the Laws of the Union, suppress Insurrections, and repel Invasions...

The word *militia* there means the local troops in states, not the nation's army. When the Framers wrote the Constitution, it was planned that we would not have much of a standing army, as armies cause trouble.

Who Has the Right To Call Up the Troops?

Militias are always available to Congress to put down insurrections (such as the 1863 Civil War), to execute Laws of the Union, and to repel invasions. Today's 'National Guard Bureau' sits in the Pentagon; its boss seems to be the executive branch. That is not cricket, per:

> Article II, section 2: "The President shall be Commander in Chief of the Army and Navy of the United States and of the Militia of the several States when called into the actual Service of the United States."

In the phrase "**when called into the actual Service of the United States,**" it is Congress that does the calling.

Note: Supreme Court decisions may modify the Constitution. In *Martin v Mott,* the Supreme Court ruled, in 1827, that the President can call up the Guard! That case dealt only with a narrow issue about a New York soldier failing to show up for duty. Still, we are stuck with it until another case comes up, or until the folks amend it. (But we don't want any constitutional conventions nowadays as they would surely be run by outsiders.)

Was 9-11 an Invasion? As far as repelling invaders is concerned, what would you advise the New York state militia to do if it were found, on 9-11, that the attacks on the WTC were being carried out by the US military or CIA? Could NY have fought them with arms? Yes, of course. That's the very point of our Second Amendment

> A well regulated militia, being necessary to the security of a free state, the right of the people to keep and bear arms, shall not be infringed.

(*Congress*, too, could have called forth the Guard on 9-11, per Article 1, section 8. It's just confusing to picture that.)

Our founding fathers were keenly aware of tyranny; we have become lax, relying on emotional bywords *freedom* and *democracy* instead of protecting the nation! No, that won't work; you have to do the heavy lifting when someone is out to kill you. Has any tribe ever been so blessed as ours, with this excellent law? Let's just use it.

chapter twenty

Posse of able-bodied men

Definition of posse from yourdictionary.com:
1 HISTORICAL
posse comitatus -- the body of men required, upon
being summoned, to assist the sheriff in keeping
the peace, pursuing felons, etc.
2 any body of persons armed with legal authority
3 b a search party

ORIGIN of the word "posse"
Medieval Latin, short for posse comitatus, power of
the county; from *possesse,* to be able
and *comitatus,* county; from *comes,* a count

20. A *Vade Mecum* for Legal Activists

Confirm they soul in self-control, thy liberty in law.
-- Katherine Lee Bates, *America the Beautiful* (1895)

Though all my law be fudge,
Yet I'll never, never budge,
But I'll live and die a judge -- and a good judge, too
-- Gilbert and Sullivan, *Trial by Jury* (1874)

This chapter is a *vade mecum* (vah-day me-koom) a handbook, "travels with me." We'll look briefly at laying an information, complaining to licensing boards, moot courts, John Doe's, Centers for Suspicious Deaths, assizes, Truth and Reconciliation Clubs, civil rights suits, jury nullification, offering to testify at a hearing, RICO suits, civil rights, amicus curiae, pre-emptive strike, outlawry, and private prosecution. (Send me more suggestions if you wish!)

This book is entitled Fraud Upon The Court, but seems to be a guide to "everything wrong with the courts." We just can't let the present situation continue. I urge folks to try anything that might work. I do not urge violence, though surely that is a normal way of dealing with miscreants, as I do not think it would succeed. To **revive community** seems to me to be a *sine qua non*.

How To Go To Court

If you plan to file a suit, first figure out if you need to go to a federal district court (if the law involved is federal, such as terrorism). If it is a state law, you usually begin at the county court house, though some matters begin at State Supreme Court. Walk into the office of the Clerk of Court; they will help you. Always be polite (and it's wise to wear your Sunday best).

Pro Se Filings and Summones

Pro se filings are available for any federal suit you wish to file. That means you operate without a lawyer. The clerk will accept your filing, and your payment of $400, at current rate, or zero if you have no ability to pay. She'll fill out the summons forms with which you must notify the defendant of the action.

You have to take these to the Post Office and pay for "return receipt requested." This is called 'service,' meaning you are serving notice on the defendant. If the defendant proves recalcitrant about answering, the US Marshal will assist you.

Note: I offer all this advice not as a lawyer but as a fellow traveler. I sued President Bush at the US District Courthouse in New Hampshire in 2006. The service postcard came back a few days later, duly signed by Alberto Gonzales for GWB. I was "suing for an injunction." I wanted the Prez to be "enjoined" against bombing Iran and Syria unless Congress declared war.

Criminal Complaints

Something else you can do if you want a crime stopped, or punished, is simply "lay an information" with the police. In the chapter on the Boston bombing, Sergeant Genck did the equivalent: he laid a complaint in court, saying that Tsarnaev should be charged with crimes. One often hears that a shopkeeper caught a shoplifter but then did not press charges. Police do not need the aggrieved party to do any pressing. They can themselves ask the district attorney to prosecute. (The FBI asks the AG. Ideally, that is.)

Licensing Boards

Every state maintains disciplinary boards for the professions. A logical punishment for a bad doctor or lawyer is the loss of his or her right to work. This has to begin with a complaint from someone. See an example later of disbarment of a lawyer for what appears to be rather minor sins. You don't have to be an aggrieved party – you are not asking for damages. You are alerting a state to the fact that so-and-so should not be in practice.

DISCIPLINING YOU-KNOW-WHOM IS *SOOO* SIMPLE

Individuals, or a group, can file a criminal complaint, which is also called 'laying an information.' As shown on this sample from Minnesota, you start by complaining and government does the rest.

Complaint and Summons Form

State of Minnesota. County of_____Court of _____

Plaintiff ____ Vs.

Name and address [That's you, Complainant]

Name, date of birth and address of defendant [your 'accused'], and any aliases.

The complainant, being duly sworn, makes complaint to the above-named court and states that there is probable cause to believe that the defendant committed the following offenses:

Charge 1 Minnesota statute___maximum sentence_____ Charge 2 (etc)_

[Note: To find "Florida law of homicide" just google for that.]

Select complaint type: summons_ or warrant_. Order for detention?

Statement of probable cause:

The complainant states that the following facts establish probable cause:_____

Complainant requests that defendant, subject to bail or conditions of release, be taken into custody pending further proceedings. Subscribed and sworn to me this day of__

****

[The rest of the form is filled out by the officials.]

Being authorized to prosecute the offenses charged, I [an official] approve this complaint. From the above sworn facts, and any supporting affidavits, I, the issuing officer have determined that probable cause exists to support defendant's arrest.

****

SUMMONS. Therefore you, the above named defendant, are hereby summoned to appear at_____on____

If you fail to appear a warrant will be issued for your arrest. [See? This very same form goes to the accused]

****

To the county sheriff. I hereby order the above named person to be apprehended and arrested without delay and to be brought before a judge not more than 36 later than the arrest.

Execute in Minnesota only   Nationwide   in bordering states   .

Any Risk of Committing Libel?

Of the two kinds of reports mentioned above – laying an information about criminal activity, or identifying a person who is unethical in professional behavior – is there a risk that you will be called a libeler? As far as I know, citizens have a right, perhaps a duty, to file these kinds of reports with the relevant authority. However if you make your case public you risk being sued. So be careful.

Moot Court and John Doe

My law school (University of Adelaide, South Australia) has a moot court, that is, a place where mock trials can be conducted for student training. A large inscription on the front wall says *"Fiat justitia, ruat caelum"* -- Let justice be done though the heavens fall! I am here to recommend the use of a moot court in law schools, or even on your front lawn, to try some of the persons who can't seem to be got at otherwise for outrageous acts against society.

Two important points. First: use the name John Doe. It will make it easy for people to attend the case and not get all nervous. Once they see the formalities being carried out, they'll better be able to realize the enormity of what is happening. Second, bend over backwards to give the accused all the due process he would have in a real case. Definitely cough up anything exculpatory.

Milder Forms: Grand Juries and Investigations

You have every right to form a grassroots grand jury. As mentioned in Chapter 3, years ago an empaneled member was expected to look around for crime and even to look around for bad roads and bridges. I doubt if anyone would be nervous today about calling City Hall to report a bad road, but to identify crime feels (and is) dangerous.

If you want to set up a Center for Suspicious Deaths, or even pursue the truth about one particular whistleblower's death, you had better first establish your power base. Certainly send notices to the mayor, the Church, the local university, the police or

FBI. Note that you must not claim any authority. And I would recommend you make up a name other than Grand Jury. Perhaps Great Jury, or Jury Wannabee, or some such. In my *Prosecution for Treason* book, I suggested that people call their local group a "Clarendon Assize," after the 12th century English model.

Truth and Reconciliation Clubs, and Immunity

As everyone knows, when South Africa de-legalized the apartheid system in 1990, there needed to be a way to call people to account for outrages committed. A way forward was found: a truth commission. Persons who admitted their crimes were given immunity from prosecution. You won't be able to offer that prize, as your group is not official. Still, you can promise co-operators that you will advocate that they be given immunity. In any case the main task is to uncover truth. Righteous anger should abound. Sheep may safely graze, etc.

Testifying at Hearings and Making Submissions

In death cases, coroners may hold an inquest. This is a good way for you to insist on their raising the possibility that a suicide was really a murder. Suggest a motive! Suggest a suspect (only to the authorities). Don't forget you can offer to testify at government inquiries, and/or send written reports.

On other matters, the executive of the state, or the US president, can appoint a commission to study this or that. All legislatures have the right to set up an inquiry. So do you! You can be a private eye and involve your neighbors. Why ever not?

Racketeer Influenced and Corrupt Organizations

The RICO Act, in force since the 1970s, deals with the fact that the higher-ups often use little guys to perform their crimes, so it's difficult to get evidence against them. A RICO case proceeds by demonstrating *a pattern of behavior*. I mocked up a RICO case in support of Troy Davis in 2009 but did not use it. I wish I had. (My make-believe case is in Chapter 23.)

Civil Rights Cases -- The Zenith of the Rule of Law

Americans associate 'civil rights' with the 1960 movement against racial discrimination. But all the rights in the 1789 Bill of Rights (displayed in Chapter 12 above) are civil rights. Moreover, there is federal legislation that helps a person sue if any of his rights were violated, whether it was by government or by a private party.

After OJ Simpson was acquitted of the crime of murder, the families of the two people he was accused of murdering sued him and won. Remarkably the law, at 42 USC 1983, says:

> Every person who, under color of any statute, ordinance, regulation, custom, or usage, of any State or Territory, ... subjects, or causes to be subjected, any citizen of the United States or other person within the jurisdiction thereof to the deprivation of any rights, privileges, or immunities secured by the Constitution and laws, shall be liable to the party injured in an action at law [or in equity].

The phrase "color of any statute" means that the person who is depriving you is claiming to do so as a government officer. It has been used in cases of police brutality.

Note: the word "equity" at the end refers to special courts of equity that allow creative remedies for problems. *Bonus judex secundum aequum et bonum judicat et aequitatemstricto juri praefert.* A good judge prefers equity to strict law. Check it out.

Coram Nobis, Amicus Curiae, Expert Witness (You)

I realize that for an individual to tackle the authorities is not easy. But the writ of "error coram nobis" described in Chapter 4 requires only that you write a letter to the court.

You are also welcome to offer, in a particular court case, a friend-of-the-court thesis, known as an amicus curiae. In it you should not stick up for either side, but only help the court to think about an aspect of the case.

You can also offer your services as an expert witness, and for this you do not have to have any special degree. You need only show special knowledge or experience.

Declaratory Relief and Jury Nullification

Two other court actions can show you as a celebrator of law. One is for you to seek an injunction for "declaratory relief " (that is, instead of asking a court to enjoin someone's bad behavior you ask the court merely to clarify that the other person is in the wrong). The other way you can participate in law-making or law-clarifying is, when you are a juror, to refuse to convict the accused if the law is unconstitutional or unconscionable. Nullify it.

Not Mild: Extreme Action, e.g., Pre-emptive Strike

To act in self-defense or on defense of another is the right of every person. If someone is coming at you with a knife you may shoot him. If arrested you plead self defense. The High Court of Australia ruled in *Zecevic v DPP* (1987):

> "The question to be asked in the end is simple. It is whether the accused believed upon reasonable grounds that it was necessary in self-defence to do what he did. If he had that belief and there were reasonable grounds for it, or if the jury is left in reasonable doubt about the matter, then he is entitled to an acquittal."

Freedom of Information Acts -- Federal and State

You can send a request to almost any agency. The federal law is at 5 USC 552. Also see the National Archives Act.

Outlawry, Citizen's Arrest, Private Prosecution

Outlawry is an old concept, still extant in common law. It means that if a criminal simply can't be caught by the authorities, he can be declared an outlaw. Anyone has the right to kill him, and persons who harbor him or feed him commit a crime! The maxim is: *Extra legem positus est civiliter mortuus*. One beyond the pale of the law is civilly dead.

For citizen's arrest see Chapter 24 below. Private prosecution is possible, but rarely used. See Veronica Michel's work on this

Legal Concepts Mentioned in Parts I-IV, Per Chapter

1. Ideals, discovery, spoliation, diminished responsibility, cross-examination, constitutions, *habeas corpus*, codification of federal law in the **USC**, obstruction of justice, abuse of process, immunity.

2. Law requiring **coroner** to investigate unusual deaths (Tillman), legislative investigations and hearings, lying to Congress, perjury.

3. Bail, extradition, political prisoner, guardianship, bench warrant, Bill Windsor's proposal for seeking an **injunction** in any state that does not permit citizens to approach their grand jury, proposal that only a jury be allowed to dismiss a vexatious litigant.

4. **Fraud upon the court** (Korematsu), Writ of Error Coram Nobis, martial law, judicial notice, plea-bargaining, *stare decisis*, exculpatory.

5. *Pacta sunt servanda* for treaties, ICJ, the impossibility of enforcing international law, the imperial nature of the WTO and the IMF, universal jurisdiction (Pinochet), ICC, Geneva Conventions,, law against torture, **war crimes**, executive as law enforcer.

6. Statute of limitations (Gallop), case dismissal, meeting of the minds, **Article III**, guilty knowledge.

7. Carrying an accusation in a person's record, then dropping the charge, **framing**, murder in jail, cover-up, fugitives.

8. Kafkaesque court (Gudbranson), child-snatching, implants (Jones), jurisprudence, common law, **accessories** after the fact.

9. Guilty plea obtained by **attorney coercion** (James Ray), trial by media, unsolved robberies, DOJ's unwillingness to prosecute, marriage of FBI-mafia-US Attorneys.

10. Recantations of witness statements (Davis) and their not being credited by the judge, a State Board's ability to grant parole, pardon, or clemency, right of anyone to attend trials, subpoena, US Marshals, material-witness law, execution, boot-strapping, perjury, **disbarring**.

11. Judaic law to keep the community balanced, care for poor, and inculcate a sense of responsibility; child's need to learn the values and rules of society, **the value of law itself**, Magna Charta, honesty.

12. Laws specifying who controls the police, Bill of Rights, joint terrorism task forces, treason, **militarization of police**, emergencies, role of national funding, *agents provocateurs*.

13. En-mod Treaty, **circumstantial evidence**, lack of law re weather-tampering or ionospheric heating, vandalism, trespass.

14. Impeaching a judge, identification of Type-1 judicial treason (parricide), and **Type-2** involving violence, contortionism in rulings.

16. The laying of a complaint, not-guilty plea as sentencing strategy (Tsarnaev), **instructions to jury**, FBI killer walks free (Todashev), rebuttable presumption.

17. Whistleblower protection law, retaliation, *qui tam* suits, relators, lack of interest by prosecutors when dissident heroes die suspiciously, such as by **more than one suicide shot** to the head (Webb).

18. Statutory bodies (FCC), anti-trust law, the crime of cover-up, genocide in mind-control cases, (Orlikow), Manchurian candidate, pedophilia, **slavery,** journalistic recidivism.

19. Constitutional provisions for a militia, state control of the national guard, the illegality of the Pentagon's control of the National Guard Bureau, the real meaning of NATO and our lack of questioning of it, restrictions on states' powers, the **Dick Act.**

20. Libel, moot court, truth and reconciliation commissions, expert witnesses, *amicus curiae*, **outlawry**, declaratory relief, private prosecution, civil rights suits, color of law, pro se filings, summons.

> To abolish the fences of laws between men -- as tyranny does -- means to take away men's liberties aand destroy freedom as a living political reality: for the space between men as it is hedged in by laws is the living space of freedom.
> -- Hannah Arendt, *Origins of Totalitarianism* (1951)

chapter twenty-one

Mary Gregory says, in her book Microwave War "As I worked at creating an aluminum tarpaulin, an aircraft buzzed overhead and perforated it with thousands of pinholes."

Do gang-stalkers get special plates?

PART V. WHERE SHOULD LAW GO NOW?

21. Cruelty and the Shklar Principle

Put cruelty first. -- Judith Shklar, *The Liberalism of Fear* (1978)

What a smart idea the late philosopher Judith Shklar had: put cruelty first. If you were asked to invent law for any society today, wouldn't you want to include some way of restraining cruelty? And if you decided to make that a first priority, wouldn't a lot of other good things tend to follow from that?

Humans are, in fact, cruel. Not everyone behaves that way but some do. Pity their family members or workmates who have to put up with them. But pity a whole nation of some of this type get to hold the reins of power.

Probably some cruel people are mentally disturbed, and one would find other aspects of their personality that are normal. But it's also likely that the behavior is present in all humans and may come out if either circumstance or cultural rules call for it. Cruelty isn't always pathological.

Other species practice cruelty: chimpanzees, dolphins, penguins. In the case of chimps, they do it only when on a raid of a neighboring troop. In other words, it may be like the instinct of a warrior. Some human warriors do not stop at killing the enemy, they make sport of him.

This chapter is concerned with the fact that cruelty can snowball. I offer an observation of Alexandr Solzhenitsyn to that effect, on the next two pages. I think I see in our society today the kind of mathematical problem described by this ex-prisoner of the Russian gulag. **Where there is no strong cultural barrier against cruelty, it starts to increase.**

Please read this amazing short excerpt about cruelty:

From Aleksandr Solzhenitsyn, *The Gulag Archipelago* (Harper and Row, 1972), translated from the Russian by Thomas P. Whitney

Cruelty. And where among all the preceding qualities was there any place left for kindheartedness? How could one possibly preserve one's kindness while pushing away the hands of those who were drowning? Once you have been steeped in blood, you can only become more cruel. And, anyway, cruelty ("class cruelty") was praised and instilled, and you would soon lose track, probably, of just where between bad and good that trait lay.

And when you add that kindness was ridiculed, that pity was ridiculed, and that mercy was ridiculed -- you'd never be able to chain all those who were drunk on blood!

My nameless woman correspondent, from Arbat No. 15, asks me "about the roots of the cruelty" characteristic of "certain Soviet people." Why is it ...proportionate to the defenselessness of the person in their power? And she cites an example – which is not at all what one might regard as the main one, but which I am going to cite here anyway.

This took place in the winter of 1943-1944 at the Chelyabinsk railroad station, under a canopy near the baggage checkroom. It was minus 13 degrees. Beneath the shed roof was a cement floor, on which was trampled sticky snow from outside. Inside the window of the baggage checkroom stood a woman in a padded jacket, and on the nearer side was a well-fed policeman in a tanned sheepskin coat.

They were absorbed in a kittenish, flirtatious conversation. Several men lay on the floor in earth-colored cotton duds and rags. Even to call them threadbare would be rank flattery. These were young fellows -- emaciated, swollen, with sores on their lips. One of them, evidently in a fever, lay with bare chest on the snow, groaning.

The woman telling the story approached him to ask who

they were, and it turned out that one of them had served out his time in camp, another had been released for illness, but that their documents had been made out incorrectly when they were released, and as a result they could not get tickets to go home on the train. And they had no strength left to return to camp either -- they were totally fagged out with diarrhea.

So then the woman telling the story began to break off pieces of bread for them. And at this point the policeman broke off his jolly conversation and said to her threateningly: "What's going on, auntie, have you recognized your relatives? You better get out of here. They will die without your help!"

And so she thought to herself: After all, they'll up and haul me in just like that and put me in prison! (And that was quite right, what was to stop them?) And . . . she went away.

How typical all this is of our society -- what she thought to herself, and how she went away, and that pitiless policeman, and that pitiless woman in the padded jacket, and that cashier at the ticket window who refused them tickets, and that nurse who refused to take them into the city hospital,
and that idiotic free employee at the camp who had made out their documents.   – end of Solzhenitsyn quote

The Shklar Principle

Judith Shklar (1928-1992) was a great intellectual who, as a child, escaped Nazi rule. She wrote a book, *Ordinary Vices* (1986), which analyzes the vice of cruelty. Shklar notes that the people who see cruelty taking place and don't do anything to stop it, **become participants in it.**

I now give the name 'Shklar principle' to that important point. We often read narratives by victims of torture who say they coped with the cruelty being inflicted on them by the baddies (the official torturers), but that it was much more hurtful if a doctor or diplomat stood by and saw what was happening and did not raise a protest.

Little Cruelties?

Until a few years ago I had not heard of the practice of gaslighting or gangstalking. The same persons who have done cruel things on a mass scale, like cause a flood or fire, do experiments on how to upset an individual in a personal way. On one of Bill Windsor's videos, a soldier named Marc Burnell recounts how he is being gaslighted. The word comes from the name of a 1944 movie, *Gaslight*, starring Ingrid Bergman, in which the husband performs very subtle hurts on his wife in order to drive her crazy.

Burnell says it's the army that is doing this to him. How cruel! Life in barracks is difficult enough, away from family, without having one's peers giving you little jibes. I assume it is all part of a deliberate program of demoralization, coming from the Top Dogs.

Gang-stalking

I have only once been the victim of gang-stalking, in 2011, in Massachusetts. I wrote up a police report, but did not submit it, as the local police car had been one of my gang stalkers. Sad, but true. Then, in 2013, I watched Gloria Canzater Wellburn mention, on a Bill Windsor video, that that the cars that stalk her, in San Diego, usually have license plates with a double letter and double number.

I went back to my police report and saw that I had written down the number of the offending car (not the police car) and, lo and behold, it started with a double letter and double number. Gave me a good laugh. A likely interpretation is that there are people out there who are paid by the state to gang-stalk, and commit who-knows-what crimes against their neighbor, and that the police will refrain from arresting them if they have the appropriate licence plate number. This is outrageous.

Is there any way law can deal with it? Naturally we don't have a rule that says "government must not gangstalk," but law can somehow deal with most things.

Massachusetts General Law, Chapter 265 Section 43 says:

> (a) Whoever (1) willfully and maliciously engages in a knowing pattern of conduct or series of acts over a period of time directed at a specific person which seriously alarms or annoys that person and would cause a reasonable person to suffer substantial emotional distress, and (2) makes a threat with the intent to place the person in imminent fear of death or bodily injury, shall be guilty of the crime of stalking and shall be punished by imprisonment in the state prison for not more than 5 years or by a fine of not more than $1,000.

Targeted Individuals ("T.I.'s")

Please believe me when I say there are targeted individuals who suffer extreme pain on a daily basis in the US and abroad. I don't ask that you accept wholesale the stories by complainants at freedonfchs.com, a website for "freedom from covert harassment and surveillance." But I know some of them are true. I have been with a friend in Boston who suffered hits *before my very eyes.*

It was rumored that during Operation Desert Storm that the US caused 100,000 Iraqi soldiers to surrender by hitting their brains. It is said they got nosebleeds. Antony Sutton said the ability is there to send radio frequencies to do specific things -- for example, cause nausea, or confusion, or aggression, or passivity!

Alex Constantine, a publisher of many excellent books about mind control and the police state, now tells us that he is being electronically tortured daily and cannot get any help. Fathom it!

On the following page is an excerpt from a book by Mary Gregory. She lives in Rego Park New York near JFK Airport. According to her, those attacked in her neighborhood are ones who have no one to help them. She says elderly, single, widowed, disabled, and Jewish, are the usual victims. I repeat the Shklar principle: If you don't help the bullied you are their co-bully. Doing nothing is positively harmful. At an absolute minimum you must listen.

DAILY LOG, in Mary Gregory, *Microwave War* (2011: 98-100).

April 5, 2009 [This is very abbreviated; the attacks go all day]:

12.09 AM. Tap on my comforter directly over my right ankle.

12:23 AM. Heavy thud on the comforter directly over my left ankle. Aircraft hovering overhead.

12:53 AM. Dagger to my left side. Aircraft hovering overhead.

1:50 AM. Circular motion over my right knee. Feels like someone is running a pencil around in a circle over my skin.

7:50 AM. I see a bright white dot on the hallway floor. I... take a closer look, discover that it is a light emanating from the apartment below. There is a brand new hole, the diameter of a pin, going straight downstairs to the apartment beneath mine.

9:40 PM. Heart palpitates. I gasp for air.

9:53 PM. Dagger beneath my left collarbone. Aircraft heard above.

10:28 PM. Heart palpitates. Five seconds later there is a loud SNAP! Off the wooden living room floor.

10:32 PM. SNAP! Off the wooden living room floor.

10:37 PM Circular motion over my left knee. Aircraft heard above.

10:57 PM. There is a circular motion on the right side of my chest. It feels like someone pressed a pencil in the comforter and is running it around in a small circle.

11:07 PM. Circular motion around left knee.

11:14 PM. My right foot involuntarily moves.

11:17 PM. A pinprick to my left shoulder. Airplane above.

11:21 PM. Pinprick to my left thigh; pinprick to my left foot. A minute later a plane flies by.

11:24 PM. RIP! It sounds like another gash has torn open in my bedroom wall.

11:25 PM. SNAP! Off the wooden hallway floor.

11:50 PM. Electronic shock shoots down my right side from the back of my head down to my right thigh. I am lying on my right side.

[Question: Is this really happening in America? Is the author joking? If you believe her, what will you do about it? Will you share this data?]

Cruelty in Prisons

Over the years we have learned that medical experiments are carried out on prisoners (as well as mental patients). Those doing the experiments ease their conscience by saying that the men volunteer, in exchange for early release. Forget it. There should be a law against using prisoners; their actions are not really voluntary.

As for the other abuses, like having prisoners wear a stun belt so the guard can jolt them from his station (in the "panopticon"), this is outrageous, no matter what. A prisoner can legally receive only the punishment that was specified in the law. That boils down to a fine, or "time behind bars." Such time means a loss of liberty, nothing else.

It was recently boasted by the builders of a new Supermax prison that each cell's window was positioned in a way that would deprive the prisoner of a view of the mountains. Very, very wrong. And there is an increased use of solitary confinement, causing psychoses. The recently condemned 19-year-old "Marathon bomber" was kept in solitary during the time it took him to "admit" guilt. Inmates need citizens to make sure that they are not being abused. Deaths in custody are legion. In Australia, Aboriginals almost expect it.

Growing up Catholic I was taught that we must "visit the sick and the imprisoned." Yet no parish ever organized a trip to the prison. Not to visit is a sin; who the hell else, if not us, will protect those men from brutality? John Ray, brother of the man who DID NOT kill Martin Luther King, says that when his father, George, was in jail at age 23, he was hung by his thumbs for 50 minutes out of every hour, and allowed to "rest" for the other ten minutes. He was in so much pain he wanted to die. Finally his Mom came to see him in prison and she "went to town" on his jailers. Soon after that, he was sent to a work farm. It pays to complain!

"Lack of training led to Bagram abuse, soldiers say"

by Tom Lasseter, *McClatchy Newspapers,* June 16, 2008. Guards at the U.S. detention center at Bagram Air Base didn't know whether Habibullah had anything to do with terrorist attacks on the US, but they knew he was defiant. On a cold December day in 2002, Spc. Brian Cammack tried to feed the Afghan clergyman in his late 20s a piece of bread by cramming it into his mouth. Habibullah's hands were chained above his head.

Later, when he eventually checked on the prisoner, Cammack said: "I took the sack off his head and his eyes looked strange." Habibullah died of a blood clot [from] the beatings. Cammack was a specialist in the 377th Military Police Company, a reserve unit based in Cincinnati. Many of his buddies were small-town police officers or, like him, blue-collar.

Senior officers who came through paid no attention to the privates and sergeants who, Cammack said, were slowly losing control of themselves in the face of the war. In the absence of supervision, he said, the same detainees were hit, over and over, by every guard shift. One soldier, former Spc. Willie Brand, told military investigators that he struck Dilawar "somewhere in the area of 37 times.... These two guys died, but I probably kneed 20 or so [detainees] total, and I just can't differentiate between the rest of the [detainees] and the ones who died," Brand testified.

The U.S. military never produced evidence showing that either Habibullah, an Islamic mullah, or clergyman, or Dilawar, a taxi driver, had any connection to the Taliban or al-Qaida.

OPINION -- What To Do about Cruelty?

I think we ought to start facing reality. The problem is ourselves. We live in the hopes that justice will occur and when we see it failing to occur we don't get angry. We say "Oh a little more of the usual solution (on paper) will fix it." People think when they have arranged for an institution to do something, it's no longer their concern. Wrong.

Why are electronically harassed people unable to get help? Because the ones doing it are the usual "protected persons," same as in 9-11. Thus, to get rid of a lot of cruelty: **halt the protecting** of our secret rulers. It may only take some publicity to persuade people that the emperor is not wearing any clothes. If one person says "By golly, he is totally in his birthday suit," others may be very relieved. Few people know how strong is our instinctive aversion to do or say what no one else is doing or saying. So say it today. Watch the bandwagon effect!

It's wired into human nature, beyond reasoning, that we respond with deference to those above us. So it is very, very hard to speak truth to power. I think we should clearly recognize that we are NOT good at banding together to deal with harm-doers. In modern society we have placed responsibility for justice in institutions such as social work and the law. See? This is a trap. Perhaps it explains how the Bozos on top — at least some of whom are pure sadists — can proceed unconcerned that we will "take up cudgels." We have bureaucratized our cudgels!

Please re-read the Solzhenitsyn story at the beginning of this chapter. The author was taken by train from one jail to another

in the 'archipelago' of secret prisons. He said the train trips were a mercy because they were dark at night while jails kept bright lights on him all the time.

This *New York Times* photo of Jose Padilla shows the prisoner being taken to the dentist, with sensory deprivation!

chapter twenty-two

All Souls College, Oxford

Site of WW1 battle of the Somme, France

Sir Edward Grey, British Foreign Secretary 1905-1916

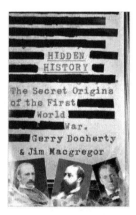

Devastating revelations in 2013

22. Hidden History: Monsters at Oxford

Yet, it was thought, the Sword she bore
Check'd but the Desp'rate and the Poor;
That, urg'd by mere Necessity,
Were tied up to the wretched Tree
For Crimes, which not deserv'd that Fate,
But to secure the Rich, and Great.

-- Bernard Mandeville, *The Fable of the Bees* (1705)

Rex est major singulis, minor universis. The king is greater than individuals, less than all the people. (Law maxim)

Behold a life-changing book: *Hidden History: the Secret Origins of the First World War.* It is massively documented by two Scots -- schoolteacher Gerry Docherty and physician Jim Macgregor. They show how "the Secret Elite" deceived Parliament by blatant lies. The deceivers saw, correctly, that human beings would look at them, upper class lords, and not be able to figure that they were liars, scoundrels.

Note: freedom to criticize leaders is constricted, not by dictators or praetorian guards, but by our own brain. We deeply fear what our neighbors will say if we criticize "the king" and, worse, we can't even perceive that the king is naughty. I am 99% certain that this is the crux of our problem. It's easy to overcome! Kids could be shown, at school, what our irrational predispositions are all about.

Britain made war against in South Africa against the Dutch-descended farmers known as the Boers. The point was to grab diamond and gold mines. Men from England, and from the colonies such as Australia, marched off with guns to fight the Boer war in 1899. It had been given a different spin by the media: the Boers were said to be depriving British settlers in South Africa of their rights, such as – wait for it – the right to vote!

Origins of WWI, by Docherty and Macgregor (2013: 342-345):

The government and opposition forces tried to end the discussion about Grey's statement at 20.15 on 3 August, but the rank and file Liberal and Labour members stood their ground. They desperately insisted on an immediate debate. Percy Molteno, the Liberal MP for Dumfriesshire was first on his feet to lament the lies that had passed as assurances from his own government over the years.

"They have brought us to the brink of disaster without our knowing, and without our being warned. I say that at the last moment, they should give the people of this country a chance to decide. This is a continuation of that old and disastrous system where a few men in charge of the State, wielding the whole force of the State, make secret engagements carefully veiled from the knowledge of the people, who are as dumb driven cattle without a voice on the question."

[They were] herded towards the global abattoir for reasons they would never properly know. A few men had unleashed the demon war and sanctioned the slaughter. Molteno pointed an accusatory finger at the now empty benches where the politicians who had fronted the decision had been sitting.

Another Liberal, W. Llewellyn Williams, accused Sir Edward Grey of disguising his motives and falsely arousing war fever: "If you had asked any man in this country, whatever his politics, whether he would calmly contemplate the entrance of his country into this quarrel, he would have said No."

As each and every contributor attacked government policy, challenged every step, asked more and more telling questions, it became ever more evident that there was a very strong body of articulate opinion ranged against Sir Edward Grey.

At which point, Arthur Balfour, rose menacingly. He had heard enough. Balfour derided their objections as the "very dregs and lees of the debate, in no way representing the various views of the Members of the House." With consummate arrogance [he said] what they were engaged in was a 'relatively impotent and evil debate'. How could this be a serious occasion, he asked, when none of the senior government ministers were present? What spurious nonsense. Senior ministers had chosen not to be present.

Whodunnit, According to Docherty and Macgregor

Back in 1966, the historian Carroll Quigley, in his book *Tragedy and Hope*, had identified various groups that carried out the wishes of the Secret Elite: Milner's Kindergarten, Royal Institute for International Affairs, the Round Table, Tavistock Institute, Council on Foreign Relations in US, and the Rhodes Scholars.

Docherty/Macgregor emphasize the role of Lord Grey and Lord Esher, and the young Winston Churchill. Surprisingly they pin a lot on the king. Queen Victoria's son had been known as Bertie the playboy. He reigned as Edward VII from 1901 to 1910. These authors show that his playboy image covered up the fact that he worked hard to plot World War I. They also say that "Natty" Rothschild supported the king's gambling addiction. (My guess would be that Natty arranged for the king to become addicted, and thus control him.)

The authors remark on the significance of the Order of Bath, but I surmise that a greater role is played by the Most Noble Order of the Garter, which began in 1348. It always includes the sovereign of Britain as its head plus a select few others. In the last 20 years there has been a new category of members: Stranger Knights and Ladies, bringing in the royalty of Sweden, Netherlands, and Japan.

The motto of the Garter is *"Honi soit qui mal y pense"* – roughly: "Don't you dare say what we do is evil." Some bishops are members of the Garter. What does that tell you? A former chief justice of Australia is there, too, Sir Ninian Stephen.

Treason Is Prospering

Docherty and Macgregor provide a long list of traitors within England, many of whom seem to have been paid for their treachery with a dukedom, a knighthood, or some other title. Recall the verse "Treason doth not prosper, what's the reason? For if it prosper, none dare call it treason." I think we had better wise up to our habit of thinking that if people dress fancy and speak nicely they are incapable of boing sociopaths. It is evident that many persons are willing to sacrifice most of the human race.

Note: The US Constitution specifies the crime of treason, and it is also a common law crime in the states. We inherited the common law from Mother England and unless a legislature has overridden a provision it is still good law. Antony Sutton wrote the *Best Enemy Money Can Buy* about the sneaky supplying of our Soviet enemy with factories to build Ford trucks. He gives an interesting quote: "The (American) businessmen who built the Soviet Kama River truck plant should be shot as traitors." That was said by Avraham Shifrin, former Soviet Defense Ministry official!

"Disregard the Screamers"

Lord Alfred Milner is seen in the Docherty-Macgregor book to be the coordinator of various international intrigues. I find it very significant that he taught his minions to "disregard the screamers" – say, any who fussed about parliament's duty or who disapproved of the Boer farmers being kept in concentration camps.

A leader who wants to accomplish an outrageous task does indeed enhance his ability to forge ahead if he acquired the moxie to *categorize decent people as screamers*. Moral of the story: keep on screaming! It's natural. Scream bloody murder! Recall the Glaspie-Saddam item above? In January, 1991, Saddam let loose his troops on Kuwait, and Congress voted to make war on him. We then continued to impose economic sanctions on Iraq for ten years. Many screamers said "Don't do that!" But Secretary of State Madeleine Albright set her face against listening to them.

Look at us today. We have identified such monstrosities as MK-Ultra, the torturing of prisoners, the judicial fiasco of the Marathon case. But as long as the powerful think they can get away with anything, **our anger has no value.**

Why Historian Robert Faurisson Can't Visit Australia

There's quite a power game being played, called "the laws against Holocaust denial." I said above that the cause of WWI (1914-1918) has only come to light in 2013. We await more revelations about WWII. (Greg Hallett's book *Hitler Was a British Agent* is worth a read.) Certainly the big Hollywood narrative of the war is propagandist; it helps men march into war.

How many Jews died in concentration camps? Was it 6 million, or only 1 million, or maybe 8 million? Don't comment; it's against the law. It's the only subject that is taboo! Ah, isn't free speech protected in nations such as US and Australia? Not exactly. The US handed a "holocaust denier" (Ernst Zundel) over to Canada, sending him to Germany and imprisonment. An Australian (Fredrick Toben) was taken off the plane in London to be extradited, for his website AdelaideInstitute.org.

Robert Faurisson, a historian in France, asked questions about Auschwitz – as a historian properly would. But this is held, in some European countries, to "offend the memory of the dead." It's criminalized! It's a crime to incite hatred, and the phrase "Less than 6 million" is alleged to incite hatred of Jews. Puh-*leeze*. All kinds of new censorship laws have appeared in 2014.

Ursula Haverbeck

Of course these laws are themselves inciting hatred of Jews, which is probably their long-run purpose. Right now a beautiful 86 year-old German lady, Ursula Haverbeck, is wining hearts and minds by calling up the suppressed story of the city of Breslau having to be depopulated of Christian Germans per the Allied decisions of 1945.

Apparently Ursula's words can be construed as criminal and the police have raided her home! Trust me: this will be blamed on Jews.

Anyway, Faurisson would like to visit Australia but he can't get a tourist visa as he has a "criminal record." See? He can't possibly be a criminal. **Any law that would make it a crime to investigate a historical fact is no genuine law.**

All over the place laws are being made that disgrace the law. I wish Jewish scholars would lead the way in decriminalizing "the defaming of the memory of the dead." The dead are crying from their graves for us to get at the truth of who has caused such horrible events -- and who, today, are planning much worse..

Statement by Britain's Chairman of Joint Intelligence
Public Record Office Document, FO 371/34551. 27 August, 1943.
"In my opinion it is incorrect to describe Polish information regarding German atrocities as "trustworthy.' The Poles, and to a far greater extent the Jews, tend to exaggerate German atrocities in order to stoke us up. They seem to have succeeded. Mr Allen and myself have both followed German atrocities quite closely. I do not believe that there is any evidence which would be accepted in a Law Court that Polish children have been killed on the spot by Germans when their parents were being deported to work in Germany, nor that Polish children have been sold to German settlers.

As regards putting Poles to death in gas chambers, I do not believe that there is any evidence that this has been done, There have been many stories to this effect, and we have played them up, in P.W.E. [Psy Warfare Executive] rumours without believing that they had any foundation. At any rate there is far less evidence than exists for the mass murder of Polish officers by the Russians at Katyn.

On the other hand we do know that the Germans are out to destroy Jews of any age unless they are fit for manual labour. I think that we weaken our case against the Germans by publicly giving credence to atrocity stories for which we have no evidence. These mass executions in gas chambers remind me of the story of employment of human corpses during the last war for the manufacture of fat, which was a grotesque lie and led to the true stories of German enormities being brushed aside as being mere propaganda....

(signed) V [Victor] Cavendish-Bentinck" [Duke of Portland]

Note: I assume the above was declassified under the 70-year rule. I found this document on the Internet and have not authenticated it.

To repeat: I find *Hidden History* life-changing, as it has finally given a clear sighting of the Top Dogs. I expand on this theme in Appendix U. We need to see the two parallel worlds we live in – one, where the Bozos have their fun on us, two where we picture "democracy" working. And not a minute too soon as we come to realize what's going on. Big thanks to the Internet and Youtube for giving us a way to "get published" without censorship. *Gracias!*

Kowtowistry

One further term is needed to handle the issues in this book, but I can't think of a name for it other than, sorry, "kowtowistry." To kowtow is to bang your own head on the floor in obeisance to the boss. During Mao's rule in China you had to bang it really loud!

What I'm saying is that *we are the problem*. The travesties in this book wouldn't flourish but for our acceptance of them. Stupid, eh? We are built this way. Selfishly we must calculate our own survival and if that means kowtowing, we kowtow. Let's acknowledge that rather than saying we are built to be egalitarian.

It remains for us to accumulate goodwill with our conspecifics to make major change a.s.a.p. I'm pretty sure this can't come about by a centralized movement. For one thing the infiltrators would be in there running it before dawn tomorrow. (I hear that the Tea Party and *Occupy!* are run by the ones they claim to oppose). You have to do whatever your talent suggests.

In the next chapter I put forth a make believe court case in which some very good legislation against racketeering comes into play. In the chapter after that, I use whatever I can think of to show how law is available to help. I do it to the point of ridiculousness, but hey, better than nuffin'.

Please watch Youtube's series "Cops Gone Wild." Why not invite the police to meet with your group and y'all can watch the flick together? Good cops will be appalled.

chapter twenty-three

Judge Roland Barnes
(killed because he was going
off the reservation?)

David Wilhelm, Customs
Officer, whose house Nichols
"randomly" chose to break into

23. A Fictional RICO Case

"Real butter pancakes!"

-- attributed to Brian Nichols (2005)

The chapter at hand describes a method by which a layperson can bring charges – by a side entrance! – against criminals. In 1970, Congress passed the Organized Crime Control Act, which contained the provisions now known as RICO. That acronym stands for Racketeer Influenced and Corrupt Organizations. (The law is codified at 18 USC 1961.)

RICO law allows someone to recognize a pattern of crime and declare the pattern to be criminal. The wrongdoer can be a business, a private person, or the government itself. You might say it's the answer to a maiden's prayer for one who finds that government engages– as it certainly does – in rackets.

Below you will find is a rough try-out of something Troy Davis could theoretically have filed in the federal district court. I made it up in cahoots with Troy Davis's sister Martina in 2009. It never got used and I want to emphasize that *this is not a case that ever got filed.* To bring a civil RICO suit you must show that the racket harmed you, you must plead economic loss. Hence, I've had to show Troy's sister listing the expense of gasoline for the car that she drove to visit the prisoner.

When I composed this draft, Troy's mother, Virginia Davis, was still alive. At the time I scribbled in the names of three co-plaintiffs: Virginia, Troy, and Martina, rather than one, because if a sole plaintiff dies, a case comes to a halt.

A wonderful thing about RICO is that you can allege an interweaving of many different crimes, so long as there is some connection. As you will see, bring in the Atlanta child murders, and Brian Nichols' case (which is the biggest fake case I have ever seen). For this I would need to demonstrate that whoever, in the state of Georgia, was able to coordinate the malicious prosecution and false conviction of Troy Davis probably did likewise to Wayne Williams and Brian Nichols. (I got ideas from the unsuccessful 9/11 RICO suit filed by Philip Berg.)

Successful litigation requires that the reality of the racketeering activity be established by a showing of relationship, and continuity over a period of time. Two acts [known as qualifying acts or 'predicate acts' – meaning the case is predicated on these] must have occurred within ten years.

The RICO list of qualifying acts includes, per 18 USC 1961:
(A) any act or threat involving murder...
(B) any act which is indictable under any of the following provisions of Title 18 United States Code: Section 201 (relating to bribery) ... section 1503 (relating to obstruction of justice), section 1511 (relating to the obstruction of State or local law enforcement), section 1512 (relating to tampering with a witness, victim, or an informant).... Persons can be found guilty of conspiring to make the Racket succeed even if they personally did not perform two acts, and even if they are not being charged with any crime.

ALERT! THE FOLLOWING IS NOT A REAL CASE!
TROY DAVIS, VIRGINIA DAVIS, AND MARTINA CORREIA, plaintiffs, Pro Se

v.

THE FEDERAL BUREAU OF INVESTIGATION, THE US DEPARTMENT OF HOMELAND SECURITY (CUSTOMS ENFORCEMENT), SPENCER LAWTON, CHATHAM COUNTY DISTRICT ATTORNEY, THURBERT E. BAKER, ATTORNEY GENERAL OF GEORGIA, THE ATLANTA JOURNAL-CONSTITUTION, PEOPLE MAGAZINE, defendants

Jury Trial Demanded

I. Introduction

Three men are in prison in Georgia having been convicted of murder, one of whom is the plaintiff Troy Davis, who is scheduled to be executed very soon at Jackson, Georgia. The other two are Brian Nichols and Wayne Williams, serving life sentences. Possibly none of the three men committed the murders for which they are charged.

Rather, the murders, totaling about 34 victims, were committed as part of a Racket. The Racket involves killing officers of the law, judges, and helpless citizens, including children. Participants include politicians, lawyers, judges, police, and the media.

The Racket has pecuniary value to some of the participants, for instance through the sale of child pornography. It is also part of a large scheme, a 'psychological operation,' or psy-op, the apparent purpose of which is to condition Americans to lawlessness so as to dispose them eventually to dictatorial control. That control would have pecuniary value to the dictators.

The RICO Act allows civil suit to be brought against racketeering enterprises by anyone whose business or property has been injured.

II. Jurisdiction and Venue

1. This Court has jurisdiction because it is a federal RICO case, under 18 USC 1961, and also involves the crimes of misprision of felony under 18 USC 4, and misprision of treason under 18 USC 2382.

2. The Atlanta venue is proper as the plaintiffs live in the state of Georgia, and most of the defendants live there, too. The RICO predicate acts took place mainly in Georgia.

III. Parties

Plaintiffs:

3. Troy Davis, born 1968, is a prisoner at Georgia Diagnostic Center in Jackson. He is on "Death Row".

4. Virginia Davis is the mother of Troy Davis. Her ex-husband stopped taking his diabetes medication when his son was given the death sentence, and died a few months later. Her son's execution will cause her a loss of income he may have lived to earn and share with her.

5. Martina Correia, born 1966, is the sister of Troy Davis. She resides at 169 [Redacted] Rd., Savannah, Georgia 31419. Almost all her time in the past 10 months has had to be given to the task of trying to win justice for the prisoner. Hence she has suffered economic loss.

Defendants:

6. The Federal Bureau of Investigation is part of the United States

Department of Justice. Its central office is at 601 4th Street NW, Washington, D.C. 20535.

7. The Customs Enforcement section of the Department of Homeland Security has its central office at 500 12th Street NW, Washington D.C. 20536.

8. Spencer Lawton is District Attorney of Chatham County, Georgia. His office is at 133 Montgomery Street, Suite 600, Savannah, Georgia. He is sued in his official capacity and in his personal capacity.

9. Thurbert E. Baker is Attorney General of Georgia. His office is at 40 Capitol Square SW, Atlanta Georgia 30334. He is sued in his official capacity and in his personal capacity.

10. The Atlanta Journal-Constitution ("AJC") is the largest daily newspaper in Georgia. Its headquarters are at Edgewood Road, SE, Atlanta, Georgia 30303.

11. People Magazine is a periodical headquartered at Sixth Avenue at 50th Street, New York NY 10019.

IV. Statute of Limitations

12. A civil RICO suit is considered to be a new species of tort claim. Federal RICO respects the statute of limitations of the respective state. In Georgia the statute of limitations for torts is one year. The injury described in this claim has two different dates from which the respective statute of limitations may run.

13. For plaintiff number one, Troy Davis, the economic injury is beginning now because of his execution (allowed to take place from today, May 18, 2009), which will deprive him of any chance to earn wealth.

14. For plaintiff number two, Virginia Davis, the economic injury will begin on the same day that her son Troy's begins.

15. For plaintiff number three, Martina Correia, the economic injury began in August 2008 when, travelling worldwide to get support for her brother Troy's case, she lost assets by having to meet the pertinent expenses (albeit much of her travel was paid for by Amnesty International).

208

V. The Racketeering Enterprise(s)

16. RICO requires that each case point to an 'enterprise.' Logic demands that crime can only thrive if the criminals have an effective way to counteract the power of the law. Throughout the world, wherever criminals have become a powerful force in society, it can be readily observed that they have neutralized the police, the courts, the legislature, and the influence of social leaders.

17. The standard methods used by these powerful criminals have been bribery, intimidation, and coercion, plus concealment of their activities. (See Professor D. Wilkes on 'copsuckery.')

18. In the present era, criminals have additional means of preventing their own arrest, namely, infiltration of the media and the use of mind-control devices. They can, and do, hypnotize people to carry out their orders in slave-like fashion.

19. In a complex society, the actual racketeers, those who operate vices such as drug running, extortion, and prostitution, have at their command a whole layer of 'subcontractors' whose work consist of thwarting the law – such as the job of delivering the bribe money, or breaking legs. The actual racketeer will be called Racketeers in this claim, and the layer of subcontractors will be called Second Tier Racketeers.

20. In Atlanta, pertinent Rackets are child abduction for purposes of child sexual abuse, prostitution, and sale of children. Additionally, Atlanta is a hub of drug trafficking.

21. Of the defendants, the two governmental organizations – FBI and Department of Homeland Security (Customs Enforcement) – are here alleged to be Racketeers. The other defendants are Second Tier Racketeers, such as persons whose job is to interfere with law enforcement.

22. Major media corporations are crucial Racketeers. They do not merely twist facts or suppress knowledge, they nowadays engage in blatant efforts to make people believe things that did not actually occur. Importantly, media give the public a strong feeling as to who committed a certain murder. They also create a general atmosphere of distrust of one's neighbors. They condition people to take for granted

that there is such a thing as a serial killer, which is highly unlikely. In American history, up until 1966, the phenomenon of 'serial killing' was simply unknown.

23. The other defendants are Second Tier Racketeers, such as persons whose job is to interfere with law enforcement.

VI. RICO Requirements of 'Continuity' and 'Relationship'

24. The Atlanta child murders began in 1979, and the killing of Judge Rowland Barnes took place in March, 2005. This 26 year spread is proof of continuity of murder and the accompanying ability of many players to cover up those murders and/or direct the function of law enforcement away from resolving the crimes and punishing the guilty.

25. As for 'relationship' it can only be deduced, from the well-coordinated results, that police, lawyers, media persons, judges, and others are working together to allow criminals to escape punishment and to force innocent people to take the rap.

REMINDER, THIS ONLY IS A MAKE-BELIEVE CASE

VII. Two (or More) Predicate Acts
26. One predicate act is the obstruction of justice that occurred when Mr. Mark MacPhail, an off-duty member of the Savannah Police, was shot in August 1989. Someone must have instructed police and media to ensure that numerous witnesses blamed person who was not a protected person within the Rackets.

Hence the following witnesses were urged in 1989 to blame Troy Davis. Eventually they signed affidavits recanting their testimony. Examples are presented here.

[Note to Reader of this exercise: To keep the story short, I shall quote only four of Troy's recanting witnesses, choosing ones that are additional to the ones discussed in an earlier chapter of this book and Appendix L.]

27. Monty Holmes: I told them I didn't know anything about who shot the officer, but they kept questioning me. I was real young at that time and here they were questioning me about the murder of a police officer like I was in trouble or something. I was scared... [I]t seemed like they wouldn't stop questioning me until I told them what they

210

wanted to hear. So I did. I signed a statement saying that Troy told me that he shot the cop.

28. Robert Grizzard: I have reviewed the transcript of my testimony from the trial of Troy Davis... During my testimony I said that the person who shot the officer was wearing a light colored shirt. The truth is that I don't recall now and I didn't recall then what the shooter was wearing, as I said in my initial statement...

29. Michael Cooper: I have had a chance to review a statement which I supposedly gave to police officers on June 25, 1991. I remember that they asked a lot of questions and typed up a statement which they told me to sign. I did not read the statement before I signed. In fact, I have not seen it before today. ...What is written in that statement is a lie.

30. Benjamin Gordon: I just kept telling them that I didn't do anything, but they weren't hearing that. After four hours, they told me to sign some papers. I just wanted to get the hell out of there. I didn't read what they told me to sign and they didn't ask me to.

31. A second predicate act also involves obstruction of justice, regarding the child murders. Four eyewitnesses saw one of the child victims, named Cater, alive on the day after he was reportedly thrown off a bridge by Wayne Williams. Such exculpatory evidence should have appeared at trial as the accused was entitled to have it heard. Such an omission can only have been intended.

32. Probably it conflicted with the bridge story that had become one of the media's focal points at the time. For that reasonalone it can be surmised that Wayne Williams is innocent of the killing of Cater. (Not that he was convicted of that child's murder. He was only ever convicted of the murder of two adults, but the bridge story added to his 'guiltiness.')

33. A third predicate act is the killing of David Wilhelm, Customs Enforcement Officer, on March 11, 2005. It is not credible that this was done by Brian Nichols. A hit-man among the Second Tier Racketeers must have done it.

34. A fourth predicate act is the obstruction of justice that consisted of Troy Davis's family being refused 'permission' to attend his first court case (They did not realize that no one in America needs permission.

VIII. Injury to Businesses and/or Property

35. Three plaintiffs have suffered or will suffer economic loss owing to the actions of the defendants. Troy Davis has already lost 20 years of what would be a normal life, by being incarcerated. The particular loss claimed here is that which will begin on the day of his execution.

36. From that moment on, he has no ability to contribute earned income to his family. In the 24 years remaining until his 65th birthday one can use a minimum-wage figure of $10,000 per year, hence he claims $240,000.

37. His mother, plaintiff Virginia Davis, asks to receive only the symbolic sum of One Dollar. The money she will lose, by way of support from her son, is already included in the $240,000 that he claims.

38. As for the plaintiff Martina Correia, she had out-of- pocket property losses and opportunity costs. This began in approximately August 2008 when she had to make almost daily efforts to contact radio channels, human rights organizations, and attorneys. Gasoline, road tolls, phone calls, etc. added up to $2000.

39. Martina Correia's intangible opportunity costs include at least some small amount of wages that she would have earned during those ten months in which she was thusly occupied. This could be expected to have been at least $100 per month net, hence $1000.

IX. Facts -- and Allegations Crime

[To the Reader, this is where one sets out the main facts. I'll leave it blank for you to do. Google for Brian Nichols'case. Re the Atlanta murders, see the helpful website: atkid.weebly.com. Families of those children can file civil RICO. The dear babes' names are: Laytonya Wilson, age 7, Yusef Bell 9, Anthony Carter 9, Jeffrey Mathis 10, Aaron Wyche 10, Earl Terrell 11, Angel Lenair 12, Chris Richardson 12, Alfred Evans 13, Edward Smith 14, Milton Harvey 14, Eric Middlebrooks 14.]

X. Possible ADDITIONAL Co-Plaintiffs

The court may wish to join other plaintiffs to this suit. For example, persons who have economic losses include Wayne Williams, Brian Nichols, Candee Wilhelm, widow of David Wilhelm, and the relatives of some of the child victims in Atlanta, such as Camille Bell, mother of 9-year-old Yusuf.

Busload of jurors inspecting the bridge where Wayne Williams "dumped bodies." The bridge story may have been invented to give media something to talk about.

XI. Prayer for Relief

Plaintiffs ask for injunctive relief, declaratory judgment, and monetary damages (trebled) as follows:

A. Court to enjoin the state of Georgia from executing Troy Davis.

B. Court to order defendants to pay 3,000.00 (trebled) to Martina Correia, $240,000 (trebled) to Troy Davis, and $1.00 to Virginia Davis, for injury to their business and property.

C. Court to give declaratory judgment, as it sees fit, regarding the enterprise described in this complaint.

D. Court to recommend that criminal charges be brought in connection with allegations in this complaint.

E. Court to consider any other way to follow Congress's advice to "construe the RICO Act liberally in order to effectuate its remedial purposes.

Respectfully submitted, on May 18, 2009, PRO SE,

In a real case, the plaintiffs would sign and date it, in front of a witness.

(To repeat: the foregoing is fictional. Alas.)

In criminalibus probationes debent esse luce clariores - In criminal cases the proofs ought to be cleared than the light. (Law maxim)

chapter twenty-four

Kay Griggs, whisleblower extraordinaire

Henry Kissinger, of "Kissinger Associates"

24. Conspiracy Museum and Citizen's Arrest (Satire)

How many thousand of my poorest subjects
Are at this hour asleep! O sleep, O gentle sleep,
Nature's soft nurse, how have I frighted thee,
That thou no more wilt weigh my eyelids down....
Uneasy lies the head that wears a crown.

   -- William Shakespeare, *Henry IV, Part II* (1597)

As was noted in the *vade mecum* of Chapter 20, legal resources are an embarrassment of riches. We've got all we need, in law, to cancel out the evil that abounds. And the previous chapter showed how to do a RICO case.

In this chapter, instead of saying "We should do this, that, and the other thing," I'll change the tense and say "We're already doing it and it's all working out great!"

The tactic of fantasizing came to me when I produced my first-ever comedy show this year for The Adelaide Fringe. My co-conspirator Dee McLachlan and I wanted to cover topics such as 9-11, Chinese immigration, geo-engineering, and the Port Arthur massacre. We knew these had to be handled diplomatically

In Port Arthur, Tasmania, 35 people were shot dead in 1996 supposedly by a "lone gunman." Aussies are reluctant to believe that Martin Bryant who is still in prison, is innocent. Everyone in Oz was told from Day One that he was the killer, and it seems too hard to turn it around. (See Appendix Y)

McLachlan and I wrote the skit, which featured a different person confessing to the crime. However, some last minute cast-and-crew problems forced us to change the script. So we wrote "Some law students went to the privatized jail in Tasmania and persuaded the CEO that the Writ of Habeas Corpus they were holding meant that Bryant had to be freed." Yay! I'll now sketch a few more such *deus ex machina* endings to our troubles.

NOTA BENE: All that follows is 100% fiction.

Retired Nurse in Detroit Opens Conspiracy Museum

Susan Larson, RN, wanted to help the failing economy of her beloved city, Detroit, by creating a tourism venture. Susan bought a warehouse and had the land re-zoned for public entertainment. It now houses six large museum rooms and a cinema. Entrance fee is $15, or $2 for kids.

The mayor of Detroit spoke at the opening ceremony, at which the governor of Michigan cut a ribbon, revealing the front foyer where you can take your choice of walking to the Watergate, 9-11, MK-Ultra, Katrina, "Dallas," or James Ray rooms.

Another room will be used only for cabaret with dining when the repertory company "Conspiracy Rules" visits. The sixth room is a library where you can read pertinent books, such as Judith Vary Baker's *Me and Lee,* or Robert Merritt's *Watergate Exposed* – both published by Trine Day Press, whose chief, Kris Millegan will be there each year on the federal holiday Conspiracy Discovery Day, May 6th.

This has made Michigan quite the tourist attraction. Carol Rutz, who lives in that state, and Cathy O'Brien, who grew up there, have said they are grateful for people's interest in what they went endured as kids in MK-Ultra.

Some of the visitors have wept when they saw the displays of torture instruments used, and when they watched the films in the on-site cinema. A psychologist is available most days for counseling members of the public.

Judge Windsor Holds Court

After his fifth sojourn in prison for such crimes as cyber-stalking and talking back to a security guard, Bill Windsor won the exoneration he had been seeking, by using the method of "coram nobis" that Mary W Maxwell had told him about. It was easy-peasy, given the amount of fraud upon the court displayed in Bill's *Lawless America* series.

Bill and fellow judges were given a mandate in each of the 50 states to re-hear any case in which a person, such as Mona

Gudbranson or Joe Lobianco, had found the ruling outrageous. This resulted in a new decision in 958 of the thousand cases! Many families were reunited and, just as had happened in South Korea when a TV show allowed long-lost relatives from North Korea to be reunited with their folks in the South, some of the *Lawless America* reunions were broadcast live.

The 9-11 Apology

A clerk named Jo-ann Sotero had been doing data-entry for the $1.8 million checks to be paid to 9-11 families at the Shanksville crash. She happened to notice her grandmother's name on the list, but Grandma had died in 1986. Jo-ann figured some of the other claimants might also be using a 'borrowed' Social Security number.

She had always doubted that a plane had gone down at Shanksville, PA, so she started to query those deaths. At one point she tracked down a photo of a passenger. In going to the home to get a signature for the claim, Jo-ann was startled to find the "passenger" in the front yard.

When confronted, he confessed, and this led to myriad other confessions related to the FBI's "investigation" of the wreck at Shanksville. The knot of lies had been described by Elias Davidsson in his superb book *Hijacking America's Mind on 9-11*. Soon, the entire 9-11 story opened up. They are still questioning if nukes were used at WTC.

(Reminder: the items here in Chapter 24 are only satire!!)

The Media. How the Mighty Have Fallen!

Rayelan Allen brought a RICO suit against Newscorp, showing that her weekly expense of $2.00 for a newspaper had caused her an economic loss, as the paper did not actually contain news. It contained nonsense, and met two of the predicate crimes, mail fraud and bribery. She prayed to the judge for relief in the form of dissolution of the corporation and forfeiture of ill-gotten gains. All other MSM quickly disbanded voluntarily.

Hurricane Katrina No Longer Considered Natural

In early 2015, residents of Louisiana prepared for the 10th anniversary of the tragic event in which the levies burst at New Orleans, during Hurricane Katrina. Together with many citizens of Mississippi and Alabama they formed a commission to inquire into the involvement of HAARP or any other technological weather-tampering device. At the same time, a younger group ran an investigation into the fate of all parcels of real estate in the Gulf Coast area.

The first thing they found was that the media had knowledge of many of the events before they happened. This could have been excellent guesswork, or it could indicate that the disaster was *planned*. At this point people began to look back at the death-by-disappearance of Rep Hale Boggs of New Orleans and Rep Nick Begich of Alaska. On October 16, 1972, both men were in a plane that has never been found. (Begich's son, Nick Jr is the top researcher on the ionospheric heart known as HAARP.) Now a group at Boston Univerity Law School has offered to take up the study of all Congressional suspicious deaths, of which there are in fact dozens.

Persons had heard explosions on the day of Katrina that indicated that the levies were blown by dynamite. They had gone to Congress with this information and been treated dismissively, despite giving sworn testimony. They were now listened to, and the Commission watched the Youtube video that clearly shows the levies breaking.

Persons throughout the country who had suspected that all recent hurricanes, such as Irene, were foul play, attended the citizens' commission meetings. A delegation came up from Haiti to talk about the apparent use of high technology to cause the earthquake of January 12, 2010. A group from Iceland decided to appear at the meetings to talk about eruption of volcanoes there in 2010 and 2011.

Reminder: Items here in Chapter 24 are only satirical, OK?

A Tuition-free College of Law

Being well-trained members of the legal profession, not to mention being scared witless about getting convicted as accessories to the crime of torture, Jay Bybee and John Yoo decided to open a fee college of law. It will be named the Alyssa Peterson School, and its Law Library will be named for Charles Gittings, who gave his life to the cause of curtailing war crimes. He was the founder of the Program for Enforcement of the Geneva Conventions.

The college will not be devoted exclusively to problems of torture and the international aggression practiced by NATO, but will stick up for the honor of the judicial system. Bybee and Yoo have recommended an end to the practice of the Department of Justice appointing public defenders. Indeed there will be an end to the Department of Justice, period. Its child, the FBI, is too problematic for the constitutionally required separation of powers.

It was seen that the DOJ thought of itself as an arm of the president (or the Pentagon, or the mafia, as the case may be), and this did not leave enough autonomy and independence for the judicial branch, per Article III, as well as the Federalist Papers, and the ratification debates.

Additional emphasis at the new Alyssa Peterson College of Law will be on whistleblower protection, coram nobis, the law maxims, courts of equity, RICO suits, and an end to SLAPP suits, in which Davids are attacked by Goliaths.

Re-examining the Dick Act

Thanks to the upheaval caused by Lou Fisher's book, *The Constitution and 9-11*, a whole review of war-related legislation had to be conducted. The first item to go was the US's unconstitutional participation in NATO. The National Guard Bureau wasn't far behind.

E.g., in 1903, Elihu Root, a buddy of Alfred Milner, got the ball rolling toward use of national Guardsmen, by sending federal funding to the states. As sooner as these newly awakened citizens of 2015 discovered what had happened back then, they undertook to review all other unconstitutional laws passed by Congress since then.

The Federal Reserve Act (1913) recommended itself for consideration, but it was decided to let that one be tackled slowly, to prevent a collapse of the economy. Ripe for the plucking on short notice, however, was the federal funding of education and health. Soon, a States Rights Organization (SRO) was formed to monitor all these developments. The chairperson is Charlotte Iserbyt.

Friends of Gary Webb and Enemies of Iran Contra

Luckily, many citizens have had their eyes on the doings of the Bush crime family for many years. According to such investigators as Wayne Madsen, Al Martin, and Robert Parry, there is much about Iran Contra that was never dealt with in the Congressional hearings. Some of the miscreants such as Oliver North got immunity, while Defense Secretary Weinberger was pardoned by Bush.

Persons who knew the Bushes had suffered torture as children came forward argued for mercy for them.

The Matter of Zionist World Control

Mary Maxwell, in Australia, had been trying to get to the bottom of the Protocols of Elders of Zion. Philip Roth's *Plot against America* had caused her to worry that we were going to be told to persecute Jews. She hosted an open conference. Hard facts about the Bank of England were revealed. Many Jews said they considered the laws against Holocaust denial to be both immoral and frightening, and were pleased to be able to debate all these things at last. It was revealed who the Mossad really works for. Amazing.

How To Send Flowers to Troy Davis

Troy asked that we not forget him if he was executed. Martina Correia had reported that prisoners in Georgia get only one free meal a day. If they want to eat more, their family must send the money. It has to go through a particular bank that charges 75 cents per meal (not for the food, just as its 'administrative fee'). You may have also heard that families often have to travel considerable distance to see their man and then are told that the visiting day has been changed. This is harassment.

It will now be possible to do something for Troy Davis. His sister Kimberly and his nephew Antone Davis-Correia were given a heartfelt apology and a huge settlement for the wrongful imprisonment and death of Troy [satire.] As a result, Kimberley and Antone now run a service in Atlanta that can be used by anyone in the nation who wants to complain about prison conditions, including medical experimentation, the use of stun belts, and rape.

Indeed there will be a special program of unannounced visits to all private prisons to check on the food quality and to make sure solitary confinement is not unjustifiably used. The visitor will also record, if the prisoner wants it recorded, that he was intimidated into plea-bargaining. A likely spinoff will be a Moot Court to see how he would have fared with a jury if he had not copped a plea.

More on Prisons: Manchurian Candidate Formation

In the Midwest, Jerry Ray, sole surviving brother of James Earl Ray, has also been paid a settlement for the murder in jail of his brother Jimmy. Jerry wants to put the money to use in a search for the making of Manchurian Candidates in jails.

This matter came to light in a 2008 book, *Truth at Last,* co-authored by Lyndon Barsten and Ray's brother John. I mean it came to light that James was trained through the MK-Ultra program to be a killer-on-cue (known as a Manchurian Candidate). But the 'work' was not done on him in prison but in the Army. James Earl Ray said "The Army put me on the road to ruin."

Oddly, *Wikipedia,* which is largely produced by the CIA, gave us the following tidbit in its write-up of the 2014 conviction of

South Boston mobster Whitey Bulger:

> "In 1956 [Bulger] was first sentenced to federal time in Atlanta Penitentiary for armed robbery and truck hijacking. There, according to mobster Kevin Weeks, he was involved in the MK-ULTRA program, the goal of which was to research mind-control drugs for the Central Intelligence Agency, headed by CIA chemist Sidney Gottlieb. For eighteen months, Bulger and eighteen other inmates, all of whom had volunteered in return for lessened sentences, were given LSD and other drugs. Bulger later complained that he and the other inmates had been 'recruited by deception,' and that they were told that they were helping to find "a cure for schizophrenia." He described his experience as "nightmarish" and said it took him "to the depths of insanity."

Most persons who went through MK-Ultra came out with a willingness to obey orders to kill or commit other crimes in such a way that it was all unconscious and secret. This method of conducting a kill was very useful to *the real killers* who ran MK-Ultra. Perhaps Ted Kaczynski (b 1942), known as the Unabomber, was such a "Manchurian candidate." If this method of investigation proves fruitful, we'll be able to know more about, say, the "terrorism" organized for Ted to carry out (if he even did carry it out). Such, of course, is treason.

The *Hosti Humani Generis* Situation

Before international law arose (around 1650), the rule was that pirates could be captured and punished by any nation that caught them. A pirate was an "enemy of mankind" – *hosti humani generis*. Yale students knew that 9-11 attackers did not come from a particular nation, so couldn't be dealt with at the ICJ. They ran a moot court, accusing the 9-11 attackers as *hosti humani generis*. Their teacher flunked them for resorting inappropriately to a judicial institution.

A Long-awaited Citizen's Arrest

Kay Griggs felt she had risked so much to tell everything on Youtube about Kissinger, yet there were no arrests. She then collaborated with folks in Virginia and Maryland to find out just what citizen's arrest is all about. They learned that it is legal in every state but some state rules vary. The following rough guide is meant only as an introduction to the Kay Griggs (fictitious) episode:

There are times when a person sees a crime being committed, or about to be committed, and there are no police around. Can he do the job himself? Cautiously, yes.

He must tell the person that he is being arrested ("arrested" only means stopped). The next part of the job is to get the person to the police. This may mean tying him down or otherwise forcibly transporting him, if, for some reason one cannot phone the cops to pick him up.

There is a risk to using force. Although it is legal, the person may later prevail if he has not committed the crime as you allege. He would then be ale to sue you for bodily injury. If no injury, he could sue you for false imprisonment even if it lasted only 5 minutes.

Some states allow you to perform the citizen's arrest if the crime was committed in the past. It must be a felony, not just a misdemeanor. In any case, in this made-up example, Kay Griggs wanted Henry Kissinger arrested for murder. She could see that he is a protected person. In other words, government would not get this criminal for his many crimes. (So we assume that he committed those crimes on behalf of the real rulers of America.)

Kay had first collected a large group of supporters, thousands of whom approached Henry that morning. He reached for his phone and called for his guards. After a time it was apparent that his guards were not going to reply to his request. They were sick of working for him.

Thus, Kay quietly stepped forward and made the arrest.

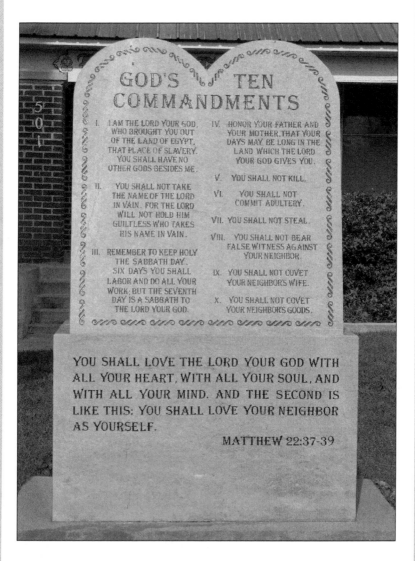

chapter twenty-five

Firmior et potentior est operatio legis quam dispositio hominis --
The operation of law is firmer and more powerful
than the will of man. (Law maxim)

25. Conclusion

The first step therefore is to make the black man come to himself; to pump back life into his empty shell; to infuse him with pride and dignity to remind him of his complicity in the crime of allowing himself to be misused and therefore letting evil reign supreme in the country of his birth.

-- Steve Biko (1946-1977) anti-apartheid leader

This chapter does not really conclude the book as there many short appendices, including ones on EO Wilson, Elvis Presley, Mae Brussell, Martin Bryant, Aunt Maret Tsarnaeva, Charlotte Iserbyt, Laurent Louis and – why not – vaccination.

Part I said "Happiness Is the Law." Indeed. Law is what can make us pretty happy, and lack of it is dreadful. Law is the human species' way of managing social life.

Part II showed "Some Stunningly Bad Court Cases." Boy, there must be quite an efficient team up there just to have pulled off the Boston Strangler case. Imagine how many news reporters, police, attorneys, and advisers had to be in on the convicting (and killing) of DeSalvo, never mind on the strangling of the women.

Part III listed "What the Law Can and Cannot Do." It said we need religious-like values to motivate community caring.

Part IV said "Get Your Hands Muddy." Why not. Just because a few whistleblowers have gone to God is no reason to stop doing what they do. The chapter called *Vade Mecum* listed a kazillion ways to tackle the problems. I went ahead and muddied my hands over matters Tsarnaev.

Part V asked "Where Should the Law Go Now?" The good news here, fantastic news, is that the Secret Pests have been identified, and so we can call Pest Control.

"Bush Administration Pays $5 Million Reward to Tipster."
by Matthew Lee and Lara Jakes Jordan, *AP News,* January 24, 2008.

The Bush administration paid a $5 million reward to a former Minnesota flight instructor who provided authorities with information that led to the arrest of **9/11 conspirator** Zacarias Moussaoui. Two colleagues questioned why he got the money.

The recipient, Clarence Prevost, was honored Thursday at a closed door ceremony at the State Department, although the payout was secretly authorized last fall by Secretary of State Condoleezza Rice and the Justice Department, U.S. officials told The Associated Press.

The reward from the State Department's "Rewards for Justice" program is…unusual because Moussaoui, who was imprisoned at the time of the attacks, was never named as a wanted suspect by the program…. The State Department would not identify the recipient, **citing privacy and security concerns**. Two administration officials, however, said the reward went to Prevost, a witness at Moussaoui's trial who has previously spoken out about involvement in the case.

The officials spoke on condition of anonymity because they were not authorized to speak publicly about the matter. Prevost, 69, is a former Navy pilot who later flew for Northwest Airlines. He was Moussaoui's flight instructor at the PanAm Flight Academy outside Minneapolis. He was one of several people who worked at the flight school that Moussaoui attended in August 2001 and who alerted the FBI to his **suspicious desire to pilot jumbo jets**.

News of the reward came as a surprise to two other Pan Am flight instructors, Tim Nelson and Hugh Sims, who also have been credited with tipping the FBI to Moussaoui. Nelson was talking with family members Thursday evening and was not available, his wife, Jodie Quinn-Nelson said. She said the reward "was given out to the wrong person" and said her husband was upset.

After his arrest, Moussaoui sat in jail for 3 1/2 weeks on an immigration violation, saying little to investigators before hijacked planes slammed into the World Trade Center and the Pentagon or **crashed in a Pennsylvania field** on Sept. 11.

But after the jury decided against sentencing him to death, Moussaoui recanted his testimony and denied any role in 9/11, saying he lied on the stand because **he assumed he had no chance of getting a fair trial.**

Rewards for **Justice**, which was created in 1984, has paid about **$77 million in rewards to more than 50 people.** [Emphasis added]

Regarding the previous page, I was surprised to learn that Congress has legislated a program that could make you (yes, you) a quinto-millionaire overnight. Just be a tipster.

Let's recommend to Congress that they pay a reward, also, to anyone who gets a "coram nobis" to succeed in setting aside a ruling where there had been fraud upon the court. You could start with the case of *Gallop v Cheney.* Yay!

Here's another thought. Let's make judgeships free. I mean the judge will work without pay. Chief Justice John Roberts has been crabbing about the low pay that SCOTUS justices receive (a quarter of a million per annum). He said that without better pay, it isn't possible to recruit top persons into the job.

I say we don't want the kind of persons who would be sad to take a pay cut from their huge earnings as lawyers. We want the kind who would be utterly humbled at the thought of serving in the US Supreme Court *gratis.*

Speaking of money, Hammurabi, 3700 years ago in Babylon (near Baghdad) had an idea. In "the Code of Hammurabi," we find, as his Rule 5:

"If a judge try a case, reach a decision, and present his judgment in writing; if later error shall appear in his decision, and it be through his own fault, then he shall pay twelve times the fine set by him in the case...."

Hammurabi's code in clay

Why not. And suffer the wrong imprisonment, too.

Welcome to the Appendices

Appendix A. Did Todd Beamer Really Say "Let's Roll"? Mary W Maxwell Interviews Elias Davidsson. Published at Gumshoenews. com, February 20, 2014. Davidsson is author of *Hijacking America's Mind on 9-11; Counterfeiting Evidence* (2013)

Elias Davidsson

Elias Davidsson lives in Germany; he is a musician and human rights scholar, and host of the website juscogens.org. The book is about the calls made from the four planes on 9-11:

-- American Airlines Flight 11, calls from Betty Ong and Madeleine Sweeney;

-- United Flight 175, from Brian Sweeney and Garnett Bailey;

-- American Flight 77, from Barbara Olson and Renee Mey;

-- United Flight 93, from Todd Beamer, Mark Bingham, Sandy Bradshaw, Thomas Burnett, Edward Felt, Jeremy Glick, Lauren Grandcola, CeeCee Lyle, and Elizabeth Wainio.

Maxwell: I would say that the most vivid section of your book is the portrait of "life on Mars" – I mean the stark emptiness of the ground at Shanksville, Pennsylvania, where the "Let's Roll" plane is said to have crashed. To any onlooker except the willfully blind, that scene has no plane wreckage in it whatsoever.

Davidsson: Whether it is the most vivid section or not, it is undeniable that many observers were amazed at the sight, but only a few dared to question what they saw (or did not see). I find it particularly revealing that the FBI did not allow any documentation of the alleged recovery of the plane from the pit and claimed after merely 12 days to have recuperated 95% of the plane.

Maxwell: When did you come to see the official story of 9-11 as not believable?

Davidsson: Gradually since 2002 but definitely around 2004.

Maxwell: Myself, I did not notice the problem until I was reading the

Hutton Inquiry into the death of David Kelly, when I was a law student in 2005. For years I've seen on your website, jusgocens.org, an offer to pay $10,000 to anyone who would prove the official 9-11 case. Have you had any nibbles?

Davidsson: No. I have removed the offer, as no one responded.

Maxwell: What is the main idea of your new book?

Davidsson: To debunk definitely the legend that a group of Muslim/Arab fanatics perpetrated the mass-murder of 9/11.

Maxwell: Your book indicates that, in the trial of Zacarias Moussaoui, the FBI presented bogus passenger seating plans that include the seats of alleged hijackers. Offering false material to a US court would constitute perjury and may also come under the federal crime of obstruction of justice. Have you tried to challenge the FBI on this?

Davidsson: No, because I have no legal standing.

Maxwell: I see that the *Wall Street Journal* of May 16, 2013 gave an unusual acknowledgement of the "conspiracy view." It said:
"During the 2006 Moussaoui Trial, the FBI (under oath) reduced the number of cell phone calls to two calls made from 5,000 feet, and presented evidence of only one (not two) "unconnected" call from Barbara Olson, lasting "0 seconds."
... [A]lthough the FBI conducted a massive investigation into the calls, none of the telephone billing, nor any of the cell phone location data stored in standard phone company records has been publicly released."

Davidsson: The *Wall Street Journal* may have been responding to my book, which had been published two weeks earlier, and to the work done by the 9-11 Consensus Panel.

Mary W Maxwell

231

Maxwell: Over what matter did you write to Judge Brinkema?

Davidsson: I wrote Judge Leonie Brinkema on March 17, 2006 as a response to alleged contradictory directions she gave to the jury in the trial of Zacarias Moussaoui. She told them first "I assume every one of you is aware of what happened on September 11, 2001, and has watched or read extensive media coverage about that day and has watched news reports or read about Al Qaeda" and then added, "Persons on trial must be judged not on the basis of what is in the news or popular media, but rather on the hard evidence presented in the courtroom during the trial." I expressed to her my concern that "the failure by your Court to establish, according to standards of evidence required in criminal law, that the crime of 9/11 was committed by the nineteen alleged hijackers, may represent a gross miscarriage of justice," and urged her to reconsider her decisions. This remained, as we now know, a futile and perhaps naive undertaking on my part.

Maxwell: I personally don't think it was either futile or naive. One has to start somewhere to put some balance and common sense back into this thing, and you are just the man to do it. Your exhaustive research into the phone calls from all the planes of 9-11 is meticulous. I am interested in this statement you made on page 14 of *Hijacking America's Mind:*

"When attempting to solve a criminal mystery, formal operations [can be] used to discover the unknown. These operations include deduction, induction, tests of logical coherence, tests of reliability and plausibility.... Where major pieces of evidence have been destroyed, the solution to a criminal mystery may not yield a precise answer but can provide an approximation...."

Davidsson: You may see that I followed that up, on page 15, by quoting approvingly the conservative approach of Nafeez Ahmed in his book *The War on Truth and the Anatomy of Terrorism* (2005: xiii). He said: "Although I attempt to outline what seem to me the obvious deductions ... the actual value of my work is in the facts themselves. The readers are...free...to draw their own overarching conclusions."

Maxwell: I agree that is the facts in your book that matter. They are stunning. Probably it helps that you are a foreigner to the US, and thus not worried about using logic in matters that Americans consider emotional. A member of Japan's parliament, Mr Yukihisa Fujita, has also demanded that his government inquire into the 9-11 "put options." By the way, most Americans don't know that the 9-11 families got a gift of approximately one million dollars each. Did you know of it?

Davidsson: They got on the average $2.1 million per family.

Maxwell: How does your book fit with your avocation as a scholar of international law?

Davidsson: The mass-murder of 9/11 was a "crime against humanity" under customary international law. This places a legal obligation on the US government to search for and prosecute the perpetrators. The crime falls also under the doctrine of universal jurisdiction, providing third states with the potential (or even duty) to arrest any person suspected of having participated in the crime. The obligation of states to adequately investigate is also a corollary of the right to the truth of victims' families. The right to the truth is one of the remedies to which victims … are entitled.

Maxwell: The part of your book I found most startling was your condemnation of the "entire academic class' for its shutting down of its brain in regard to 9-11. What do you think the academic class needs to do now?

Davidsson: It does not need to know anything. It needs to think rationally. Then it will seek knowledge, as required.

Appendix B. Academics Assassinated in Baghdad, small excerpt (about 12%) from a list at cara1933.org. Date: 2005.

"Abbas Al-Attar: PhD in humanities, lecturer at Baghdad University. Abdel Razak Al-Naas: Lecturer in information and international mass media at Baghdad University's College of Information Sciences. He was a regular analyst for Arabic satellite TV channels, he was killed in his car at Baghdad University on 28 January 2005. His assassination led to confrontations between students and police, and journalists went on strike. Ahmed Al-Nassiri: PhD in education sciences, Baghdad University, assassinated February 2005. Ali Abdul-Hussein Kamil: PhD in physical sciences.

Amir Al-Jazragi: PhD in medicine, and consultant at the Iraqi Ministry of Health, assassinated November 17, 2005. Basil Al-Karji: PhD in chemistry. Essam Sharif Mohammed: PhD in history, professor in Department of History and head of the College of Humanities. Faidhi Al-Faidhi: PhD in education sciences, lecturer at Baghdad University, assassinated in 2005.

Fuad Abrahim Mohammed Al-Bayaty: PhD in German philology, professor and head of College of Philology, Baghdad University. Haifa Alwan Al-Hil: PhD in physics, College of Science for Women. Heikel Mohammed Al-Musawi: PhD in medicine, assassinated 17 November 2005. Hassan Abd Ali Dawood Al-Rubai: PhD in stomatology, dean of the College of Stomatology. Assassinated 20 December 2005. Hazim Abdul Hadi: PhD in medicine, lecturer. Khalel Ismail Abd Al-Dahri: PhD in physical education, lecturer at the College of Physical Education, Baghdad University.

Kilan Mahmoud Ramez: PhD lecturer at Baghdad University. Maha Abdel Kadira: PhD, lecturer at Baghdad University's College of Humanities. Majed Nasser Hussein Al-Maamoori: Professor of veterinary medicine at Baghdad University's College of Veterinary Medicine, assassinated 17 February 2007. Marwan Al-Raawi: PhD in engineering and lecturer at Baghdad University."

Appendix C. Persons Who Could Be Involved in 9-11.
From the website whodidit.org (no evidence provided)

Note: the researchers do not give their name. They list 103 persons who had some connection to 9-11. I have picked every 7th name. The point seems to be that these persons were in relevant positions of control – MM

1. **Dov Zakheim**. Pentagon comptroller, former CEO of fly-by-remote manufacturer

2. **John Ashcroft**. US Attorney General, protected Abdussatar Shaik from subpoena

3. **Jerome Hauer**. Manager of Kroll, put John O'Neill at WTC that day, worked in Emergency Management 1996-2000.

4. **Andrew Card**. Was with President Bush at Florida School.

5. **Richard Miles**. Former admiral, ran the Global Guardian 'war game' out of Offutt Air Force Base that day.

6. **Philip Odeen**. Director of Program Analysis for National Security Council, provided staff support to Henry Kissinger, 1971-73, former president of BDM International.

7. **Lewis Eisenberg**. Chairman of Port Authority of New York and New Jersey, later chaired Republican National Ctee.

8. **Abdullah Noman**. Worked for US Consulate in Jeddah, Saudi Arabia, used visa express program for patsy hijackers.

9. **William Baker**. In FEMA probe team. Contributed to the flawed NIST* report as to why the WTC towers collapsed.

10. **Charles Thornton**. Part of ASCE** team that investigated both the WTC and Murrah federal building in Oklahoma City.

11. **Larry Silverstein**. With Frank Lowy made billions of dollars from insurance when WTC attacked. Pulled Building 7.

12. **Jules Kroll**. His firm was in charge of security at the WTC on 9-11. He is a private military contractor in Iraq.

11. **Michael Cherkasky**. CEO of Kroll on 9-11. Was investigator for Manhattan District Attorney from 1978-1994.

13. **George HW Bush**. Member of Skull and Bones secret society. President of the US (and Reagan's VP 1981-1989)

*National Institute for Standards and Technology
**American Society of Civil Engineers

Appendix D. A Parliament of Puppies. Speech by Laurent Louis, Member of Belgian Parliament, January 17, 2013

Belgium is indeed the land of surrealism. This morning… we decide to help France in its war against "Terror" by providing logistical support for its operation in Mali. What wouldn't we do in order to fight against terrorism outside our borders? …

I seem to be joking, but what is going on in the world today does not make me laugh at all.

Preventive war has become the rule. And today, in the name of democracy and the fight against terrorism our states grant themselves the right to violate the sovereignty of independent countries and to overthrow legitimate leaders. There has been Iraq and Afghanistan, the wars of the American lie. Came later, Tunisia, Egypt, Libya where thanks to your decisions, our country has been "first in line" to participate in crimes against humanity…

Well, our Minister of Foreign Affairs decided **to offer the Syrian rebels** 9 million euros! Our country is only participating to put in place Islamic regimes in North Africa and the Middle East. So, when they come and pretend to go to war in order to fight against terrorism in Mali, well … I feel like laughing. It's false! Under the appearance of good actions, **we only intervene to defend financial interests** and to complete a neo-colonialist mindset.

The time has come to tell the truth. Arming the Islamist Rebels, as Westerners have in the past armed Bin Laden, western countries are taking the opportunity to place military bases in the newly conquered countries while favoring domestic companies.

Everything is therefore strategic. In Iraq, our American allies have put their hands on oil wealth. **In Afghanistan, it was its opium and drugs.** In Libya, in Tunisia, in Egypt or Syria, the aim was and still is today to overthrow moderate powers, **to replace them by Islamist powers** who very quickly will become troublesome and that **we will shamelessly attack.** Thus the next targets are already known. Within a few months I **bet that our eyes will turn to Algeria** and eventually to Iran. To go to war, to free people from an outside aggressor is noble. But to go to war to defend the interests of the USA … To go to war to defend the interests of big corporations such as AREVA … To go to war to put our hands on gold mines, has nothing noble at all and **it reveals our countries to be attackers and thugs!**

No one dares to speak, but I will not shut up! ...I don't have much respect either for the journalists... Finally, I despise at the highest point those who believe they are the kings of the world and who are dictating their laws because I am on the side of the truth, the side of justice, the side of innocent victims of looting.

Opposing the pro-war resolution

And it is for this reason that I have decided to clearly oppose this resolution. Since the beginning of the French operation, the lie has been organized. **We are told that France is only answering the call for help** of a Malian president. We almost forget that this president has no legitimacy. The French president, François Hollande dares to pretend to wage this war to fight against jihadists who threaten (Ohhh do you realize!) who threaten the French and European territory! ... By taking increasing the terror alert level, implementing the Vigipirate plan, our leaders and media are demonstrating an un-imaginable outrage!

The pretext hides strategic and economic purposes. Our countries are no longer fearing inconsistency because everything is done to hide it. But the inconsistency is well present. It is not tomorrow that you'll see a Malian citizen commit an act of terrorism in Europe. **No, unless we suddenly create one so we can justify this military operation**. Haven't we created September 11th, after all, to justify the invasions, torture and massacre of innocent populations? Thus, to create a Malian terrorist is no big deal!

So let's be clear, the primary beneficiaries of this military operation will be the owners and shareholders of the French giant AREVA who has been trying for years to obtain a uranium mine in Falea, a town of 17,000 inhabitants ....

Time to get Belgium out of UN, NATO & EU

For all these reasons and in order to not fall into the traps of lies they are telling us, I've decided not to give my support to that intervention in Mali. I never supported in the past our criminal interventions in Libya or in Syria, and so being the only MP in this country to defend the non-interference and the fight against obscure interests. **I really think it is about time to put an end to our participation in the UN or NATO** and get out of EU.

In conclusion, let me emphasize how lightly we decide to go to war. First, the government acts without any consent from the Parliament.. It sends equipment, men to Mali. The Parliament subsequently reacts. This is coming from a Parliament of Puppies, submitted to the dictates of political parties. Thank you. -- *Translation: Geraldine Feuillie*

Appendix E: Dismissal of Appeal of *Gallop v Cheney*

U.S. Court of Appeals, Second Circuit 10-1241-cv
Before: Winter, Walker, and Cabranes.

Decided: April 27, 2011

April Gallop appeals from a March 18, 2010 judgment of dismissing her complaint asserting violations of her constitutional rights ...a common law tort of

April Gallop conspiracy to cause death and great bodily harm, and a violation of the Antiterrorism Act... Gallop alleged that defendants, former senior government officials, caused the September 11, 2001 attacks in order to create a political atmosphere in which they could pursue domestic and international policy objectives and to conceal the misallocation of $2.3 trillion ...We hold that the District Court did not err in concluding that Gallop's claims were frivolous, and affirm.

Background. As the sentient world well recalls, on the morning of September 11, 2001, "agents of the al Qaeda terrorist organization hijacked commercial airplanes and attacked the World Trade Center and the national headquarters of the Department of Defense" See, e.g., The 9/11 Commission Report: Final Report

.... Apart from these factual allegations, the Complaint hypothesizes a fantastical alternative history to the widely accepted account of the "explosion" that injured Gallop and killed hundreds of other men and women inside the Pentagon. Among other things, Gallop's complaint alleges that American Airlines Flight 77 did not crash into the Pentagon indeed... Instead, the Complaint alleges that the United States" most senior military and civilian leaders cause[d] and arrange[d] for high explosive charges to be detonated inside the Pentagon, and/ or a missile of some sort to be fired at the building... to give the false impression that hijackers had crashed into the building....

On May 6, 2009, defendants moved to dismiss Gallop's complaint on the following bases: (1) that defendants are entitled to qualified immunity; (2) that the Antiterrorism Act fails to provide a cause of action against U.S. government officials; (3) that Gallop's constitutional claim is untimely, and, in any event, fails to state a claim upon which relief can be granted; (4) that all of her claims are barred under the doctrine of judicial estoppel; and (5) that all of her claims are frivolous.

To survive dismissal, Gallop "must provide the grounds upon which [her] claim rests through factual allegations sufficient 'to raise a right to relief above the speculative level." As the Supreme Court explained in *Ashcroft v. Iqbal*, a complaint that merely "tenders naked assertions devoid of further factual enhancement" fails to meet standard.

A court may dismiss a claim as "factually frivolous" if the sufficiently well-pleaded facts are "clearly baseless" that is, if they are "fanciful," "fantastic," or "delusional."

While, as a general matter, Gallop or any other plaintiff certainly may allege that the most senior members of the United States government conspired to commit acts of terrorism against the Untied States, the courts have no obligation to entertain pure speculation and conjecture. Indeed .... the complaint utterly fails to set forth a consistent, much less plausible, theory for what actually happened that morning in Arlington. We therefore agree with the District Court that Gallop's allegations of conspiracy are baseless and spun entirely of "cynical delusion and fantasy."

(Note: German Federal Judge Deiter Dieseroth stated in 2009: *"No independent court has applied legal procedures to review the available evidence on who was responsible for the attacks."* -- MM)

POSTSCRIPT. Gallop's Attorney Veale then requested a re-hearing, based on the judges being prejudiced (in part because one of the three judges is a first-cousin of George W Bush). In reply, the Court, on July 7, 2011, ordered Veale to show cause why he should not pay sanctions. Said the judges:

"Indeed, rather than pursuing his client's interests, Veale's actions appear to be malicious – intended, in bad faith, to use his position as an attorney of record to harass and disparage the court.... Such conduct, in our view, is ground for consideration of further appellate sanctions."

NOTE FROM MM TO ANYONE WHO MISSED IT IN THE COURSE OF THIS BOOK. THE MESSAGE IS: YOU CAN'T AFFORD TO LET THEM GET AWAY WITH THIS. THEY NEED TO BE LOCKED UP RIGHT NOW.

Appendix F. Ahoy, Men under Age 30: What's the Real Purpose of War? from Goldstein' view, in Orwell's *1984*.

The world of today is a bare, hungry, dilapidated place compared with the world that existed before *1914*, and still more so if compared with the imaginary future to which the people of that period looked forward. [It was assumed that science] would go on developing.

This failed to happen, partly because of the impoverishment caused by a long series of wars and revolutions, partly because scientific and technical progress depended on the empirical habit of thought, which could not survive in a strictly regimented society....

From the moment when the machine first made its appearance, it was clear to all thinking people that the need for human drudgery, and therefore to a great extent for human inequality, had disappeared ...

But it was also clear that an all-round increase in wealth threatened the destruction ... of a hierarchical society. In a world in which everyone worked short hours, had enough to eat, lived in a house with a bathroom and a refrigerator ... the most obvious and perhaps the most important form of inequality would already have disappeared....

If it became general, wealth would confer no distinction ... the great mass of human beings who are stupefied by poverty would become literate and would learn to think for themselves; once they had done this, they would realize that the privileged minority had no function, and they would sweep it away.

In the long run, a hierarchical society was only possible on a basis of poverty and ignorance. To return to the agricultural past ... was not a practicable solution. It conflicted with the tendency towards mechanization which had become quasi- instinctive throughout almost the whole world... Nor was it a satisfactory solution to keep the masses in poverty by restricting the output of goods... since the privations it inflicted [would be] obviously unnecessary, it [would make] opposition. The problem was how to keep the wheels of industry turning without increasing the real wealth of the world. ... In practice the only way of achieving this was by continuous warfare.

The essential act of war is destruction, not necessarily of human lives, but of the products of human labour. War is a way of shattering to pieces ... materials which might otherwise be used to make the masses too comfortable, and hence, in the long run, too intelligent....

It is deliberate policy to keep even the favoured groups somewhere near the brink of hardship, because a general state of scarcity increases the importance of small privileges and thus magnifies the distinction between one group and another. And at the same time the consciousness of being at war, and therefore in danger, makes the handing-over of all power to a small caste seem the natural, unavoidable condition of survival.

In principle it would be quite simple to waste the surplus labour of the world by building temples and pyramids, or even by producing vast quantities of goods and then setting fire to them. But this would provide only the economic and not the emotional basis for a hierarchical society.

What is concerned here is not the morale of masses, whose attitude is unimportant so long as they are kept steadily at work, but the morale of the Party itself. All that is needed is that a state of war should exist. The higher up the ranks one goes, the more marked it becomes.

It is precisely in the Inner Party that war hysteria and hatred of the enemy are strongest.... it is often necessary for a member of the Inner Party to know that this or that item of war news is untruthful, and he may often be aware that the entire war is spurious but such knowledge is easily neutralized by the technique of doublethink.

Meanwhile no Inner Party [man] wavers for an instant in his mystical belief that the war is real... Technological progress only happens when its products can in some way be used for the diminution of human liberty. In all the useful arts the world is standing still or going backwards. [Emphasis added]

Appendix G.   OFFICIAL HANDBOOK FOR CHAPLAINS

1978 Department of Army pamphlet no 165-13

CHURCH OF SATAN, PO Box 7633 San Francisco, Cal.   Anton S. LaVey, High Priest.   Church formed in US in 1966.

HISTORICAL ROOTS: The Church of Satan is an *eclectic* body that traces its origin to many sources - classical voodoo, the Hell-Fire Club of eighteenth century England, the ritual magic of Aleister Crowley, and the Black Order of Germany.

ORGANIZATIONAL STRUCTURE: The Church of Satan is focused in the Central Grotto. Power to regulate members is in hands of the Head of the Church.

WORSHIP REQUIREMENTS: Worship consists of magical rituals and there are three basic kinds: sexual rituals, to fulfill a desire; compassionate rituals, to help another; and destructive rituals, used for anger, annoyance, or hate. Gather on Friday.

MINIMUM EQUIPMENT FOR WORSHIP: Varies with the type of ritual performed but is likely to include a black robe, an altar, the symbol of the Baphomet (Satan), candles, a bell, a *chalice*, elixir, a sword, a model phallus, a gong, and parchment.

SPECIAL RELIGIOUS HOLIDAYS: Halloween. *Solstices* and *equinoxes* -- which fall in March, June, September, December.

BASIC TEACHINGS OR BELIEFS: To the Satanist, the self is the highest embodiment of human life and is sacred. The Church of Satan is essentially a human potential movement, and members are encouraged to develop whatever capabilities they can by which they might excel. They are, however, cautioned to recognize their limitations -- an important factor in this philosophy of rational self-interest. Satanists practice magick, the art of changing situations in accordance with one's will, which would, using accepted methods, be impossible.

CREEDAL STATEMENTS and Authoritative Literature: The writings of Anton S. LaVey provide the direction for the Satanists -- *The Satanic Bible*, *The Compleat Witch*, and *The Satanic Rituals*. (See also "Ethical Practices.") Members are encouraged to study pertinent writings which serve as guidelines for Satanic thought, such as works of Mark Twain, Machiavelli, G.Bernard Shaw, Ayn Rand, Freidrich Nietzsche.

Appendix H. Why NATO's Attack on Libya Is Illegal

by Mary W Maxwell, PhD, published at juscogens.org, May, 2011.

1. Q. What is the presumed 'legal basis' for the attack on Libya?
A. It is Resolution 1973 (of March 17, 2011) of the United Nations Security Council.

2. Q. Who has the right to vote in the UN Security Council?
A. The UNSC has 15 members, of which 5 are permanent and hold veto power: US, UK, France, China, Russia, and ten others that are elected to two-year terms.

3. Q. How many votes are required to pass a UNSC resolution?
A. Any nine votes suffice, but if one of the Big Five casts a veto, the resolution fails.

4. Q. Did Resolution 1973 pass 'unanimously'?
A. Technically yes, because no one voted against it. There were 9 yes's. Two of the Big Five abstained, namely Russia and China, and three of the others: Germany, Brazil, and India.

5. Q. Which nations cast the yes votes?
A. Technically it is not nations but 'states,' i.e., governments, that vote. The yes's were: US, UK, France, Portugal, Bosnia and Herzegovina, South Africa, Gabon, Lebanon, Nigeria, and Colombia (Colombia is the current chair of the UNSC).

6. Q. Did any Arab states object?
A. No. Only one Arab state sits on the Security Council, Lebanon. The Security Council received written encouragement from the Arab League.

7. Q. What does Resolution 1973 say?
A. It demands such things as a ceasefire and "a complete end to violence and all attacks against, and abuses of, civilians...." It imposes a no fly zone over Libya, and an arms embargo. It calls for a freeze on the assets of certain Libyans. It does not offer evidence as to what Libya had allegedly done.

8. Q. Was there a lead-up to this Security Council Resolution?
A. Yes and No. On February 26, 2001, Resolution 1970 mentioned such things as "concern at the plight of refugees" and "the need

to respect the freedoms of peaceful assembly and of expression, including freedom of the media."

9. Q. Where does the United Nations get the authority to use force against a member?

A. Article 39 of the UN Charter says "The Security Council shall determine the existence of any threat to the peace... or any act of aggression and shall...decide what measures shall be taken in accordance with Articles 41 and 42."

10. Q. What is the content of those Articles, 41 and 42?

A. Article 41 is about measures that can be taken that do not involve the use of armed force, such as sanctions. Article 42 says: "Should the Security Council consider that measures provided for in Article 41 would be inadequate... It may take such action by air, sea, or land forces... to maintain and restore international peace and security."

11. Q. Does this mean that the UN will call out its troops?

A. The UN doesn't have troops. Article 48 says: "The action required to carry out the decisions of the Security Council for the maintenance of international peace and security shall be taken by all the Members of the United Nations or by some of them, as the Security Council may determine."

12. Q. Who has provided the military force against Libya?

A. NATO, which is headquartered at Boulevard Leopold in Brussels, Belgium.

13. Q. What is NATO?

A. The North Atlantic Treaty Organization. It was an alliance formed during the Cold War, ostensibly against the Soviet threat. But following the 1990 collapse of 'world communism,' NATO has started to look like the mailed fist of World Government.

14. Q. How did the United States become part of NATO?

A. It joined when a two-thirds senate vote ratified the NATO treaty, sometimes called the Washington Treaty, in 1949. Lately, some former Communist states have joined, e.g., Albania and Bulgaria.

15. Q. Legally, how does NATO relate to the UN?

A. NATO's Article 1 says: "The Parties undertake, as set forth in the Charter of the United Nations, to settle any international dispute in which they may be involved by peaceful means in such a manner that international peace and security and justice are not endangered...."

16. Q. What about the rights of a nation that is being attacked?
A. NATO's Article 4 says: "The Parties will consult together whenever, in the opinion of any of them, the territorial integrity, political independence or security if any of the Parties is threatened."

17. Q. Isn't the territorial integrity of Libya is being threatened today?.
A. Yes, but Libya is not a 'Party"; the member states of NATO are European countries plus the US and Canada.

18. Q. As a member of the UN, is Libya entitled to protection from attack?
A. Yes. The quotes above from Articles 39, 41, 42, and 48 of the UN Charter have only to do with extraordinary Security Council action. Earlier in the UN Charter we find the famous Article 2(4), which says: "All members shall refrain in their international relations from the threat or use of force against the territorial integrity or political independence of any state."

Such an obligation to refrain from international aggression is best conveyed in the opening words of the UN Charter's preamble: "We the peoples of the United Nations determined to save succeeding generations from the scourge of war, which twice in our lifetime has brought untold sorrow to mankind...."

19. Q. So the UN Charter implies in one breath that members can expect protection from attack, and in the next breath it makes the Security Council itself an attacker?
A. The UN Charter condemns forcible measures, but justifies them in instances where "it determines [fairly or otherwise] the existence of any threat to the peace, breach of the peace, or act of aggression." However, before military force can be used, other means such as conciliation or sanctions must be tried.

20. Q. Is Libya attacking other nations?
A. No. Resolution 1973 alleges only internal conflict. The UNSC says it is:

"*Expressing* grave concern at the deteriorating situation, the escalation of violence, and the heavy civilian casualties... *Reiterating* the responsibility of the Libyan authorities to protect the Libyan population ... *Condemning* the gross and systematic violation of human rights, including arbitrary detentions, enforced disappearances, torture and summary executions... *Considering* that the widespread and systematic attacks currently taking place in the Libyan Arab Jamahiriya against the civilian population may amount to crimes against humanity ..."

21. Q. Does 'crimes against humanity' mean that "international humanitarian law' is being invoked?

A. Not exactly. Some treaties, such as the Geneva Conventions, regulate certain acts of war. This is known as International Humanitarian Law. Based on the Rome Statute of 1998, a person accused of war crimes and/or 'crimes against humanity' can be hauled before the International Criminal Court at The Hague, as was the Serbian leader Slobodan Milosevic.

In fact, the UN Security Council, which is the body that asks the ICC to indict a criminal, has already referred Muammar Qadhafi to the ICC.

22. Q. What happened to Milosevic?

A. He died in jail at The Hague, Netherlands, awaiting trial.

23. Q. Has NATO ever forcibly attacked a nation for supposedly humanitarian reasons?

A. Yes. For example, in the late 1990s it attacked Serbia, which was part of the Federal Republic of Yugoslavia. The basis for its current role in Afghanistan is unclear.

24. Q. What legal basis was there for NATO's attack on Serbia?

A. None has yet come to light. NATO did not go through the UN Security Council. The US construed its participation as having been a creature of 'presidential policy.'

25. Q. How is that the United States is legally bound to follow UNSC's orders?

A. The US joined the United Nations in 1945 by signing a treaty, namely, the UN Charter. The Constitution of the United States says in its Article VI: "... all treaties made or which shall be made, under the Authority of the United States, shall be the supreme Law of the Land...anything in the Constitution or Laws of any state to the Contrary notwithstanding."

26. Q. Does that mean that the constitutional requirement for Congress to declare a war could be overruled by way of a treaty?

A. No. Changing the Constitution of 1787 can only be done by amendment and none has ever been proposed that would change the Legislature's allocation of power. Congress, back in days when it was jealous of its turf, passed legislation, The UN Participation Act (1945), to underscore the need for Congress to approve of any use of American troops under Article 42 of the UN Charter.

27. Q. What exactly does the US Constitution say about Congress declaring war?

A. Article I, Section 8 says: "The Congress shall have Power... to declare War...."

28. Q. Does the President also have that power?

No. The part of the Constitution that lays out the powers of the Executive branch, namely, Article II, does not say anything about a power to declare war. It does say: "The President shall be Commander in Chief of the Army and Navy of the United States," meaning that once a war is declared he or she is on charge of it.

See the website of Louis Fisher, the US's most 'with-it' constitutional scholar: loufisher.org.

29. Q. Do you mean Congress would have to legislate, to authorize participation of American Military in any action requested by the UN or by NATO?

A. Yes. A joint resolution by the House and Senate would be the ticket.

30. Q. Has Congress in fact approved of the attack on Libya?

A. No. Two members proposed a bill to prevent it; most of the other 433 representatives are playing dumb. Ten senators opposed it: Collins, Snowe, DeMint, Ensign, Johnson, Lee, Moran, Sessions, Toomey, and Paul.

31. Q. Without Congress's formal approval, is the US attack on Libya illegal?

A. Yes. Domestically it is illegal. Senator Barack Obama stated the law correctly when interviewed by the Boston Globe in 2007, during the presidency of George W Bush : "The President does not have power under the Constitution to unilaterally authorize a military attack in a situation that does not involve stopping an actual or imminent threat to the nation."

32. Q. But in international law is the United States bound to attack Libya?

A. Of course not. As Professor Alfred Rubin clearly shows in his 1997 book, "Ethics and Authority in International Law," no such subjection of one sovereign state to another, or to a multilateral group, is legally possible.

33. Q. Does anything legally prevent Congress from authorizing an attack on a nation that has not 'deserved' it?

A. If we look only at Article I of the Constitution, the answer would be: "Congress can declare war against any nation anytime." However, Article VI is a reminder that if the US has signed a treaty to restrain itself from attacking – as indeed it did in Article 2 of the UN Charter, that puts a restriction on Congress's freedom. The treaty is the supreme law of the land "any Thing in the Constitution.... to the Contrary notwithstanding."

34. Q. But doesn't Rubin say "Nothing restricts the US"?

A. He means no one outside can do the restricting, but the Constitution itself does the restricting, domestically. Such is the main point of 'rule of law.'

35. Q. Does anything in the 1945 treaty known as the United Nations Charter go against the kind of attack now being made on Libya?

A. Yes. Article 2(7) of that Charter says: "Nothing contained in the present Charter shall authorize the United Nations to intervene on matters which are essentially with in the domestic jurisdiction of any state..." This '2(7)' item was called the 'Stay out of my backyard principle' and was virtually sacred from 1945 to the 1990s.

Granted, that item does end with the phrase "but this principle shall not prejudice the application of enforcement measures under Chapter VII" (Chapter VII being Articles 39 – 51). But Article 24, which sets out the role of the Security Council, reminds it to "act in accordance with the Purposes and the Principles of the United Nations." The SC is not a tribunal with a mandate to judge the behavior of sovereign states.

36. Q. What about the fact that Resolution 1973 condemns torture, yet certain other nations do the same? Isn't that a double standard?

A. It is up to individuals to maintain cerebral ground against such double-standard talk, as the diplomats steadfastly treat language as something to be 'called into service.'

37. Q. UNSC Resolution 1973 mentions: "Reiterating the responsibility of the Libyan authorities to protect the Libyan population." Isn't that a 'Stay out of my backyard' sort of thing?

A. Yes, it is a surprisingly clear example of flouting 2(7). Years ago it would have been considered unwise for powerful nations to put such a remark in writing lest it come back to haunt.

38. Q. UNSC resolution 1973 calls for a freezing of the assets of Libyan authorities. Is that normal? Could it constitute plain theft?

A. Courts have allowed it, as with some of the wealth of the Philippines leader Ferdinand Marcos. Domestically, the US has legislated for seizing the property of Americans in many circumstances, known as 'asset forfeiture.' It is a bit surprising, however, that in the order to freeze the assets of "Muammar Qadhafi" one of the justifications given is his "Responsibility for ordering repression of demonstrations…"

As to the question of 'plain theft,' it is noteworthy that the UNSC has not tried to show how the freezing of assets would restore peace. The SC appears to be ultra vires, going beyond its authority, in naming specific people who should be deprived of their property. The SC also names some who are to be placed under a travel ban.

39. Q. Let's say Qadhafi felt aggrieved. To whom could he make his plaint?

A. One possibility is for him to bring a lawsuit. Qadhafi may not succeed in a US Court, in so far as his suit, for the US killing of his adopted daughter Hanna, was dismissed as frivolous. (Her death occurred in 1986 when President Reagan ordered a retaliatory strike for the bombing of a disco in Germany, allegedly by Libyans, in which two American soldiers were killed. The UN General Assembly passed a resolution condemning that retaliatory strike as "a violation of the Charter of the United Nations.")

As a state, Libya can always go to the International Court of Justice to sue other states.

40. Q. At that court, can Libya sue the collective entity known as NATO, or even sue the United Nations Security Council?

A. Either of those would make an interesting exercise. At the very least, Libya could ask the ICJ for an advisory opinion about Article 39 with regard to aspects of the current situation. In 1996, the General Assembly put a question to the ICJ, about nuclear weapons, and got an advisory opinion. Qadhafi would need to hurry, though, as the outside powers are discussing 'regime change,' and the ICJ will only listen to the 'state of Libya'; it does not deal with individuals. One can easily locate the Statute of the ICJ, as it is formally annexed to the UN Charter.

41. Q. Is there scope for Libya to say that war crimes have been committed against it?

A. Canadian economist Professor Michel Chossudovsky has already suggested it. He said, at globalresearch.ca, that we see the evidence in NATO's own dispatch dated April 23, 2011 from Naples: " NATO has conducted the following activities associated with Operation UNIFIED PROTECTOR: Since the beginning of the NATO operation (31 March 2011), a total of 3,438 sorties and 1,432 strike sorties."

Presumably Chossudovsky means that these bombings are criminal under the general crime of aggression. That crime was declared at Nuremberg, at that time called "crimes against peace", but has never been added to the Geneva Conventions.

42. Q. Can war criminals in NATO, if there be such, get indicted?

A. Yes. Most nations have domestic laws that permit the bringing to justice of one's own war criminals or those of other states. The crime of *aggression*, which always reflects a government's decision, rather than the actions of low-rank soldiers, has recently been added to the jurisdiction of the International Criminal Court – with the proviso, however, that it will not come into force until 2017.

43. Q. Does the United States have any way to punish war criminals?

A. Oh yes, of course. The War Crimes Act of 1996, as codified at 18 USC 2441, says: "Whoever, whether inside or outside the United States, commits a war crime [if he is a member of the armed forces of the US] shall be fined under this title or imprisoned for life or any term of years, or both...." This includes someone who "willfully kills or causes serious injury to civilians."

There is also law against genocide at 18 USC 1091.

44. Q. Is there any Neutrality Act in the United States?

A. Yes. It can be found on the Internet. It's at 18 USC 960: "Whoever... knowingly begins...or prepares a means for...any military ... enterprise to be carried on from thence against the territory or dominion of any foreign prince...with whom the United States is at peace, shall be fined...or imprisoned...."

45. Q. Please state, once again: is the current NATO action against Libya illegal?

A. Yes. For the US, it is unconstitutional. For all members of the UN, it does not meet the legal intent of Article 39, which is that the Security Council must find the offending nation to be disturbing international peace, and it also arrogates to the Security Council some new powers to which the treaty signers never agreed (such as the ban on travel for some Libyans).

As for NATO, it is disobeying its own Article 1, "The Parties undertake...to settle any international dispute in which they may be involved by peaceful means in such a manner that international peace and security and justice are not endangered...." – and, more generally, it has no legitimate basis for acting as 'world government" and is thus acting ultra vires (beyond power).

Appendix I. "Kissinger Out of the Closet" by Charlotte Iserbyt, November 27, 2002, at NewsWithViews.com.

Today, the day before Thanksgiving, it is snowing here in Maine, and very beautiful. I had decided to live my other life, the normal one which finds me staring out the window at the gorgeous ship captains' houses on our street, enjoying the smells of the woodstove and my husband's pumpkin pies ...

Charlotte Iserbyt

Today I was just going to pretend I live in the America of yesteryear... I was going to try to forget how our country is being taken from us, without firing a shot. (This stealing of our free political and economic system can perhaps be attributed to the deliberate dumbing down of America since if one does not know what form of economic and political system one has one doesn't care if it is taken away from him.)

And then, all of a sudden, I was jolted by news that our born-again Christian (member of The Order...Skull and Bones..) President Bush has appointed "enemy of all enemies of America", former Secretary of State Henry Kissinger, to lead an investigation of the September 11 attacks. Of all people!

In 1974 a very important little book entitled "Henry Kissinger... Soviet Agent" was written by the late Frank A. Capell. For the benefit of younger readers who know little about Kissinger, let me give them some background information. He advocated a "United Europe with federal supranational institutions" (Capell, p 21). Professor Henry Paolucci wrote in the Congressional Record of August 4, 1971: "Henry Kissinger, too, expressed as recently as 1965 the conviction that the time was at hand for a surrender of nationhood because 'institutions based on present concepts of national sovereignty are not enough.'"

The official magazine of the American Jewish Committee in New York, *Commentary,* stated in 1958: "The international government of the United Nations, stripped of its legal trimming, then is really the international government of the United States and the Soviet Union acting in unison."

That comment by the AJC in N.Y. reflects clearly what Norman

Dodd was told in 1953 by Rowan Gaither, President of the Ford Foundation: "Mr. Dodd, all of us here at the policy making level of the foundation have at one time or another served in the OSS (Office of Strategic Services, (CIA forerunner) or the European Economic Administration, operating under directives from the White House. The substance under which we operate is that we shall use our grant making power to so alter life in the United States that we can be comfortably merged with the Soviet Union."

President Ronald Reagan and the Carnegie Corporation signed extensive agreements with the Soviet Union merging the United States and Soviet education systems. Now to the meat of this story, from Capell. "An anti-Communist who infiltrated Polish Communist Intelligence and rose to the equivalent rank of general has now named Henry Kissinger as a Soviet agent, recruited while he was a sergeant in the U.S. Armed Forces in Germany during World War II."

"In 1961 and 1962 our source informed the CIA about Kissinger who at that time appeared to be an unimportant Harvard professor. In 1973 he again brought the matter to the attention of the British Security Service since Kissinger [had] become President Nixon's National Security Adviser."

In the mid-seventies when a Strategic Arms Limitation Treaty was being discussed by the U.S. Senate, I (Iserbyt) arranged for a Soviet defector by the name of Igor Glagolev to come to Maine to participate in a debate with Secretary of Defense Paul Warnke. Glagolev did a superb job presenting reasons why the US should not sign onto this Treaty.

At dinner the same evening Glagolev informed me that prior to his defection, when he held a very high position in the **Kremlin, he sat in on meetings at which David Rockefeller Sr. and Henry Kissinger were often present.** At one of these meetings Kissinger shocked his Soviet audience by informing it that the United States was planning to pull out of Vietnam. This information, of course, was transferred to the North Vietnamese and put United States military forces at a great disadvantage. [Emphasis added]

Appendix J. " Jeff Bradstreet, MD, Was a Loving, Happy Man," by Mary W Maxwell, Gumshoenews.com, July 14, 2015.

This is a followup to my Gumshoe report of 2 July, 2015. The amazing news is that 528 individuals so far have sent a donation to the GoFundMe site, asking that the death of Jeff Bradstreet be investigated. I have never known anything like this to happen. I rejoice that the GoFundMe phenomenon exists. We know of many murders paraded as suicides, but normally there is no way for folks to state their suspicions. Since it was his bro, Thomas, that set up the fund, all Jeff's previous patients – his autistic alumni – are eager to express their love by donating. Thank you, Jeff, for being such an admirable doctor that everyone trusted you.

Jeff Bradstreet, MD

Now here's a shocking comment from a colleague, John Reinhold, Sr, MD. He wrote: "Jeff's research was a threat to many representing huge financial losses if the direction his research was validating came to be accepted as 'fact.' We discussed this when he was in the earliest stages of his work. The public is unaware of how easy it is for someone to make a phone call and simply state, 'He's an annoyance we don't need right now,' and that putting plans in motion. If Jeff's strong suspicions are right regarding cause and causes of autism, legal actions against those corporations implicated would be staggering. Jeff was brilliant and had every reason to live."

At this moment the bad news is that several doctors have died inexplicably in the US and Mexico in the last few weeks, all of them studying alternative science. I don't agree that money is what caused the murders. As I argue in *Consider the Lilies,* many diseases, including cancer and autism, are genocidal. The extreme boldness of the murdering of several doctors can't compare with the boldness of the way in which diseases have been handed out to us all, since around 1950, but increasing greatly around 1990. I see that Jeff Bradstreet was criticized on Quackwatch.com by the late Stephen Barrett. My research showed many outstanding doctors coming under the sword of Barrett.

To repeat: this is a great day. People have woken up and are demanding the truth. This will make all the difference!

Appendix K.   Mary Maxwell's *Coram Nobis* for Troy Davis

To Chatham County Superior Court, Savannah, Georgia

From Mary Maxwell, PhD, LLB, United States citizen and friend of the court [street address provided], Toorak Gardens SA 5065, Australia. Telephone number [provided].

I hereby respectfully ask the Court that convicted Troy Davis for murder in 1991, and sentenced him to death, to grant a Writ of Coram Nobis based on an error that occurred at trial, an error that constitutes a fraud upon the court.

I cite Judge Marilyn Patel's opinion of 1984 in the Federal District Court of Northern California, in which she set aside the 1942 conviction of Fred Korematsu, based on the fact that the prosecutor, the federal government, misled that court by not letting the court hear available information about the loyalty of Japanese-Americans during World War II.

In Troy Davis' case, the Court was similarly misled: information was withheld from it. The Court was not allowed to know that the accused came from a good family. As stated by one of the surviving members of the family, Martina Correia, the family was forbidden to attend the trial! Thus the jurors could therefore not avail themselves of the relevant information that the young man (age 22 at the time) had a devoted mother and father and supportive siblings.

Moreover, not seeing family in the courtroom would suggest that the family chose to 'stay away' and that would help the jury sense 'guilt' on the part of Troy Davis. That constitutes fraud-upon-the-Court.

The Court was also defrauded by the media's naming Davis as "the wanted cop killer." Jurors may have seen photos of officers making high-fives at his arraignment. Worse, the police showed photos of Davis to witnesses, instead of having them identify him at a line-up.

In 2007 the Associated Press tracked down seven of the jurors from the Chatham County Court, trial. They were shown the recantations by witnesses. One witness, Ms Ferrell, signed an affidavit saying she was coerced into blaming Troy because she was on parole for a shoplifting charge at that time. This has caused a juror, Brenda Forrest to remark,

"If I had known the young lady had issues in her past that made her susceptible to being pushed into something, I would not have put so much emphasis on what she said." Three other jurors also said they would have acted differently if they knew then what they know now.

I humbly petition the Court to set aside the conviction that was obtained by such errors. My reason for not acting sooner is that it seemed to me that a pardon for Troy Davis was in the offing, given the fact that 3,000 clergy and 663,000 individuals have signed petitions on his behalf.

On the matter of my standing, as a citizen, to petition the court, I note that Wilson M. Brown III, of Drinker Biddle petitioned the US Supreme Court in 2003 re *Reynolds*.

We see, in Federal Rules of Civil Procedure 60(b) Grounds for Relief from a Final Judgment, Order, or Proceeding: On motion and just terms, the court may relieve a party… from a final judgment, order, or proceeding for the following reasons:

… (3) fraud (whether previously called intrinsic or extrinsic), misrepresentation, or misconduct by an opposing party…

In respect to authority, I note Tyler v. Magwire, 17 Wall. 253, 84 U. S. 283:

"Repeated decisions of this court have established the rule that a final judgment or decree of this court is conclusive upon the parties, and that it cannot be reexamined at a subsequent term, **except in cases of fraud**…". (emphasis added)

In the 1944 United States Supreme Court ruling in *Hazel-Atlas Co. v Hartford Co.,* Justice Black opened with the words:

"This case involves the power of a Circuit Court of Appeals, upon proof that fraud was perpetrated on it by a successful litigant, to vacate its own judgment entered at a prior term."

In concurring, Justice Owen Roberts wrote:

"No fraud is more odious than an attempt to subvert the administration of justice. The court is unanimous in condemning the transaction disclosed by this record.... The resources of the law are ample to undo the wrong and to pursue the wrongdoer.... It is complained that members of the bar have knowingly participated in the fraud. Remedies are available to purge recreant officers from the tribunals on whom the fraud was practiced. Finally..., to nullify the judgment if the fraud procured it, ...This is a suit in equity in the District Court to set aside or amend the judgment. Such a proceeding is required by settled federal law, and would be tried, as it should be, in open court with living witnesses...."

Although it may seem that I am acting on behalf of Mr Davis, with this petition for a Writ of Coram Nobis, I am not. I am acting on behalf of the court, of society, and of rightness.

Signed on this 19th day of September, 2011, Mary Maxwell, widow, of [address provided], Toorak Gardens, SA 5065, Australia. Witnessed by Justice of peace, Burnside, SA

Reply received from Mr Dan Massey, Clerk of Court, Chatham County, dated September 20, 2011:

"I am sorry but your e-mail is not sufficient for a court filing. Likewise a fax has the same shortcomings."

Comment by Antone Davis-Correia: My uncle, Troy Davis, was sentenced to death in 1991, three years before I was born. He was in jail my whole life, but I knew him very well. I visited him in prison every other week and he became a father figure to me. Troy was wise, respectful, motivated and a great listener. He didn't like

the position he was in but said he had to learn from it, and used that experience to give me advice. He told me to pick the right friends and not to run away when things got rough; to keep my head up in school and take criticism positively.

Appendix L. Judge William T Moore Jr's Ruling on Witness Recantations, US District Court for Southern District of Georgia, re Troy Davis' Appeal for Federal Habeas Corpus. March 25, 2011

(Full text of section viii, except citations are deleted. Note: This judge was doing the work of the United States Supreme Court on this occasion.)

Antoine Williams

Antoine Williams was the night porter at the Burger King on the night of the shooting. At trial, his testimony was used to establish that the person in the white shirt both struck Larry Young with the pistol and shot Officer MacPhail, and to directly identify Mr. Davis as the person in the white shirt. Mr. Davis contends that Mr. Williams has since recanted his direct identification.

The earliest statements from Antoine Williams are two statements given to the police in the days following the murder. In his first statement, he explains that the same person struck Larry Young and shot Officer MacPhail, and that this person was wearing a white shirt. In his second statement, Antoine Williams identified Mr. Davis as the shooter from a photo array with a sixty percent certainty. He also stated that he could distinguish yellow and white on the night in question, despite watching the events through the tinted windows of his car.

At trial, Mr. Williams identified Mr. Davis as the shooter and testified that the same person who struck Larry Young shot Officer MacPhail. (However, he initially backed off his earlier statement about his ability to distinguish the yellow and white shirts.) Mr. Williams nextstatement, the recantation affidavit,[date?] stated that he was unsure of his direct identification of Mr. Davis as the shooter.

At the evidentiary hearing, Mr. Williams testified that he was not sure who shot the police officer and that he felt pressure to identify Mr. Davis as the shooter at trial. However, Mr. Williams never testified that his earlier statement or testimony were false, only that he could not remember what he said. Despite initially recanting his statement regarding the shirt colors, Mr. Williams ultimately reaffirmed his statement to the police, explaining that his memory would have been better closer to the events in question. In his affidavit and at the   does not contest the accuracy of their contents. For example, with respect to his initial identification of Mr. Davis, Mr. Williams testified: 'Q: Do you remember telling [Detective Ramsey] you were 60 percent sure that Troy Davis was the person that shot Officer MacPhail? A: I maybe did, ma'am. I can't remember. Being honest, I can't.'

Saying that one cannot remember his prior testimony is different from admitting that it is false. He also contradicted his [?] testimony regarding feeling pressured at trial during cross-examination: Q: But it's your testimony the police never pressured you to say anything in those two statements from August 19th or August -- A -- Ma'am, nobody never pressured me, ma'am. just.. Q: And nobody suggested for you to say anything specific? A: No, ma'am, never.

Mr. Williams's testimony does not diminish the State's case. First, it is not proper to consider Mr. Williams's testimony a recantation— he never indicated that his earlier statements were false, only that he can no longer remember what he said. And, to the extent that his present testimony is inconsistent with what he had previously said, he indicated that his memory would have been better at the time of the crime. Second, Mr. Williams testified that his prior testimony was never coerced by state officials. This testimony accords with the record; Mr. Williams's statements were far from ideal and if the State was to coerce testimony, it surely would have coerced testimony more favorable than that actually provided by Mr. Williams.

Although Mr. Williams's own testimony undermines allegations of coercion, there was also credible testimony by the officers and prosecutors [!] that Mr. Williams was not coerced. (Accordingly, Mr. Williams's testimony established only that his statements were never coerced and that he can no longer remember his previous statements—not that his prior testimony was false or, more importantly, that Mr. Davis was not the shooter.

Kevin McQueen

Kevin McQueen was the "jailhouse snitch."

At trial, Mr. McQueen claimed that Mr. Davis confessed the following events to him. Mr. Davis began his night by shooting at the group from Yarnacraw – the Cloverdale shooting. Mr. Davis then went to his girlfriend's house for a time, and later to the Burger King to eat breakfast. While at Burger King, Mr. Davis ran into someone who "owed [him] money to buy dope." There was a fight regarding the drug money, and when Officer MacPhail came over, Mr. Davis shot him. Other than claiming that Mr. Davis was guilty of both the MacPhail murder and Cloverdale shooting, Mr. McQueen's trial testimony totally contradicts the events of the night as described by numerous other State witnesses while other witnesses claimed Mr. Davis went to shoot pool immediately prior to the murder, Mr. McQueen claimed Mr. Davis went to get breakfast.

These inconsistencies make it clear that Mr. McQueen's trial testimony was false, a fact confirmed by Mr. McQueen's recantation. Given that Mr. McQueen's trial testimony was so clearly fabricated, and was actually contrary to the State's theory of the case, it is unclear why the State persists in trying to support its veracity. Regardless, the recantation is credible, with the exception of the allegation of prosecutorial inducements, but only minimally reduces the State's showing at trial given the obviously false nature of the trial testimony. While the Court credits Mr. McQueen's recantation, it does not credit the portion of his testimony claiming that he received inducements to testify at trial. As Mr. Lock credibility testified, Mr. McQueen received no favorable treatment for his testimony. ("Q: So my question to you, Mr. Lock, is: to your knowledge as the chief assistant district attorney at this time did Mr. McQueen get any benefit for the information that he was giving … regarding Mr. Davis? A: No, and I'm relatively certain that any assistant district attorney that contemplated doing that would have come to me about doing it.") That is to say, if a witness testified credibly at trial and then recanted, that recantation would obviously be much more damaging to the State's case than a recantation by a witness who only confirmed what should have been apparent to all at the time of trial—that the testimony was fabricated. [Couldn't the jurors have included McQueen's allegations in the cumulative picture of guilt?]

Jeffrey Sapp

Jeffery Sapp was a long-time friend of Mr. Davis. At trial, Mr. Sapp's testimony was used to relate Mr. Davis's confession to the MacPhail shooting. Mr. Davis contends that Mr. Sapp has "recanted his testimony in full" and that his false trial testimony was "the result of police pressure." Jeffery Sapp testified twice in this case, first at Recorder's Court and then at trial. Both times he testified that Mr. Davis confessed to shooting Officer MacPhail, but that Mr. Davis claimed the shooting was in self-defense. Under direct-examination at trial, Mr. Sapp further testified that he had made up a portion of Mr. Davis's confession. In his recantation affidavit, Mr. Sapp claimed that he fabricated the entire confession due to police harassment.

Monty Holmes provided similar statements to the police regarding a confession by Mr. Davis. Monty Holmes, who did not testify at trial, has since recanted his police statement, claiming police coercion. Because Mr. Holmes's testimony did not form a portion of the evidence presented to the jury, his recantation does not diminish the proof at trial. Moreover, the State provided credible, live [self-serving?] testimony from Officers Ramsey and Oglesby that Mr. Holmes was not coerced by police pressure.

In addition to this testimony, Mr. Sapp attempted to lie about other facts regarding this case to exculpate Mr. Davis. For example, he attempted to hide his knowledge of Mr. Davis's street name: Rough as Hell ("RAH"). Jeffery Sapp's recantation is valueless because it is not credible. First, as noted above, his false [?] exculpatory testimony at the hearing indicates that he was not a credible witness. Second, the truth of his trial testimony is corroborated by [whose?] other statements given to police. [and therefore...?] Third, his claims of state coercion are impossible to square with various aspects of his allegedly false testimony, such as claiming that Mr. Davis acted in self-defense. Ironically, at the hearing there was credible testimony from Officer Ramsey that Mr. Davis's mother threatened Mr. Sapp [non-sequitur?] Indeed, if the State wanted to coerce false testimony, they would not include within it an affirmative defense. Also, Mr. Sapp felt comfortable enough at trial to claim that a portion of his police statement was false, dealing with some details of Mr. Davis's confession, but still testified that Mr. Davis confessed to the MacPhail shooting Even if Mr. Sapp's claims of fabricating a confession were credible, they are not new evidence that was unavailable prior to trial. At trial he testified:

Q: Do you recall making a statement to the police about this matter?
A: Yeah.
Q: Do you recall making the statement on August 21 in the middle of the afternoon?
A: No, they came to my house that morning, about two o'clock in the morning.
Q: Two o'clock in the morning?
A: Yeah, beating on my door, woke me up, so you know, I just said a lot of stuff that I ain't even meant. A lot of stuff he didn't even tell me, I just made up.
Q: Do you remember what you said in that statement?
A: No, I can't remember what I said.
A: He shot the officer and got a good look at him, and it was self-defense. And all the rest, I just said. He never did tell me any of that.

Fourth, his claims of state coercion are refuted by credible, contrary testimony from both prosecutors and Officer Ramsey. In sum, neither Mr. Sapp's recantation nor his claims of police coercion are credible. Accordingly, his recantation does not diminish the State's case.

Darrell Collins
Darrell Collins was the third individual involved in the altercation with Larry Young. At trial, he testified that Mr. Davis was wearing the white shirt and assaulted Larry Young. According to Mr. Davis, Darrell Collins has since recanted the latter portion of that testimony, which was originally secured through police coercion. In statements that Mr. Collins gave to the police in the days following the shootings, he stated that Mr. Davis was responsible for the Cloverdale shooting, struck Larry Young on the head, and wore a white shirt on the night of the incidents.

At the trial, Mr. Collins reaffirmed that Mr. Davis was wearing the white shirt and assaulted Mr. Young. His present recantation is a second attempt at recantation in which he goes further than he did at trial; it is new only in its breadth and rationale, not in its existence. Moreover, it is unclear why, if Mr. Sapp was being coerced to testify, he felt comfortable testifying that his previous inculpatory testimony was largely false. Mr. Collins also told the police that Mr. Davis was responsible for the Cloverdale shooting, but recanted this testimony at trial. He also testified at trial that he included this in his police statement due to police coercion. However, Mr. Collins testified that he lied about Mr. Davis's involvement in the Cloverdale shooting due to police intimidation. In his recantation affidavit, Mr. Collins claimed a second lie—that he never saw Mr. Davis strike Larry Young. He averred that he was comfortable revealing the first lie at trial but not the second because he felt the police cared more about whether Mr. Davis assaulted Mr. Young than Mr. Davis's responsibility for the Cloverdale shooting.

At the hearing, Mr. Collins again claimed that he lied about both the assault on Larry Young and the Cloverdale incident due to police coercion. Specifically, he claims that he simply parroted what the police told him to say. However, he did not recant his earlier testimony that Mr. Davis was wearing the white shirt on the night of the shootings." At the hearing, Mr. Collins did not recant his testimony regarding the white shirt. Instead, he testified that he presently had no memory of what color shirt Mr. Davis was wearing that night, but would assume that whatever he told the police about the color of Mr. Davis's shirt would have been a lie because all inculpatory testimony he provided is presumptively false in his mind. Of course, that statement is very different from stating that, as a matter of his own knowledge, he is sure that he was lying when he placed Mr. Davis in the white shirt.

Mr. Collins testimony is neither credible nor a full recantation. First, regardless of the recantation, Mr. Collins's previous testimony, that has never been unequivocally recanted, still provides significant evidence of Mr. Davis's guilt by placing him in the white shirt. Second, if Mr. Collins's claim that he simply parroted false statements fed to him by police is truthful, query why Mr. Collins never directly identified Mr. Davis as Officer MacPhail's murderer. Surely, this would have been the best available false testimony, and given Mr.Collins's proximity to the murder it would have been as reasonable as any other false testimony.

Third, there was credible testimony from Officer Sweeney and Mr. Lock that Mr. Collins's testimony was not coerced. Further, even if Mr. Collins's allegations regarding coercion and false testimony are true, they are not new. Mr. Collins testified at trial that he was coerced and that his statements regarding Mr. Davis's involvement in the Cloverdale shooting were fabricated.

Moreover, his explanation as to why he revealed only the lie regarding the Cloverdale shooting at trial is not believable (explaining that Mr. Collins believed the police cared more about his false testimony regarding Mr. Young than the Cloverdale incident). Indeed, it would be puzzling to think that the police would not find Mr. Collins's accusations of harassment in the context of the Cloverdale shooting offensive but would be bothered by the exact same allegations with respect to the assault on Larry Young.

Fourth, Mr. Collins generally lacked credibility, testifying to an implausible version of events: that he was less than ten feet from Larry Young when the assault occurred and did not turn away from the confrontation until Officer MacPhail arrived, but saw nothing. Given the close proximity, (Mr. Collins testified that he was as close to the assault as he was to the court reporter while he was on the witness stand – a distance of approximately five feet) it would be safe to assume that surely Mr. Collins saw either Mr. Coles or Mr. Davis strike Mr. Young—not that [he] simply saw nothing. Because Mr. Collins continues to provide evidence of Mr. Davis's guilt and his recantation is not credible, his testimony does not diminish the State's case.

Harriett Murray

Harriett Murray was Larry Young's girlfriend. At trial, her testimony was used to place Mr. Davis in the white shirt and to directly identify him as the gunman in the MacPhail shooting. Mr. Davis contends that Ms. Murray's "recantation" affidavit is important because it described Mr. Coles and not Mr. Davis as the shooter. Ms. Murray is deceased and did not testify at the evidentiary hearing. The first recorded statements by Ms. Murray are two police statements; one on August 19, 1989 and one on August 24, 1989. In the former, she described Officer MacPhail's shooter as wearing a white shirt. In the latter, Ms. Murray identified Troy Davis as the shooter by first identifying Mr. Davis as one of the three men at the shooting, and then using a process of elimination—she eliminated Mr. Coles as the shooter because she recognized him as the person in the yellow shirt and Mr. Collins because he was too short to be the person in the white shirt.

During her Recorder's Court and trial testimony, Ms. Murray testified that the shooter was wearing a white shirt and was the same person who assaulted Mr. Young. At trial, Ms. Murray also directly identified Mr. Davis as the gunman. Ms. Murray was also thoroughly crossexamined at trial as to discrepancies between her various statements regarding the assault on Larry Young, and her difficulty in indentifying Mr. Davis as Officer MacPhail's murderer. Ms. Murray's "recantation" is an unnotarized affidavit, begrudgingly obtained. [perhaps most affidavits are begrudgingly given] ("Q: Mr. Hanusz, can you explain why the affidavit was not notarized. A: The affidavit was not notarized because neither Mr. Mack nor myself are South Carolina notaries, and Ms. Murray would not allow us time to get a notary or accompany us to a notary to have it sworn.") It does not contain any direct recantation, any admission that Ms. Murray lied under oath, or even a statement that Ms. Murray was aware that her affidavit varied from her trial testimony. The only "recantation" in the affidavit is an indirect one—Ms. Murray states that she saw the "man who was arguing with Larry, chasing him from the Time- Saver, and who slapped Larry shoot the police officer."

Mr. Davis finds this change important because Ms. Murray indicated that Mr. Coles was arguing with Mr. Young, despite testifying that Mr. Davis slapped Larry Young and shot Officer MacPhail. On this basis, Mr. Davis reasons that Ms. Murray has now identified Mr. Coles as the shooter instead of Mr. Davis. This affidavit is not helpful to Mr. Davis's showing because it seems unlikely that it was intended to recant or alter Ms. Murray's testimony regarding who shot Officer MacPhail. It would have been a simple matter for Ms. Murray to directly state that her identification at trial of Mr. Davis as the murderer was mistaken, but she chose not to do so. To the contrary, her affidavit, at first blush, actually appears to affirm her trial testimony; only a close examination reveals the minor inconsistency—that the same person who shot Officer MacPhail and assaulted Larry Young, also argued with Larry Young. Given that Ms. Murray spent a minimal amount of time reviewing the affidavit, even refusing to wait to have it notarized, it seems likely that she was unaware of this inconsistency.

The affidavit does not allege police coercion. However, it bears noting that there was credible testimony at the hearing that Ms. Murray was not coerced. This reading is confirmed by her behavior regarding the securing of the affidavit. Surely if Ms. Murray believed her testimony placed an innocent man on death row, she would havefound time to wait for a notary public to validate her Statement. More importantly, it is not obvious that the implication of this 'recantation" even exculpates Mr. Davis. Ms. Murray's affidavit simply states that the same individual who assaulted Larry Young and shot Officer MacPhail, also argued with Larry Young. Nowhere does it provide any identifying information as to who took all three actions. That is, there is no way to know whether Ms. Murray believed that Mr. Coles or Mr. Davis took all three actions. Moreover, the affidavit states that the individual argued with Larry Young, it does not attribute any specific threats to him. It could easily be that Ms. Murray considered all three of the individuals to have been "arguing" with Larry Young, [?] an interpretation that does not require any implied recantation of Ms. Murray's prior testimony. Accordingly, the Court finds this affidavit valueless to Mr. Davis's showing.

Dorothy Ferrell

Dorothy Ferrell was a guest at the Thunderbird Motel, located across Oglethorpe Avenue from the Burger King parking lot. At trial, Ms. Ferrell's testimony was used to show that the shooter was wearing a white shirt and to directly identify Mr. Davis as the gunman. Mr. Davis contends that Ms. Ferrell has clearly disavowed her prior statement, stating that she lied at his trial based on promises of favorable treatment by the District Attorney. Mr. Davis intentionally declined to allow Ms. Ferrell to testify, preventing her testimony from being challenged on cross-examination and denying this Court the opportunity to personally assess her credibility.

Even it this Court adopted Mr. Davis's reading of this affidavit, it would be valueless because it contains no new evidence. As Mr. Davis notes, the only way to understand this affidavit as a recantation is by reference to inconsistencies between her initial police statements and later testimony. These same inconsistencies were known to Mr. Davis at trial and were put before the jury. At the hearing, the admission of Ms. Ferrell's affidavit was discussed, but never decided due to an intervening discussion Ms. Ferrell gave two statements to the police: one on August 19, 1989 and one on August 24, 1989. In the former, she described the shooter as wearing a white shirt. In the latter, she again related that the shooter was wearing a white shirt. She also identified Mr. Davis from a photo line-up and discussed a prior identification of Mr. Davis based on a picture she saw in a police cruiser; however, she admitted to seeing a picture of Mr. Davis on the news between the two identifications. Both at the probable cause hearing and at trial, Ms. Ferrell testified that that shooter was wearing a white shirt and directly identified Mr. Davis as the shooter.

At trial, a number of inconsistencies between her trial testimony and prior testimony were pointed out for the jury during crossexamination. In her recantation affidavit, Ms. Ferrell claims that she never saw who shot the police officer and that her testimony was coerced. Mr. Davis has also submitted a letter from Ms. Ferrell to District Attorney Spencer Lawton, asking for special treatment for her trial testimony. Ms. Ferrell did not testify at the evidentiary hearing. Unlike Ms. Murray, Ms. Ferrell was available to testify and, in fact, was sitting just outside the courtroom waiting to be called to testify. Despite her ready availability, Mr. Davis made the tactical decision not to call her to the witness stand. This decision is especially curious because, based upon the contents of her affidavit and her lack of any obvious connections to Mr. Davis, it would appear she should have been his star witness. Ms. Ferrell's affidavit is a clear recantation, but Mr. Davis's intentional decision to keep Ms. Ferrell from testifying destroys nearly its entire value. In determining actual innocence, affidavits are disfavored because the affiants' "statements are obtained without the benefit of cross-examination and an opportunity to make credibility determinations." Herrera, 506 U.S. at 417.

At the evidentiary hearing, Ms. Ferrell did not testify at all, and Mr. Lawton was never questioned regarding inducements to Dorothy Ferrell. Even if the letter was sent, there is no evidence [!] that Mr. Lawton offered any inducement to Ms. Ferrell in exchange for her testimony. Given that Mr. Davis specifically requested this hearing, claiming that a determination based on affidavits was insufficient his decision to rely on an affidavit where live testimony was readily available strongly suggests his belief that this recantation would not have held up under cross-examination. Mr. Davis explained the decision not to call Ms. Ferrell as based upon "the circumstances under which she's been avoiding the Petitioner made us reluctant to call her, even though she was perfectly willing to meet with the state yesterday. Surely, this general antipathy towards affidavit testimony counts double where the affiant is available, and the affidavit is submitted in lieu of live testimony to prevent cross-examination and credibility determinations. Moreover, much of Ms. Ferrell's affidavit testimony was directly contradicted by credible, live testimony at the hearing. Officer Ramsey testified that he never coerced her testimony in any way or suggested what the contents of her testimony should be, and that Ms. Ferrell actually approached a different officer without solicitation and identified Mr. Davis as the shooter. And, Mr. Lock credibly testified that he never attempted xxx....to which this recantation was presented and the credible live testimony contradicting it, the recantation holds very little weight. This Court made very clear to Mr. Davis that presenting the affidavit instead of live testimony would severely diminish the value of its contents because he was intentionally preventing the State from cross-examining the witness. Mr. Davis was apparently so concerned as to what Ms. Ferrell would say on the stand that he explained, " [w]e understand that her testimony is not going to be afforded as much weight. We're okay with that."

Larry Young

Larry Young was the individual assaulted in the Burger King parking lot. At trial, his testimony was used to establish that his assailant was definitely not the person in the yellow shirt, that the person in the yellow shirt was Mr. Coles, and that the person in the white shirt struck him. Mr. Davis contends that Mr. Young has recanted his trial testimony. Mr. Young gave a statement to the police on August 19, He stated that he was not sure, but that he believed his assailant was the man in the white shirt. He also gave a detailed description of the man in the yellow shirt. At the probable cause hearing, Mr. Young testified that the person in the yellow shirt was Mr. Coles, and that he was assaulted by someone other than Mr. Coles, likely the person in the white shirt.

At trial, Mr. Young testified that he was arguing with the person in the yellow shirt, that the person in the yellow shirt was not Mr. Davis, and that he was not sure who struck him but did not believe it was the person in the yellow shirt. In his recantation affidavit, he claims that the police refused to allow him medical treatment and that his testimony was coerced. Like Mr. Collins, Mr. Young claims he testified by simply stating what the police wanted him to say.

While Mr. Young's testimony indicated that he did not know exactly who struck him, in closing argument the prosecutor did treat Mr. Young's testimony as claiming that the individual in the white shirt assaulted him. "Accordingly, the Court will treat Mr. Young's testimony as if it was used to help establish that the white shirt assaulted him." Mr. Young was included on Mr. Davis's witness list and was expected to testify at the evidentiary hearing. However, Mr. Young was never called to the stand. Like the affidavit of Ms. Ferrell, the value of Mr. Young's affidavit is minimal.

First, affidavits are disfavored in this context because they do not allow for cross-examination and credibility determinations. Herrera, 506 U.S. at 417. Just as with Ms. Ferrell, Mr. Davis chose to present less reliable affidavit evidence of Mr. Young's testimony to avoid cross examination. Second, Officer Whitcomb testified credibly that he neither coerced Mr. Young's testimony nor suggested to him what to say. Mr. Young was not present to contradict this testimony, and his affidavit is insufficient for the task. Moreover, as with many other witnesses, if the State was prepared to coerce false testimony, they could have coerced much more inculpatory information. Mr. Young was at the scene of the murder and was the victim of the assault. Surely the State would have had Mr. Young directly identify Mr. Davis at trial if they were looking to coerce false testimony.

 I am concerned about the judge's practice of methodically accepting the police versions of disputed events while simultaneously rejecting citizens' versions of these events. This verges on what is called "copsuckery" -- slavish or excessive deference to law enforcement personnel -- and may be another manifestation of regulatory capture in the criminal justice system, under which many judges view themselves not as protectors of the rights of citizens but as cheerleaders for police and prosecutors.

-- Donald E Wilkes, Jr, Emirtus Professor of Law, University of Georgia

Appendix M. Strip Search, Magna Charta Anniversary Essay #3.

Mary W Maxwell, *Gumshoenews.com,* June 15, 2015.

One day, in 2003, Mr Albert Florence did something he shouldn't have done in New Jersey. Namely, he was DWB, "driving while Black." This led to a fine, which he paid promptly, in 2003. Again in 2005 he committed DWB. The state trooper phoned HQ, and was told there was an arrest warrant for Albert for that unpaid fine (which he had paid).

He was taken to jail and asked to strip. Humiliation and trauma are part of the case he presented to US Supreme Court. Fourth Amendment "The right of the people to be secure in their persons, houses, papers, against unreasonable searches and seizures, shall not be violated... Fully 800 years ago, people had decided that such an incursion by government was not to be tolerated. Magna Charta put it this way (in Latin, but later translated): "No free man shall be seized or imprisoned except by the lawful judgment of his equals...."

Ever since *Marbury v Madison* in 1803, the role of the Supreme Court has been "to state what the law is." In *Bell v Wolfish*, the court said there ARE times when a strip-search is allowable. It's "for the good of all" that a prisoner be searched if he is coming in from the outside. He may be bringing in contraband, such as drugs. Or he may have a weapon up his kazoo, with which to harm other prisoners or staff. What rubbish. The purpose of power is power.

Albert Florence sued. He'd already 'won' in the federal district court, insofar as they noted that he had no charges pending against him so he shouldn't have been arrested. His attorneys then asked the Supremes to rule on one question: *the constitutionality of strip searches of people accused of minor offenses.* One judge is on record that a prisoner has diminished expectations of privacy. I don't think 'loss of privacy' would have to extend to orifices of my body, thank you.

Forget the 'diminished-expectations' logic; the Bill of Rights cries out "Never let your expectations be diminished, Boys and Girls. That is a slippery slope you mustn't get on."

Now please consider that a court case has more than just its legal factors. We shall look around at the surrounding social and political factors. Here are seven such "context" items:

Context Item 1. Everybody knows there is major drug trafficking in jail. Well, then, it must be something the prison system condones. No point dramatizing make-believe horror about it.

Context Item 2. Everybody knows that weapons can be tiny and concealed. Not every weapon is a shoulder-held missile. Might the prisoner be bringing in one of those cute poisons that the CIA uses? He could sew it into the hem of his jeans.

Context Item 3. There is no need to adhere to *Bell v Wolfish*. It mattereth not what the justices said in that case. The highest court in the land is never bound by any other court's precedents, not even its own.

Context Item 4. Speaking of drugs-in-jail, how would the prisoner on furlough have acquired them from the street? Sure, we know heroin comes from Asia and cocaine from Latin America, but how do those things pass through Customs? Reporters have discovered how it is done: Bush and Clinton personally arranged it! So why not issue a bench warrant for the arrest of those two? (Come on, Sonia, do it!)

Context Item 5. Back to the worry that a prisoner, harboring a gun up his kazoo, might use it to harm staff, don't staff carry Tasers? Aren't many prisoners forced to wear stun belts so they can be electroshocked remotely by the guard in the Panopticon?

Context Item 6. Everybody knows that the 'sexual humiliation' we practice in Abu Ghraib has nothing to do with eliciting information, as the CIA standardly uses sodium amytal for that. Orwell: the point of humiliation is humiliation. (WayneMadsen.com says the searches are filmed for porn). I think the day cometh when it will be necessary to break us all down by demoralization. SCOTUS is merely greasing the skids. The Great Nine decided 5-4 in Albert Florence's case. Judge Anthony Kennedy, writing the majority opinion, said:

"People detained for minor offenses can turn out to be the most devious and dangerous criminals." Guess whom he named as an example of that? The late Timothy McVeigh, the "OKC bomber," who was stopped by cops for a bad licence plate.

Context Item 7: McVeigh didn't do the OKC bombing. So…

Appendix N. State Constitution of Massachusetts of 1780

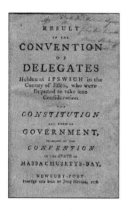

PREAMBLE. The end of the institution, maintenance, and administration of government is to secure the existence of the body politic, to protect it, and to furnish the individuals who compose it with the power of enjoying, in safety and tranquility, their natural rights and the blessings of life....

The body politic is formed by a voluntary association of individuals; it is a social compact by which the whole people covenants with each citizen and each citizen with the whole people that all shall be governed ...for the common good. ...

PART THE FIRST ... A DECLARATION OF RIGHTS

Art. III. As the happiness of a people and the good order and
... essentially depend upon piety, religion, and morality, and as these cannot be generally diffused through a community but by the institution of the public worship of God...Therefore... the people of this commonwealth have a right to invest their legislature with power to authorize and require, ... the several towns, parishes, precincts... for the support and maintenance of public Protestant teachers of piety, religion, and morality

Art. V. All power residing originally in the people, and being derived from them, the several magistrates and officers of government vested with authority, whether legislative, executive, or judicial, are the substitutes and agents, and are at all times accountable to them.

Art. VI. No man nor corporation or association of men have any title to obtain advantages, or particular and exclusive privileges distinct from those of the community, than what rises from the consideration of services rendered to the public, ...the idea of a man born a magistrate, lawgiver, or judge is absurd and unnatural.

Art. VII. Government is instituted for the common good, for the protection, safety, prosperity, and happiness of the people, and not for the profit, honor, or private interest of any one man, family, or class of men; therefore the people alone have an incontestable ...

right to institute government, and to reform, alter, or totally change the same when their protection, safety, prosperity, and happiness require it.

Art. VIII. In order to prevent those who are vested with authority from becoming oppressors, the people have a right ... to cause their public officers to return to private life....

Art. X..... In fine, the people of this commonwealth are not controllable by any other laws than those to which their constitutional representative body have given their consent.

Art. XI. Every subject of the commonwealth ought to find a certain remedy, by having recourse to the laws, for all injuries or wrongs which he may receive in his person, property, or character. He ought to obtain right and justice and without being obliged to purchase it.

Art. XII. No subject shall be held to answer for any crimes or no offence until the same if fully and plainly, substantially and formally, described to him; or be compelled to accuse, or furnish evidence against himself; and every subject shall have a right to produce all proofs that may be favorable to him; to meet the witnesses against him face to face... And the legislature shall not make any law that shall subject any person to a capital ... punishment, excepting for the government of the army and navy, without trial by jury.

Art. XIII. In criminal prosecutions, the verification of facts, in the vicinity where they happen, is one of the greatest securities of the life, liberty, and property of the citizen.

Art. XIV. Every subject has a right to be secure from all unreasonable searches and seizures of his person, his houses...

Art. XVII. The people have a right to keep and to bear arms for the common defence. And as, in time of peace, armies are dangerous to liberty, they ought not to be maintained without the consent of the legislature; and the military power shall always be held in an exact subordination to the civil authority

Art. XVIII. A frequent recurrence to the fundamental principles of the constitution, and a constant adherence to those of piety, justice, moderation, temperance, industry, and frugality, are absolutely necessary to preserve the advantages of liberty and to maintain a free government. The people ... have a right to require of their lawgivers and magistrates an exact and constant observation of them.

Appendix O. "Tsarnaev's Aunt." Mary W Maxwell, June 19, 2015 at Gumshoenews.com, Last of the Magna Charta Anniversary Essays.

What has this to do with Magna Charta? Well, just about everything. The barons who got King John to sign that parchment in 1215 were "modern" enough to demand freedom from thuggery by the rulers. Apparently the people of Massachusetts in 2015 aren't modern. They seem to think it's OK for police to shoot anybody dead on a whim.

Look at this boat. The story is that these are bullet holes. I suppose it's true. The police believed their quarry was inside, as indeed he was.

So why shoot? How about a nice little "Come out with your hands up"? How about spraying him with Mace? Or doing what Bush Sr did to Manuel Noreiga when he was "resisting arrest" (as heads of state tend to do) in the Vatican embassy in Panama City. We forced him out with loud music.

The "new way" started in 2005 when the London police shot dead a 27 year-old Brazilian, Jean Charles de Menezes, in the tube station because… well… just because, that's all.

When police shot at Jahar, who had been decorating the walls of the boat with religious philosophy (he weren't the type, said article in Rolling Stone), all that the cops had on him was that the faces of Jahar and his older brother Tamerlan were recorded at the Marathon and at an ATM. Wow.

Enter the aunt. Maret Tsarneva of Toronto, a lawyer. She has evidence that Tamerlan (what a name!) did not get killed in a shootout, as the whole world was informed. She saw the video of a naked man being put into a police car, not dead or even wounded, and she says that is her nephew. Being a lawyer she asks "Why was I not asked to identify the body?"

There's a journalist named Dan Dicks of pressfortruth.ca who looks trustworthy to me. He has made a video of his conversation with Auntie, in which she says she fears she will be killed. She said that before any of us heard of the death of Igraham Todashev, a friend of the brothers.

Reminder: the FBI men went to the home of this Chechen, lad, Todashev, in Florida to "take a statement" and then simply murdered him. It's not even on of the many cases where the FBI denies what it had done. They brazenly said they did it.

Consider this. By doing that, they don't seem to get in trouble. Rather, the public voluntarily yields up some of its manhood. We all think, "Oh yes the FBI can get away with that sort of thing." Excuse me, wait a minute. Who is letting them get away with it? What is the alternative to "letting them."

Note the word "impunity". I used to think it meant bravado or cheek -- a person could "act with impunity." No, that is not the definition! It is the onlookers, us, who provide the impunity. The dictionary says impunity is "exemption from punishment."

Today Jahar is in prison appealing his death sentence. The court behavior was shocking; it deviated in every way from the spirit of the law. But as for Tamerlan, he is gone. No one is talking about it. See how smart the aunt is. She knew it would all be this bad, cuz she grew up in Soviet Union, and has since been an ethnic "other" – as they are called – in Russia.

We've got Tamerlan dead and Todashev dead. NO ONE IS TALKING ABOUT IT.

Here is a frightening thing. Amaitai Etzioni, a moralist at George Washington University, wrote in *Commentary* (albeit only nine days after the 2013 Marathon, and in response to people saying the lad should have been "miranda-ized"): "The commitment to the Constitution and the Bill of Rights, even in the wake of such vicious attacks, is one of most laudable features of American society. Yet one wishes it would evolve to a fuller understanding of what our founding document entails. It seeks to balance individual rights and the protection of the public. So far there is no indication that this balance has been violated by the authorities in dealing with the Marathon bombers. This is what should make us proud."

Oh boy. Count me out. I am not proud. I am furious. And you are wrong, Amitai. The Bill of Rights is not trying to protect the public from Jahar Tsarnaev, Sirhan Sirhan, James Earl Ray, Arthur Bremer and all the other WELL-KNOWN patsies. The Magna Charta had the picture right. The individual is no match for the authorities.

They win every time. You ought to look into the way they have crucified three generation of Malcolm X's family. What was Malcolm's sin? He was a moralist like you. He head his head screwed on properly. That was his sin.

It takes brains and guts to figure a way around this dreadful imbalance of power. Amitai, are you working for the wrong team? I know your writings; they are sharp and inspiring. You once invited me to join your Communitarian Summit. Recall? Has someone brainwashed you since then? Why can't you see what is happening? It could not be plainer!

To repeat: the aunt has a photo (from regular news channel, I think) showing the boy being escorted, in the buff – but we won't worry about buffness today, or about stupid Miranda's – over to a patrol car. So he was NOT SHOT.

How then is he dead? Did he get Todasheved, if I may call it that? Did he get Menezesed? Are we all going to get Todasheved? Orwell has promised us that we will. And Judge George O'Toole did his best to see we are not protected from the maniacs who actually did organize "the Boston bombing." O'Toole graduated from BC and Harvard Law. Would the thousands of alumni now living in Boston please send him a letter? Offer to help him if he is being coerced. Strength in numbers.

Fancy him letting the defense attorney present a not-guilty plea, and yet say that her client did it! None of the liars got cross-examined. Nobody even mentioned the aunt's claim that Tamerlan did not die in a shootout.

Bostonians, get a grip, will you? All you need do is sashay down to any local police station and report the murder of Tamerlan Tsarnaev. I recommend you be white to do this, as ethnic minorities at the moment are all "suspects."

If you're black, take two elderly white companions – EWC's -- with you. If you're white, take two EBC's. Make an outing of it. Have some fun!

It's simple. Tell the cops you want to fill out a complaint form; believe me they do stock them. If they ask to strip-search you, just say "Yes, I'd love it." It's time to be creative and not fall for all the clever schemes of intimidation.

274

Appendix P. Cathy O'Brien 'Sells' Education Envelope

In Cathy O'Brien *Trance Formation of America* (1995: 179-183, 215)

I recognized Governor X [names of politicians redacted here by Maxwell], and was well aware of Michigan's ranking first in the nation in education. "That little sister of yours (Kimmy) is coming to Mackinac to further her skills. Your whole family is a prime example of how good Education 2000 works."

I finally met up with Bonnie again in Lamar [redacted]'s room as the night came to a close. "Bonnie, how's that snake of yours?" he asked. Bonnie, who had been filmed pornographically by CIA commercial photographer Jimmy Walker with Dick Flood's snakes, had a pet boa constricter. "Great!" Bonnie laughed. "How's yours?" "Constricted," he replied, Lamar Redacted began removing his pants.

Referring to me in Project Monarch terms he said, "When I first saw you, you were a worm with no hint of being a butterfly." "Daddy (Alex Houston) said she was a diamond in the rough," Bonnie volunteered, "She shines now." Turning to me he said, "I know you are a shoe shiner, and mine need a shine." Bonnie, also familiar with the Stockyard booth and Lamar's meaning, laughed when he said, "Why don't you both take a foot."

Task complete, I went to Byrd's nearby room as instructed. He was in the bathroom preparing himself for bed. Drying his hands on a towel, he turned to me and said, "Looks like you've had your wings spread a bit tonight." "I wore a path up and down the stairs," I stated. Much to my relief he said, "I'm not going to fiddle with you I'll just give you something to remember me by-Bye." He compartmentalized my memory with his stun gun.

Soon thereafter, Kelly and I were transported to Mackinac Island, Michigan, to meet with Canadian Prime Minister Redacted at then-Governor Redacted's mansion. Houston led Kelly and me as quickly as we stepped off the ferryboat onto the timeless, antiquated island, I noticed that the Canadian flags were again flying at the Grand Hotel, but was of no mind to question.

Kelly sat quietly beside me, apparently drugged as our carriage took us through the woods to the Governor's mansion. The guests in the mansion were reminiscent of the recent Tennessee Governor's convention: Governor X, Ohio Governor Dick X, and Pennsylvania

Governor X [later a US Attorney General]. Guy Vander X and Jerry Redacted were also present.

Mulroney appeared to be the guest of honor. He reached out his hands and greeted me, "I slipped time, space, and distance to be here this evening. You and I have some ground to cover."

"Yes, Sir. President Reagan's Global Education Secretary Bill Bennett has sent me to deliver this education packet directly to you." I was to deliver a large, brown envelope of documents. Blanchard excused himself. "I've already heard the schpiel," he said, leaving Mulroney and me alone.

"Global Education is the wave of the future," I recited as programmed. "As the world gets smaller and smaller due to higher technology spanning the globe, our children must be educated in the ways of the world. Education as it is, barely equips them for life in their own backyard. We need to become involved. Global education is the only way. Look into it…"

I handed him the envelope. "Peer into the future." Mulroney said "I am interested in the children and the way we shape their future. Tell Mr Bennett(sss), he hissed cryptically, revealing his knowledge that Bill and Bob Bennett work together, that I am already sold on Global 2000. Redacted then triggered my sex programming and led me upstairs where Kelly was robotically waiting, entranced under the Orders of the Rose. Two guards ushered us down the hall, through an ornately carved door, and into bedroom [of a New England senator]. The room was highly effeminate for a man, decorated in pastels, white eyelet, and huge billowy pillows. When the Senator walked in, Kelly groaned, "Noooo, not you again," He signalled with his hand, switching her into total silence and submission.

Then he accessed specific personality fragments that previously recompartmentalized in my mind from constitutional scholar's sexual abuse of Kelly. His torturous abuse complete, he ordered us to follow him downstairs to his "torture lab." I had experienced basement "spy conditioning" torture chambers before both in the U.S. and Mexico, and this "torture lab" looked more like a NASA lab with the latest advances in electronic/drug mind-control technology was consistent with his ability to use it. I was strapped to a cold, chrome, stainless steel table by guards.

He began reciting, "Cross your heart and hope to die, Stick aneedle in your eye." A wiry "needle" was pushed slowly into my right eye while Kelly was forced to watch.... He continued with me, "Each word you speak, each breath you sigh, Your eye trance-mits to the Eye in the Sky." Kelly believed it, which locked her into silence. While I was literally out of my mind from intense pain, Redacted utilized the opportunity to program me with what he said was financial information to deliver to Senator Y.

This was not the first time he transferred apparently sensitive US Government intelligence information to Y through me. I had photographically recorded numbers in my mind's "computer banks" ever since he prepared me for the task some months before at White Sands Missile Base in New Mexico. It was there in the TOP SECRET mind-control area of the base that X subjected me to extreme tortures and high-tech programming.

"Funding will continue to be approved as long as (mind-control) Projects such as this continue to receive your full attention." I was treated like a lab animal with no apparent regard for whether I lived or died. I was put in an electrified metal walled and floored cell, referred to by some as the woodpecker grid.

He did succeed in causing Kelly and me to be hospitalized from his torturous abuses upon our return to Tennessee. I had suffered damage to my right eye, while Kelly psychosomatically suffered respiratory failure due to his extreme traumas. The physical manifestations of the devastation wreaked on us by Senator So-and-So failed to raise questions from outsiders as to the cause. Equally worthy of mention, are other high profile perpetrators.

These individual were in positions to be knowledgeable of Kelly's and my victimizations. All of them accessed our programming either for drug distribution, banking/message delivery, mind-control demonstrations, or, most often, for their perverse sexual gratification. ...

Therefore, a list of perpe-Traitors has been compiled and strategically distributed for posterity, as well as to prevent these individuals from interfering in any Congressional hearings that should be forthcoming as a result of this exposure.

Black LL Bean Swiss Army Knives were a coded indicator of White House-level operations. Red LL Bean Swiss Army Knives, and regular Swiss Army Knives were a standard CIA indicator. Please support us in this effort by writing your Congressmen.

Appendix Q. Janine Jones Petitions The Crown Re Implant
-- published at randomcollection.info / mcf

Note: Like Mary Gregory in NY, Ms Jones of New Zealand receives electronic hits on a regular basis. Like Blanche Chavoustie, she has an unwanted brain implant. Luckily she was able to get the following verification:

Janine Jones

Letter from Dr. M. E. Godfrey M.B.B.S., F.A.C.A.M., Environmental & Preventive Medicine Mrs. Janine Jones, Holdens Bay, Rotorua 28 June 1998 Dear Mrs. Jones,

Having seen copies of your x-rays and the Radiologist's report, I am sure that you do indeed have two identical looking foreign objects, centrally placed deep to the frontal bones and in close proximity to the frontal lobes of the brain. I have never seen anything like these objects on an x-ray. They are radio-opaque, metallic, and certainly could be "electronic". I will do whatever I can to help you find a surgeon who could either remove them or prevent them from stimulating your brain, if the latter is, indeed, the more appropriate course of action. [signature] M. E. Godfrey

---

This is her petition to the Crown of New Zealand:

I, Janine Francis Jones of Rotorua, allege that the crown of this country has authorized a secret medical experiment and the use of torture upon a citizen. I write this petition seeking Justice. I write with urgency seeking an absolute halt to the persecution I am suffering. I turn to you because the Human Rights Commission and Privacy Commission, both lack capacity to deliver Justice in my case.   In 1989, I graduated with a Bachelor of Arts. My academic record was sound with mostly A grade passes to my credit. I had two daughters in my care. In 1989, I went on to specialise in Policing. In 1991, I graduated with a Master of Arts (Honours).

It was during my three years of postgraduate study that official interference in my life first became manifest. These operatives befriended me and began to follow me, gaining access to my private life and the research I was undertaking. The interference was progressive. They were subtle, well trained and did not respond and after a time I was afraid to cross them. Initially, the intrusions ranged from knocking at my door uninvited, to trailing me on campus. One particular agent nearly always appeared wherever I went. Royal Police Training College at Manley, NSW, [told] me I was at the top of their list of applicants for the job of police educator. In 1992 I failed to secure employment due to the continuous meddling in my life. This external source with the power to do so, interfered with my bank account, continuously tampered with my mails and broke into my private documents held in Safe Custody at the Bank of NZ. Friends I had known for years began asking me strange questions, quite out of character, as if they had been asked to act for others.

My daughters were also sad and disillusioned by the interference process. This included damage to my car and threatening behavior on the roads. My home and later on that of my mother, was entered and articles of clothing were switched from house to house. I felt like prey as the behavior was relentless and intimidating and I grew very stressed. If I went into a coffee house, one or more of these agents would enter and sit down next to me. They would proceed to stare doing nothing else. On all occasions these persons dressed in suits and looked professional. I began to fear for my life.

One evening it was quite late when I finished jogging. My friend had gone on another route and I returned to my car, which was at the College. As I stood by my car, another car appeared and the driver began circling the carpark, slowing near me and shining the headlights into my face. In consequence, I began having nightmares and felt near breaking point. I withdrew from the community. Of those who witnessed my deterioration, some knew the cause.

I had nowhere to go for help anymore. It was terrible to experience a blanket abandonment and I felt like a pariah left to face an officially endorsed persecution. I also realised that those acting against me must be extremely powerful to tie official hands thus. This country which embraces democratic principles, has stooped so very low.

As the harassment steadily continued I began to internalise the shame of being an unwitting party. My final efforts to counter it were directed to the Council for Civil Liberties and Amnesty New Zealand. But no response came back from either.

I curtailed normal, daily activities and worried for my children. I stopped writing and ceased forever to contemplate a career. Because I have had to contain a deep fear and disillusionment, I have come to loathe this country I grew up in and once appreciated. For almost a decade I have lived with a moral outrage at my treatment. By early November 1994 I must have been passed on to the military as the harassment intensified and changed its form to become no less than torture. This torture was to be conducted unrestrained, for two years, the military deploying sophisticated electronic weaponry to cripple, maim and punish. The so-called "soft kill" weapons currently in vogue is torture. I suggest that there is no limit to its cruelty.

For night after night over months, sleep was replaced with sheer terror. This was produced by the radiations flooding my bedroom. I quickly became disorientated, fearful and confused. My skin reddened and became excruciatingly itchy around the eyes and nose. My hands became blotchy and raw. My vision blurred as excessive light was pulsed around my bedroom and blinded my eyes. My whole head throbbed with a continuous barrage of electronic noise.

I was subjected to alternating frequencies, from piercing screams to low droning noises. A continuous static pounded my left ear, while the rest drove through my right ear. I have been thrown unconscious and brought to my knees, unable to balance or put one foot in front of the other to walk. I was subject to a terrible pressure; it gripped my head like 'pincers'.

As further, more intensive noise is applied, the victim sees sparks and white light arcing behind the eyelids. I was subject to sudden voltages ripping through my body, firing first at my head, the electronic shocks causing my kidneys to fill, my muscles to convulse and my feet to twitch and jump. Often, this went on all night. With this in view I cannot forgive these people. My torturers, while distant and hidden from view, are known by their methods. This only abated when I moved away from Palmerston. I now live with my mother in Rotorua. The attacks against me continue but at a reduced level. However, my mother's home is now a target for radiation because I am here. She is in her eighties and is recovering from cancer. Directed energy disrupts our power and splatters each night, over the roof, windows and walls. Fire is the risk we live with as our blinds and curtains have already been shredded by laser.

I have long ceased to pose the question "doesn't anyone care?" Historically, those who torture, have gone to great lengths to shield its shame from public view. For as long as there is secrecy to ensure its survival, it will persist. In New Zealand, there is a pervasive normalcy that guarantees its practice.

I close this petition by disclosing the reason for the crimes above. This was revealed to me during the course of my struggle and is: I was born in January 1949 at Lower Hutt Hospital and subsequently adopted. While still in hospital care I was subjected to a medical experiment know as psychosurgery. In this, a stereotaxic procedure was utilized to implant in depth electrodes inside my head. These electrodes (known as stimoceivers) were to become connected to my senses, brain and nervous system. This psychosurgery using in- depth electrodes was perfected by the neurophysiologist from Yale, Doctor José Manuel R. Delgado and initial experiments using human subjects were conducted successfully as early as 1947. I was one such guinea pig and I know of another victim of this early operation to implant electrodes. Bengt was born in 1947 and lives in Sweden. But, while still alive today, he is severely disabled from the procedure. The electrodes planted in his head and mine, have served as radio transceivers connecting us to computers, throughout our lives. In this way, a continuous, monitoring of my body functions, behavior, emotions and neurological processes, has been underway.

Appendix R. Elvis, Our Elvis. Brice Taylor, *Thanks for the Memories: The Memoirs of Kissinger's Mind Controlled Slave.* (1999: 136)

I was used with Elvis until he died. The last time they sent me in to be with him he was nearly unconscious. I don't know what they did to him but they used him up and then felt afraid he could "crack" and spill what he knew so they kept him drugged. Of course it wasn't an accident or a natural death, he had a lot of help from his controllers. Elvis was targeted heavily by these men. When I was given messages to deliver to Elvis or others, they would inject my arm with some drug and then unless I had been pre-programmed, they quickly whispered the message into my mind files and sent me off to deliver them to Elvis. Then Elvis would use the phrases he was told as he introduced his songs or in the early days they might have become a part of new song lyrics.

Just a single key phrase was enough to keep the programmed individuals, who later hear the introducing or song, under control. Then many slaves were "drawn to him," or they did things as a result of the effects of the various harmonics in his voice, in his music, and in the orchestration. But at concerts the messages were often delivered directly through words he would use to introduce his songs. He was no different than Michael Jackson, who replaced him in many ways.

My controllers often gave me the key to his suite and sent me there late at night with a message to deliver after sex with "the king." In the beginning, when I was 18, 19, and 20, he was more receptive and we had sex, and then I would whisper the message in his ear. Sometimes the messages to him were in the form of words from his own songs, but all the words weren't there and it would take on a different meaning. Like,

"Wise men say, only fools rush in," and then there would be words, numbers, or codes that I delivered that I didn't even understand. He was told certain 'lines' to say in between certain songs and I feel he may have been keeping many women 'in line' and programmed by these phrases. When he slipped the messages in between songs, as pre-instructed, the messages went deeply into the subconscious minds of the audience, especially to those individuals who were programmed to react to universal. They are simple words that when put into a certain sequence have a great impact on people who have been pre-conditioned with programming. In later years, when I was in my early 20s, Elvis became more and more 'out of it' when I went into his suite. Elvis had tons of pill bottles on the nightstand, and groggily said he needed them all.

It was late at night when I entered Elvis's room. He was lying in bed, still adorned with the gold jewelry and white suit he wore in concert. I watched as he finished his room service dinner and then I waited while he threw up in the bathroom. He was very mad at himself because he was so fat. I guess he made himself throw up. He cried as he stood in front of the mirror, and hitting the counter with both hands he screamed, "I hate my life! Everything's out of control. I'm ruined! I'm a failure!" I put my hand on his back in support and then on the back of his neck. As he felt my touch, his head hung down even further over the sink and he cried, "God, I'm a mess. I don't know what happened, just all of a sudden, I'm destroyed."

Then he screamed, "What is wrong? What is wrong with me!" and he started pulling his hair. I pulled him up. When he turned around I hugged him and he just kept crying and crying and almost collapsed in my arms. I guided him back to bed and helped him lay down.

My father was standing outside, just down the hallway. He was wearing a beige suit and when he snapped his fingers, with the hand wearing the diamond pinky ring, I listened intently to all the directions he commanded before he hit me high in my back with a stun gun.

I felt exhausted and nauseated, but had no way to access my own brain in order to know why. After a while Elvis couldn't function any longer. Henry [Kissinger] and his buddies laughed, and said that Elvis was like the tin man, all rusted up and ready for the junkyard.

Elvis Presley

Appendix S. The Purpose of Violent Videogames, from Mary Efrosini Gregory, *The Science Behind Microwave War*, Oregon: Trine Day Press, 2011, pages 42-44.

In 1990 HAARP was established, jointly run by the Air Force and Navy. Its 180 antennae are radio telescopes in reverse: rather than receive, they transmit electromagnetic waves to induce changes in the temperature of the ionosphere so that subsequent physical reactions can be studied... An unclassified Air Force document devotes considerable material to the weaponization of the ionosphere. It indicates that by the year 2025, manipulation of the ionosphere will be an integral tool in the US military's arsenal. This is available on the Internet and is subject to scrutiny by every country on earth...

Tension will be exacerbated as world population increases and natural resources become depleted. The research paper is entitled, "Weather as a Force Multiplier" in a 5 volume set. Volume 3 contains such documents as "Star Tek – Exploiting the Final Frontier," and "A Hypersonic Attack Platform."

The titles of these documents indicate that the military is appealing to young recruits, just out of high school, who have been raised playing computer games after school. These chapter titles also do what is necessary in warfare, they dehumanize the enemy and make it just another target in a science fiction-based computer game on a monitor...

The pathways in the brain have already been laid down regarding the enjoyment of computer games, becoming totally immersed in them for hours, and responding spontaneously to events on the screen. Humans are creatures of habit. Psychologists have known for a long time that people spend their lives recreating events that they experienced in their childhood, over and over again. Today's recruits have spent their earliest years from toddlerhood perhaps, operating a mouse and responding quickly to visual stimuli.

Appendix T. The Vexatious Litigant, by Stephen White, Ph.D., Fall 2011 *Newsletter of Work Trauma Services Inc.*

"The company has refused to address my appeals and is hiding behind lies of eliminating my job due to a reorganization. This is patently false and I will show that the CEO himself is behind this conspiracy to silence me and trample on the rights of suffering employees. SOMEONE MUST CHAMPION THEIR CAUSE. LET IT BE ME! When the time is right I will reveal all the names of those behind this criminal conduct. Heads will roll in high places!!!" ... From our case files.

Everyone has a right to his or her complaints being properly investigated. [But] "querulous vexatious litigants" raise concerns about violence risk [!] given their fixation, demands to be recognized, and increasingly grandiose list of complaints and accompanying insults. On rare occasions these cases can indeed eventuate in violence.... The angry, overtly paranoid or delusional litigant poses monitoring and security issues over an extended period of time.

We frequently consult on these cases to [e.g., to] academia, involving subjects who come to attention due to their threats, bizarre presentations, or increasing agitation and desperation. Even in cases that do not appear to pose a risk, it is important to understand the mentality and course of the puzzling vexatious litigant, as well as some case management principles.

A typical scenario
Anyone in the professions concerned with dispute resolution will eventually encounter the claimant – rigid and suspicious but perhaps initially ingratiating – who often appears with many documents, pleading or demanding that they be read. On inspection the arguments are poorly constructed and often confusing and rambling. Excessive highlighting [!] and underlining are common, as well as many attachments, often of no relevance to the case or touting broad principles of human rights. They may utterly deny obvious undisputed facts known to others. Although they certainly may engage in conscious lying, fundamentally it is more the case of a passionate belief in the truth of their perceptions.

Personal blogs, chat room dialogue reinforcing their perceptions, and other internet activity will accompany their quest. ... Usually those engaged with them very quickly have their competence challenged and their patience sorely tried. Some litigants may appear at corporate or legal offices, dramatically presenting their self-authored "briefs" to receptionists or support staff – a very disturbing or frightening occurrence for an office. [?]

According to Australian psychiatrists Paul Mullen and Grant Lester... querulous describes "a pattern of behavior involving the unusually persistent pursuit of a personal grievance in a manner seriously damaging to the individual's economic, social, and personal interests, and disruptive to the functioning of the courts [?] or other agencies attempting to resolve the claims."

The querulous litigant is different than simply a difficult complainant.

Querulousness falls along a continuum, and is not generally considered to include those campaigning for social reform, or most whistle blowers seeking to uncover real or perceived corruption, however mistrustful and disruptive such individuals or groups may be. These subjects generally remain within normal legal structures, have a reasonably legitimate or at least understandable social agenda (such as economic reform), and/or ultimately accept some settlement.

Querulous behavior, according to Mullen and Lester, involves a "totally disproportionate investment of time and resources in grievances that grow steadily from the mundane to the grandiose." Resolutions not only require "an apology, and/or compensation but retribution and personal vindication" – objectives beyond what courts can bestow. [?] As Western society and organizations have expanded the opportunities and avenues for individuals to present or appeal grievances and pursue justice, a side effect may be the enabling of abuse. [!] In our experience these individuals often reveal grand fantasies of their ultimate vindication unveiled dramatically at the highest judicial levels, accompanied by criminal punishment and public humiliation of their wrong doers. It can start with a relatively minor issue. Being bypassed for a promotion can eventually lead to a bizarre, life-engrossing campaign to uncover and bring down "global conspiracies." [Oh-oh] In meetings the querulous may insist on taking notes or recording the session.

They may even call for the disbarring of attorneys [!] and the dismissal or prosecution of other officials. In the courtroom they may make unruly remarks to the judge, inviting sanctions. Some may show a keen awareness of the lines not to cross so as to avoid contempt charges or jail terms. If an individual is declared a vexatious litigant by the courts, due to their accumulated frivolous lawsuits, they can be prohibited from filing further actions unless granted permission.

In the workplace or in academia these individuals will exhaust internal appeals processes, and are often eventually terminated for poor performance or misconduct, or denied tenure. They are typically very suspicious of the option to resign or benevolent severance offerings designed to preserve their dignity [?] and provide transitional support. To accept them would be an act of weakness and a further humiliation. (It is true that some paranoids, usually in the midst of a dispute with the employer, will resign, as a way to reduce their anxiety.)

Querulous behavior is likely rooted in a mental disorder. In practice, without benefit of a direct assessment, diagnostic distinctions are often difficult to make. [?] In our case [?] experience, paranoia and delusions are common. *Paranoia* can range from vague feelings of being persecuted in the absence of any facts that support such perceptions, to a highly developed, organized, and fantastic set of beliefs that are clearly delusional. Many of these persons are otherwise functional. A good number have families and at least some friends, and careers, and may even be technically [?] talented. However, the felt insult from their real or perceived grievance stimulates and reveals their underlying hypersensitivity and vulnerability, leading them to become completely consumed in a self-destructive quest for vindication.

[Note: this is the same Paul Mullen, MD, who advised the court of the mental state of Martin Bryant, in regard to the Port Arthur massacre.

Outrageously, Bryant has been in prison for 19 years. Mullen also just happened to be in NZ when a similar diagnosis was needed for a killer.]

Appendix U. Why Is Police Violence Increasing Like Mad? How Does This Connect to Bill Windsor's Lawless America?
Mary W Maxwell, RumormillNews. August 9, 2015.

In my August 7, 2015 GumshoeNews.com article, "We Need More Bill Windsors, and Urgently," I included a two-minute video by Irene Holmes, whose kids had been snatched by the state. Gumshoe's editor suggested that I use a more exciting video than the one by Irene Holmes.

I am indeed interested in telling the more gritty stories of violence that Bill Windsor has included in his Lawless America video series. To Irene, though, the loss of her children is biologically violent; and to them, the loss of their mom is almost certain to be permanently damaging.

I see the increasing police violence as "of a piece" with the judicial corruption that Bill has uncovered in the US. Just go to Youtube and search "Police violence," you will be shocked. Commonly now a cop "takes someone down" which mean arresting them by throwing them on the ground.

It seems this is the policy of the police, as is, of course, the use of the Taser gun. Both men and women get thrown to the ground. If the arrest occurs in your house, there too, you may be thrown to the floor! (Note: a friend of mine in Canada says she sees, almost once a week, homeless persons being "taken down" in the street.)

When this happens in America, a lawyer might suggest that the legal solution is to file a lawsuit under the amazingly generous civil-rights provisions found in codified federal law at 42 USC 1983. In other words, the individual was wronged and can bring a civil action, a type of tort.

There are two things wrong with that approach (though it's much better than nothing). First, when compensation is awarded it is the public that has to pay the bill. Huh?

Second, it is a personal solution for the plaintiff, but does not counteract the police policy. That is, the tort action itself does not oppose what is done in any case other than the individual's case. ("I want my client to win money, period.") What about the fact that the assault made on the person's body is plainly a crime? Nobody goes there.

So let's ask: why are police becoming more violent? I will give a 'local' answer first, and then give a Big Picture answer.

The local reason why a cop ventures past the proper cop-citizen interaction is that he is trained to do so. Naturally a cop carries out the instructions he is given. Today he is given a strong line about the badness of people. They are terrorists. They are child neglecters. They are…etc.

This is connected to the normal "labor union" approach of police forces, which is nudged along by, say, a Police Benevolent Association (meaning benevolent to any member). That is, they state loudly that all policepersons live under danger, and advocate measures of self-protection.

African-Americans say the reason drivers get killed during a car-pullover by police is that cops are taught that if the man at the wheel appears to reach for something in the glove compartment it may be a gun, intended for use against the cop. Therefore the cop should take pre-emptive action of self-defense. Bang, you're dead, for speeding.

The Big Picture

Put aside for now the proximate cause of police violence, as just described, and consider the ultimate cause. I'm pretty sure I've got this right, and I credit a book called "Hidden History" for my Eureka moment.

The gist of that book, by Gerry Docherty and Jim Macgregor, is that the Great War of 1914-1918, later known as World War I, was cooked up in the halls of Oxford by Lord This and Lord That, and foisted on the Parliament with amazing deceit. (Nothing like we were taught, that the assassination of the Archduke Ferdinand instigated the war.)

Has this anything to do with police brutality as such? No. It has to do with the fact that since at least 1913 (if not late 1700s), England was purportedly run by Parliament but was really run by men operating behind the scenes.

I now make the claim that this is the normal position of the human race. Powerful persons run the show and all the others more or less follow obediently. An important thing to notice is that cultures that say they have conquered this problem are probably not being accurate. I repeat: it is normal in human life for some persons to be controlled by others. The controlling may be subtle or be violent. The controlees generally capitulate and cooperate. And now I add: they often don't realize they are doing so.

My America

I was born in 1947 and grew up in almost magical circumstances. By the time I was old enough to think, in the late Sixties, there were wonderful Supreme Court cases offering nuanced legal protections to everyone. It did seem that this law was a force that could act against the powerful.

Until quite recently I felt protected by the law. I failed to notice -- and here is where the Docherty/Macgregor book comes in – that the apparent rulers are not the real rulers. In England in 1913 the apparent rulers were the elected members of parliament. But the real rulers were hidden; they did not have a position of authority and were therefore not held accountable by the public.

The hidden rulers did whatever they had to do by bribery, persuasion, intimidation, etc. If a troublemaker needed to be removed he could be removed via a heart attack, a train wreck, a fall from a horse, or whatever. In this sense the rulers were a mafia. They had hit men. But with most mafias, the people know who the mafioso are. In England, it was not apparent.

Off went the boys to World War I. Millions died for "a cause" that the people believed in. Nobody even smelled a rat.

In my America it was definitely not apparent that a few men behind the scenes were running everything. We spoke of the two parties in Congress as each having an agenda that may win or be defeated – based on the tallying up of the vote. In reality, though, some very clever masters were dictating to Congressional leaders, and to appointed officials.

Did they dictate to the Supreme Court? I now think so. But didn't I claim above that this Court was handing out all sort of beautiful rulings in favor of the people? Well, yes, but that could mean that the Secret Rulers wanted this. They may have considered it a good tactic for folks to be mis-educated about law's ability to protect! I assume they also wanted us to be mis-educated about the so-called competitive spirit of the two main political parties. I sure fell for it hook, line, and sinker.

Looking back on it, I can see that the media and school textbooks were the man sources of our knowledge of 'politics,' and both those sources could have been under tight control.

A few years ago I read an intriguing comment that President Kennedy, during his first week in office, had to be introduced to his Cabinet. In other words he did not already know them; he did not pick them. (Allen Dulles, McGeorge Bundy, Robert McNamara, etc.) So then who does pick each president's cabinet members? Presumably the men who really run things.

Actually, the "Bozos" who mis-educated me, by teaching me that the law works against the powerful, did themselves a bad turn. I can use my sociobiological toolkit in conjunction with my legal idealism and come up with something that is really threatening to the powerful. That is, I really do understand that folks today are powerless against the new police brutality. I've got not the slightest illusion that "goodness will win out." But I know how informed peeps can act in enlightened self-interest.

Back to Mae Brussell

It's pretty annoying to think that more than 40 years ago, Mae Brussell had collected the key information that we need today!

Among the things she noticed were the personnel connections between "Dallas '63" and Watergate 73, and between the use of mind-control at Vacaville prison and the Patty Hearst affair. Mae also noted the influx of Nazi's to the US in the 1950s and said to herself:

"When you think of Hitler, you think of prisons And when I thought about the killing of Kennedy and all the Nazis involved, I realized that the prison system had to be directly related to it. That's when I began to correspond with prisoners and get more information about prison deaths and mind-control experiments." In 1978, Paul Krassner writing "The Mind of Mae Brussell," noted that a turning point in her research occurred when she attended the trial of Hugo Pinell, accused of killing a guard at Soledad prison. "The whole trial was rigged. I was just outraged. It was then that I decided … to find the relationship between the corruption, political prisoners in this country, and the assassinations and conspiracies."

The Way Out

Go to Youtube and watch videos on Police Brutality in India. I can't claim any understanding of Hindu culture and won't attempt to figure out how the violence cold be reduced. But in US we have big traditions of controlling the police. To the extent that we've let police get away with murder it was due to:

1. failure of peeps to find out about the violence and injustice,

2. our ignorance of the real chain of command, particularly our naïve belief that the legislature acts freely and cares for us,

3. our bafflement at how to deal with the current takeover by brazen liars and genocidal idiots.

One and Two on that list no longer register. It is only Three that we need to get stuck into. I think the over-50 set would know how to respond. They had better do something about teaching the younger ones. Yuri Bezmenov, who defected from the Soviet Union, gave Ed Griffin an interview in 1983. He said our enemies, as led by himself, went for our youngest.

Yuri says demoralization was the main goal. What young person do you know who has hopes and dreams? Most have been taught to "move on" when they are dissatisfied with the present. But move on to where? They are given a steady diet of junk on the screen and are not even taught the lessons of history. They can't connect past and present. Like the field mouse whose nest Robert Burns accidentally overturned with his plow:

But, Mousie, thou art no thy lane
In proving foresight may be vain;
The best laid schemes o' mice an' men gang aft a-gley.
Still thou art blest compared wi' me!
The present only toucheth thee:
But, oh! I backward cast my e'e
On prospects drear!
An' forward, tho' I canna see, I guess an' fear!

Well, the mouse may be 'blest' by its intellectual limitations, but a child is not.

Appendix V. Review of EO Wilson's *The Meaning of Human Existence.* Mary W Maxwell, Rumormill News, July 14, 2015.

EO Wilson

A blank piece of paper and a pen is a good thing. It makes you figure things out. (Ditto a blank screen.) Edward O Wilson likes to figure things out. I'd like to know exactly where that drive exists in his brain. It's been carrying him along for seventy years or more. (He's just turned 86.)

Ed has now come out with a Youtube video (and book) to explain "the meaning of human existence." Here's his pitch: You know we're in trouble over the fact that we are destroying the planet. (Wilson is the inventor of the word "biodiversity;" he'd like to make us go to bed without supper for having destroyed so many species.) He points out that our foolishness – really it's suicidal – is but a typical manifestation of the way we evolved.

Animals evolve the specialized behaviors that help survival. For us humans, a major specialization has to do with social relations and social intelligence. As the theory of sociobiology shows, we calculate what we need for our individual ego, but we're also intensely concerned with *groups.* We make sacrifices for our own group (the family, the tribe, colleagues) and are ever at the ready to fight other groups.

Alas, this concern with strictly human affairs, he says, means we are blind to much of what goes on around us, the things that tie us to the biosphere. (In 1984, Wilson produced an amazingly poetic volume: *Biophilia.*) In sum, as a species we are "narcissistic" – concerned only with what humans are doing. We should be paying attention to the bigger picture.

Once, when asked what he would like us to have done differently, back at the beginning, he said he'd have wanted us – "before we left Africa" – to know our relationship to other species. I think Ed has absolutely nailed it this time. Admittedly I've said that some of his other works were the ultimate ultimate – e.g., *Genes, Mind and Culture,* and *Consilience.*

Hmm. Let's see if he can outshine himself, down the road, by following on from "the meaning of human existence."

Bet he can.

Appendix W. An Open Letter to the Privy Council, by Mary W Maxwell. Published at Gumshoenews.com, June 2, 2105.

From Mary W Maxwell, Marblehead MA, USA, October 19, 2013

To the Lords of the Judicial Committee of Her Majesty Queen Elizabeth's Most Honourable Privy Council,

I respectfully ask for your attention to an urgent, very urgent, matter. The matter arose last month when Mrs Justice Theis of the Family Division of the High Court ruled, surprisingly, that two sisters, age 11 and 15, must be given the MMR vaccination (measles, mumps, and rubella) against their mother's wishes. The urgency to which I refer is not based on any danger to those two girls. They are past the age at which MMR has allegedly caused developmental problems. I refer, rather, to the way we seem to be bounding down the slippery slope to a point where law and reasoning simply disappear….

I happened to read Salon.com's critical report of the Simpsonwood conference, held in the US by the Centers for Disease Control and Prevention in 2000. … I noted that someone at Simpsonwood said "It's what Walt wants." The word "it" there refers to a certain interpretation of the results of research into thimerosal. "Walt" refers to CDC official Walter A Orenstein, MD. In other words, it was said that researchers were asked to find that thimerosal does not cause autism. One would be curious about anyone wanting a finding that such-and-such a substance doesn't cause autism. What if the substance did cause autism? Should we deduce that someone wants to withhold this knowledge in order that more children would receive the substance and come down with autism?

Lately I have been looking into protests against mandatory vaccination that took place in the 19th and 20th centuries. Courts actually sentenced to prison parents who had already lost a child, if they refused to let the sibling be vaccinated! The protestors, who included many physicians, couldn't get governments to budge. What is not widely known is that the original inoculations against smallpox were utter fakes. Writing in 1889, Charles Creighton, MD, exposed Edward Jenner, MD, as a fraud. In 1898, Alfred Russel Wallace, FRS, used a Royal Commission report to show that smallpox vaccines gave no protection, and that the unvaccinated fared better during epidemics than the vaccinated. Still, the Commission managed to find that vaccination should remain mandatory.

In 1803 the King of Spain sponsored the Balmis Expedition to inoculate every man, woman, and child in the Spanish colonies of South America and Philippines. Wouldn't that be an unlikely concern for Spain at a time when the Napoleonic wars were starting? It's possible the plan had more to do with harming the natives...

In 1998, Drs Andrew Wakefield and John Walker-Smith discovered that a few children with bowel disease, who also had autism, were carrying some measles material in their body. They wrote that up, quite properly, as a "series of cases" in The Lancet. Their article clearly states that they have not proved any causal link between MMR and autism.

Wakefield recommended that doctors use single shots of measles, mumps, and rubella until the combined MMR could be inspected. (The single-shot was subsequently taken off the market by UK authorities!)

Since 1998, it has been constantly said by the media that Wakefield caused "a vaccine scare." Of course it was the media itself that caused the scare.... The decision to hold a press conference to announce Wakefield's findings was not a decision made by Wakefield. It was made by the Royal Free Hospital Medical School dean, Professor Ariel Zuckerman. So if someone should be "blamed" for warning parents about the MMR it should be the dean. But of course blame is not appropriate – telling the public that there is reason to be cautious about something is perfectly OK.

Years later, at a General Medical Council hearing, the dean kept contradicting himself about that press conference, wanting to blame Wakefield for it. On page 98 of his book, *Callous Disregard* (2010), Wakefield suggests that Zuckerman was pressured to do this by the WHO as well as the UK Department of Health. Here is an excerpt from the hearing:

Coonan (Wakefield's defense lawyer): The fact is that, knowing what you did from this correspondence (of Wakefield and Walker-Smith) ... you did not stop the press conference.

Zuckerman: No, I did not. I should have done but I was assured that this would not arise. So there we are.

Coonan: At the press conference, ... at some stage a particular journalist raised the question... of what parents should do in relation to MMR and you directed the journalist to Dr Wakefield for an answer.

Zuckerman: ...Yes.

Coonan: After Dr Wakefield gave his answer you explained... the basis of Dr Wakefield's theory, namely by which the immune system is challenged by the combination of vaccines.

Zuckerman: What I recall happened is as follows. The question was asked. I certainly directed the question to Dr Wakefield for an answer. When he gave his answer, which I did not expect... single measles vaccines were not available in the UK.... I knew that Dr Wakefield had a young family. It therefore was inevitable that they were protected with MMR and the expectation was that he would say "Yes I used the MMR to vaccinate my children". When he replied in the way that he did, I immediately directed the question to Dr Simon Murch... who rejected that completely and said that he had full confidence in MMR...

On page 97 of his book *Callous Disregard*, Andrew Wakefield tells us: "In fact, the video of the press briefing was played to the GMC. It bore little, if any, resemblance to Zuckerman's recollection.... Captured on the video was the inevitable question of what parents should do about vaccination.... The truth was that Zuckerman had known for some weeks exactly what my position on MMR was. According to Hutchinson, Zuckerman had called for a press briefing precisely to reflect the differing opinions on MMR, and as she said in her witness statement, "He controlled who spoke and when." If he had had the concerns that he protested to the GMC, he could have …at the very least, directed the question to someone else who continued to support MMR."

Probably most doctors today are not aware of all the deceit involved in "the Wakefield affair," but they will have made a mental note that Wakefield lost his right to practice and so its best to keep one's head down. I find that when I broach the subject of autism to physicians, as gently as possible, they change the subject in a millisecond. Happily, Professor John Walker-Smith has been fully exonerated by the High Court. Meanwhile, the number of childhood immunizations keeps going up. The US CDC website, retrieved on July 30, 2013, recommended 24 doses of vaccines by the age of 18 months!

Some US soldiers have tried legal action to stop anti-anthrax shots. In 2008 US District Judge Rosemary Collyer ruled "[The FDA] considered the relevant data and articulated an explanation establishing a rational connection between the facts found and the choice made. The court will not substitute its own judgment when the FDA made no clear error of judgment." I believe the Judge could have taken judicial notice of "regulatory capture," of which every man and his dog is aware, not blessing a "good-faith decision."

The new ruling about the 11 and 15-year-old sisters is sad. (Was the case set up to engender powerlessness? It's pretty odd that a father would go to court to demand that his daughters be vaccinated.) The courts are being used. These outrages must stop. Law is precious and law has got to have at least something to do with truth and reality.

The courts have the ability and the power to put us back on track.

With thanks for any consideration given to this letter, I am,
Yours sincerely,

Mary Maxwell

Appendix X. Do You Resist Jade Helm? 'Tude Is All, by Mary W
Maxwell, PhD, LLB, GumshoeNews, July 31, 2015.

So far I have not heard of anyone resisting Jade Helm. It is good to
see, however, that there are Youtube videos of citizens resisting pull-
overs by cops. Some have had 4 million hits.

You know, it takes a lot of work to find out how to resist. I discovered
a good piece the other day written by an Australianized American, Terry
Shulze. As a barrister he was defending an egg farmer from having to
have his business dictated to by a monopoly. Give me ten minutes of
your time to see how he ran the case. It's 'Tude City, believe me.

Here's an idea that Shulze drew from the Case of Monopolies -- of
1602! "It was recognized at page 1263 of the Case of Monopolies
"that every man's trade maintains his life and the high value placed
upon this aspect of personal liberty."

That happily reminds me of Judaic law. See Meir Tamari's coverage
of rabbinic court rulings in *The Challenge of Wealth*: a monopoly goes
against a man's right to make a living.

Moving along to the very next page, Page 1264 of the Case of
Monopolies, Shulze reports: "Further is the recognition of the
**deception of the sovereign in granting such a monopoly as for
the public good,** when it will actually be employed for private gain of
the monopoly to the prejudice of the public."

Who can say today whether a company that is so big, such as
Microsoft, is not perforce a monopoly? Our Sherman anti-trust law
is very "Judaic" and, amazingly, it has not been encumbered with
the slightest amendment since it was enacted in 1890. Which wasn't
yesterday.

The Office of the Attorney General has a branch devoted to enforcing
the Sherman anti-trust law, but its workers are just so many Maytag
repairmen. They twiddle their thumbs; they nap. Sure there are private
cases in which one company sues another for breach of "Sherman,"
but your basic well-paid US Attorneys just aren't there for you.

Now here is where Shulze goes deeper than deep. He asks Why
should there not be monopolies? Is it because the law so states? If you

think the essence of law consists of "whatever Parliament or Congress has decided to impose," **you're only on the surface**. You're a believer in Legal Positivism, he says. Nah, dump that wimpy stuff. Go for the deeper, Magna Charta type stuff.

In defending his New South Wales client, an egg farmer, Shulze argued that "The appellant submits that the Egg Industry Act 1983 [is] unconstitutional. That is, it is ultra vires the constitution of NSW." How so? Shulze starts with observations as to the continued validity of "natural law" and fundamental rights of the people.

Whoa, hang on there. I – the undersigned, Mary Maxwell, have mucho skepticism that there's such a thing as "natural law." For me, a committed sociobiologist, the real law of nature includes killing, deception and all those fun things. Stalwartly I have also opposed, and still do oppose, the word "rights" if it means something that exists *in* the person.

To the extent that I, or any mammal, desires freedom – and I think every creature desires to move around freely – it is only that, a DESIRE. If one is successfully opposed by stronger others, the "RIGHT" does not exist. I claim that in animals, "rights" can never exist but they exist in humans to the extent, and only to the extent, that humans band together to make it a reality.

Back to Terry Shulze, and natural law which – he says – is based on reason. The first thing you have to apprehend about him is his love for Coke. You know that I'm referring to Sir Edward Coke of "The Institutes of the Laws of England" (1628). What a guy! Shulze believes that "The fundamental documents such as the Magna Charta (thirteenth century) and Bill of Rights of 1688 were considered paramount to statutes and judicial decision when they were produced."

Cokian stuff: **Those documents were products of the people to dictate to the government of the day the conditions under which the government took power.**... "They and the principles they expound have never been overruled." In other words those original declarations of the true relationship of king and people were already residing "in" the people of the colony of NSW. Yes, even BEFORE those English-rights-bearing folk got around to making a NSW constitution.

AN EARLY MASSACHUSETTS CASE

So can the same be said for that other famous British colony? In *Bowman v Middleton* (1787), the judge knew his Coke. The plaintiff had complained that an Act of the assembly had transferred his freehold property to another without trial or compensation. (Hmm, in *Kelo v New London* there was at least the appearance of a trial.) In Bowman, the Court ruled that the transfer of property was not kosher, as:

"It was against common right, as well as Magna Charta, to take away the freehold of one man and vest it in another...without even a trial by jury of the country, to determine the right in question. The Act was therefore, ipso facto, void."

Wow. Ipso facto. That's what I was trying to say about the Homeland Security Act in *Prosecution for Treason* but I lacked the phrase.

(At this point, Shulze recommends you read *The Higher Background of American Constitutional Law* by Corwin, 1984, and I recommend Nelson's *The Americanization of the Common Law*, 1982. Gosh, I'd never noticed that the Eighties were so hot.)

Shulze says, about the Homeland Security Act, or, pardon me, the Egg Industry Act:

"It would be a design offensive to the rational mind if the NSW Parliament sought to take principles which had a pre-existence and declare them on a piece of paper only to destroy the paper later in the hope of destroying the principles."

As said, Terry Schulze is a Yankee in King Arthur's court, or, as we would say here in Oz, he is a Seppo in Steak and Kidney (i.e., Sydney). (US-trained but migrated here.) He tips his hat to *Marbury v Madison* but says the proof of his claim that his Australian client is entitled to Magna Charta, etc., is to be found in the Imperial Acts Application Act, 1969.

Note: The separation of Australian law from Mother England has occurred gradually. The Australia Act of 1986 more or less cut the apron stings -- but that Act was itself an Act of UK Parliament! Slightly embarrassing, but oh well, it's done.

Shulze: "Taking a despotic NSW Parliament [John Ashcroft, anyone?] at its highest, if the Parliament should wish to abrogate the fundamental rights of the citizens of NSW, it would first need to abrogate the fundamental documents that were declared in the Imperial Applications Act."

SPOILING FOR A FIGHT? GREAT.

I must point out here that we're not living in a society that jumps to support principles. As Charlotte Iserbyt laments, the young are not taught the Constitution, so they don't get upset about having it taken away from them. Oldies to the rescue!

The sociobiologist in me says that the new oppression by legislatures, and courts, is a normal manifestation of the power struggle in society. "Those who can, do." Or as Thucydides put it pretty baldly in his funeral oration to Pericles, "The strong exact what they can and the poor grant what they must."

Shulze is saying "Yep, the strong can do that, so let the people develop some 'tude that will make them strong enough to squelch the Bozos." He reminds me of one of my beloved mentors, Philip Allott, who says "Once human rights has been thought, it can't be un-thought." Well, OK, Allott, but it takes more than thinking. It takes an armed fight. Armed? Sure, the arms can be thoughts and words, but the fight has to be a *fight*.

None of this falling asleep for twenty years like Rip Van Winkle, hoping when you wake up all will be resolved. In fact there is a dark age coming, says the wise old Jane Jacobs (*Dark Age Ahead*) in which skills and manners will be lost and we'll regress Oh you who think you have to have every luxury and comfort today, beware. There won't even be toilet paper.

I believe all of the above paean to Englishmen should be taken with awareness that the Brits screwed the Chinese in the opium "wars," and went so far as to smash the fingers of textile spinners in India, for the benefit of "Manchester."

Maybe there is a brainiac out there today who could figure how to pin down the "rights of man" in all their glory while also figuring out how not to take delight in genocide. Chances are it could be done. And why? Because we are, by the grace of God selfish, and want to preserve our life.

Appendix Y. Port Arthur Massacre and Martin Bryant's Innocence: A New Perspective from Tasmania by Mary W Maxwell, PhD, LLB, at RumorMillNews.com, July 8, 2015.

In reply to my article on GumshoeNews, which talked about Naomi Wolf and the media handling of "Port Arthur," I received a surprising email. It was from an elderly chap who said he knows (or at least can surmise) who did the shooting that day, and it wasn't Martin Bryant.

At first I doubted this Australian's claim, but he provides clues that have not previously appeared in the literature. So I offered to interview him under the pseudonym Shane Gingkotree and he graciously agreed. "Shane" was living in Tasmania on that famous day April 28, 1996, but he was not near the site of the shootings (thank God).

Mary Maxwell: Thank you for sending me that old newspaper clipping about David Everett (from an article in the *Launceston Examiner,* dated July 5, 2008). I have to agree with you that he looks a lot like Martin.

Shane Gingkotree: Yes, and one of the Port Arthur witnesses said the gunman had hair parted in the middle, which is the way David Everett wore his hair.

Mary: Oh, but that would negate the famous allegation that the Martin impostor wore a wig.

Shane: I see what you mean. Anyway, Martin doesn't part his hair in the middle.

Mary: You have told me that on the day of the massacre, David Everett was supposedly in prison for another crime. That gives him an alibi.

Shane: Yes, it's a matter of public record that Davis Everett was in prison, from 1991 to 2002.

Mary: The first thing that came to my mind was that, in 1967, James Earl Ray was in prison in America, but the authorities needed him to be outside so he could (allegedly) shoot Martin Luther King. Hence they helped him make an escape. Sort of the reverse of David Everett, if you are correct. Now please tell me your story.

Shane: I suspect that the massacre involved SAS people. Although David, who was born in 1962, had quit the service by the time of the Port Arthur massacre, you can't really be sure these guys are not still attached to the SAS.

Mary: You also told me that David appeared to have been struck in the face, before the event at Broad Arrow Café.

Shane: I had read that he got beat up in prison around that time, but I really don't know.

Mary: Didn't Wendy Scurr say that she saw a man who looked like a "boxer"?

Shane: Yes, and by the way I attended Officer Macgregor's talk in Devenport and he hinted at an SAS presence. He has written a big DVD book about the innocence of Martin Bryant, called *Deceit and Terrorism in Port Arthur.*

Mary: I regret that Wendy Scurr is in hiding or at least does not make herself available for questions. Her hour-long talk on Youtube is very helpful however. I have no hesitation in trusting her. She's a hero. And she was on the premises the whole day.

Shane: She wasn't in the café when the shooting occurred; she was further down toward the gate where the tourist buses come in.

Mary: Tourism reminds me that my husband and I visited Port Arthur in 1981. It was so sad to learn of the way the convicts were treated. And they had a sadistic guard who taunted them. Many years later he came back to visit and was so arrogant that he walked among the men unarmed. They ganged up on him and finished him off.

Shane: There are two parts to my story. One is that as soon as I heard about the massacre I "twigged" that it was David's work, simply because I had already been following his exploits, as mentioned above.

In fact I was so sure he did it, that when a neighbor of mine said to me, right after April 29, 1996, "They ought to take Martin Bryant out to a tree and hang him," I said "He didn't do it." Boy, did I get a funny look from my neighbor.

Mary: If you had said it to me in 1996, I would have given you a funny look, too. I didn't get clued in till 2005, first about 9-11, and then, thanks to links on the Internet, to many other "conspiracies." By the way, an Australian girl named "Shizzaa" uploaded a video sympathetic to Martin, but she hasn't checked into her Youtube channel "Opinion Hour" for the last 8 years. I worry about her.

Shane: I don't know her. I have read some of Keith Noble's book, *Mass Murder*, online. It is very thorough. He provides a lot of testimony.

Mary: I like the way Noble lashes into the legal system. Surely there is not a judge anywhere in the world who could read the details of Martin's "court case" and not realize it was unethical. But why don't they comment?

Shane: They might be killed.

Mary: You, too, might be killed, so thanks for speaking out. Now what is the second part of your story?

Shane: In 1996, I was living in a town near Devenport, which is where the ferry comes in. On the Monday before the massacre there was a small mention in the local paper that a troop of SAS had come across from the mainland, and would be camping in West Tasmania. That is actually why, when we were told Martin did it, I figured it was the SAS.

Mary: you realize a critic would say "The presence of the SAS in Tassie at the right time does not prove anything."

Shane: I don't claim it is proof. It is enough to satisfy me, and since I am getting old I want to get the word out there.

Mary: Legally I would say "the opportunity was there" for David Everett, if he were in that group that came over.

Shane: No, "officially" he wasn't there. As I said, he was in prison.

Mary: Do you know what crime he was convicted of? I thought in the military you get court martialled and serve time in the brig.

Shane: It was a robbery of a cinema, plus the home invasion of the cinema owner, and, later, an IGA shop. In 1991 he got caught, then escaped for 10 months, and so he was "Australia's Most Wanted Criminal." The media reporting of his crimes is what made me aware of his existence.

Mary: Ah, I see he's got a page in Wikipedia. It says he was in the Air Services Regiment and that his job took him to Burma. He decided to help the oppressed Karen people there after he finished his military service. How unusual. He was teaching marksmanship to soldiers there!

Shane: Did you know that a former head of the SAS – I forget his name -- said he thought he himself was one of the world's best shots, but that after he saw the results of Port Arthur he would rate that gunman as even better?

Mary: No I didn't know that. As for the part about Everett becoming a volunteer to the folk of Burma, it's more likely he was a covert agent. I'm speculating that he was "programmed" to be a helper in Burma, to do the robberies in Perth, and then, maybe, to use his shooting skills at Port Arthur.

Shane: Yes, I similarly consider David to have been probably as much a victim as Martin. Poor things. I think they might be told what to do under hypnosis.

Mary: I speculate that all manner of experts – singers, sports heroes, scientists, have been brain-enhanced. I am an amateur singer and I miss a note every now and then, but professional entertainers absolutely never fail. How is that possible?

Shane: Like you, I don't want to blame David Everett. Anyway he is deceased. I am only interested in seeing Australia do the right thing by Martin Bryant.

Mary: Although I know I should care about Martin, I have to say that my main interest here is selfish. It makes me nervous to live in a country where the entire legal profession is mum on the subject. Any schoolchild knows the correct way for a trial to proceed. As I said in an earlier Gumshoe article, even the coroner broke the law, by not having an inquest.

Shane: The coroner said no inquest was needed because "everyone knows what happened."

Mary: Yes, as I am ashamed to say, for the first nine years I "knew" that Martin did it.

Shane: I know a really good lawyer in Hobart; they're not all bad.

Mary: I know two in Adelaide. Maybe we should publicize a register of all lawyers who support Martin. Then when folks are looking for an honest lawyer they can choose one of those.

Shane: OK. I am glad you're on the case for Martin.

Mary: I got on it because Dee McLachlan and I produced a show for the Adelaide Fringe, "Puppetry of the Watermelons." We tried to spoof some of these mysteries.

Shane: Port Arthur is not really a mystery.

Mary: OK. I agree. When a coroner refuses to look into the cause of death of 35 people, and gets away with that breach of the law, it's no mystery. It is bare, plain, obvious: some people "high up" must be the killers. Isn't that awful?

Shane: Yes. I will send you more information if I obtain any.

Mary: OK, thanks a mil for your info. I invite anyone to copy this Gumshoe interview and to be brave and do the right thing.

POSTSCRIPT. David Everett wrote a book, *Shadow Warrior:* Here is the publisher's blurb: "Renegade soldier, outlaw, and fugitive. An SAS soldier bored with life in the Regiment during peacetime, Dave was lured to the jungles or Burma. There, he became swept up in a war between the military junta and the oppressed Karen people. Back in Australia on a mission to raise funds for the Karen, he soon became every government's nightmare; a highly skilled commando on a crime spree. Dave had every cop in the country on the lookout for him."

I wondered if my library has a copy of that book, so I looked it up at Worldcat.org. Turns out 70 libraries in Australia have it. The author, David Everett, died in 2013, age 51. In the review article, sent to me by "Shane Gingkotree," there is mention that David at age 46 was on a pension for Post Traumatic Stress Disorder, and possible neurological damage "which his Dad died from." When are we going to stop treating each other this way?

Note: I can't say that David did the Port Arthur massacre, just that the shooter must have had SAS-like skills. Does the fact that a retarded man, Bryant, is now unfairly incarcerated mean that the justice system of Oz is bought? Surely every barrister and judge can see the truth. -- MM

Appendix Z. John Brown to the Virginia court after he was condemned to death for state treason, in 1859.

"I have, may it please the court, a few words to say.

In the first place, I deny everything but what I have all along admitted, the design on my part to free the slaves. I intended, ...as I did last winter, when I went into Missouri and there took slaves without the snapping of a gun on either side, moved them through the country, and finally left them in Canada. I designed to have done the same thing again, on a larger scale. I never did intend murder, or treason, or the destruction of property, or to excite or incite slaves to rebellion....

It is unjust that I should suffer such a penalty. Had I interfered in the manner which I admit, ... had I so interfered in behalf of the rich, the powerful, the intelligent, the so-called great, or in behalf of any of their friends... or children, or any of that class, and suffered and sacrificed what I have in this interference,... every man in this court would have deemed it an act worthy of reward rather than punishment.

This court acknowledges, as I suppose, the validity of the law of God. I see a book kissed here which I suppose to be the Bible.... That teaches me that all things whatsoever I would that men should do to me, I should do even so to them. It teaches me, further, to **"remember them that are in bonds, as bound with them."** I endeavored to act to that instruction. I am yet too young to understand that God is any respecter of persons. I believe that to have interfered as I have done in behalf of His despised poor, was not wrong, but right.

Now, if it is deemed necessary that I should forfeit my life for the furtherance of the ends of justice, and mingle my blood further with the blood of my children and with the blood of millions in this slave country whose rights are disregarded by wicked, cruel, and unjust enactments, I submit; so let it be done!"

John Brown was hanged on December 2, 1859. He left a note: "I, John Brown, am now quite certain that the crimes of **this guilty land** will never be purged away; but with Blood. I had, as I now think, vainly flattered myself that without very much bloodshed it might be done." [Emphasis added]

Bibliography

Allen, Gary. *Kissinger.* Seal Beach, CA, Spirit of '76 Press, 1976.

Bezmenov, Yuri. *Deception Was My Job.* Youtube.com.

Carter, Tamara. *A Memoir of Injustice: as Told by Jerry Ray* Walterville, OR: Trine Day, 2011

Chaitkin, Anton. *Treason in America from Aaron Burr to Averill Harriman.* Executive Intelligence Review, 1999.

Coleman, John. *Conspirators' Hierarchy: Committee of 300.* 1994.

Constantine, Alex. *The Essential Mae Brussell.* Feral House, 2014.

Creighton, Chas, *Jenner and Vaccination: A Strange Chapter.* 1889.

Daviddson, Elias. *Hijacking America's Mind 9/11.* Algora 2013.

Dillon, Emile. *The Inside Story of the Peace Conference.* 1920.

Docherty, Gerry and Jim Macgregor, *Hidden History: The Secret Origins of the First World War.* Edinburgh: Mainstream, 2013.

Dreyfuss, Robert with Thierry LeMarc. *Hostage to Khomeini.* NYC: New Benjamin Franklin Publishing House, 1980.

Emery, Carla. *Encyclopedia of Hypnotism.* 1998.

Estulin, Daniel. *Tavistock Institute.* OR: Trine Day, 2015.

Fisher, Louis. *The Constitution and 9/11: Recurring Threats to America's Freedoms.* Kansas: U. Press of Kansas, 2008.

Fotheringham, Trish. "Dissociation," at MoreThanAnIdea.ca.

Freeland, Elana. *Chemtrails, HAARP.* WA: Feral House, 2014.

Gibney, Alex and Eugene Jarecki. *The Trials of Henry Kissinger* (DVD). Sundance. 2003.

Hallett, Greg. *Stalin's British Training.* Auckland. NZ, 2008.

Hopsicker, Daniel. *New American Drug Lords.* Trine Day, 2012.

Hoffman, Michael. *Secret Societies and Psychological Warfare.* 2001.

Iserbyt, Charlote. *The Deliberate Dumbing Down of America,* 2011.

Martin, Al. *Conspirators: Secrets of an Iran-Contra Insider.* 2002.

Maxwell, Mary. *Prosecution For Treason: Epidemics, Weather War, Mind Control, and the Surrender of Sovereignty.* Trine Day, 2011.

Maxwell, Mary W. *Consider the Lilies; A Review of 18 Cures for Cancer and Their Legal Status.* Walterville OR: Trine Day, 2013.

Maxwell, Mary W. *A Balm in Gilead: Curing Autism and Awakening the Physicians.* 2014. Online at maryWmaxwell.com

McGowan, David. *Programmed To Kill,* iUniverse.com, 2004.

McLachlan, Dee and Maxwell, Mary. *Truth in Journalism.* 2015.

Merritt, Robert. *Watergate Exposed.* OR: Trine Day, 2010.

Noble, Keith. *Mass Murder at Port Arthur. Witnesses.* 2014.

Peck, MS. *People of the Lie: Hope for Healing Human Evil.* 1990.

Rappoport, Jon. *Aids, Inc: Scandal of the Century.* 1988.

Ray, John, and Lyndon Barsten, *Truth At Last.* 2008.

Rockefeller, Eileen. *Being a Rockefeller.* NYC: Penguin, 2013.

Ryan, Richard. *Another Nineteen: Investigating Legitimate 9/11 Suspects.* 2013.

Schwitzgebel, Robert and Schwitzgebel, Ralph. *Psychotechnology: Electronic Control of Mind and Behavior.* NY: Holt, Rinehart. 1973.

Shklar, Judith. *Legalism.* Cambridge, MA: Harvard U Press, 1964.

Skolnick, Sherman. *Overthrow of the American Republic.* 2006.

Skolnick, S. *Ahead of the Parade: a Who's Who of Treason.* 2003.

Stauffer, Vernon. *The Bavarian Illuminati in New England.* 1918.

Stich, Rodney. Wikileaksusa.org and Defraudingamerica.com.

Sullivan, Kathleen A. *Unshackled.* 2003 (online at scribd.com).

Tamari, Meir. *The Challenge of Wealth.* NJ: Aronson, 1995.

Tamari, Meir. *Al Chet: Sins in the Marketplace.* NJ: Aronson, 1996.

Taylor, Brice. *Thanks for the Memories... the Memoirs of Bob Hope's and Henry Kissinger's Mind-Controlled Slave.* 1999. Online.

Taylor, Greg. "Parliament's Power To Require the Production of Documents." *Deakin Law Review,* Vol 13, No. 2, 2008.

Thomas M. *Monarch: The New Phoenix Program.* iuniverse, 2007.

Uttley, Sandra. *Dunblane Unburied.* UK: Cromwell Press, 2006.

West, Nigel, ed., *British Security Coordination: a Secret History of British Intelligence in the Americas, 1940-1945.* London, 1998.

Wilkes, Donald E. "Final Chapter of the Troy Davis Case" University of Georgia Law, Digital Commons, uga.edu. 2010.

Windsor, Bill, "Lawless America" videos, Youtube.com.

INDEX